GOA INDICA
A Critical Portrait of Postcolonial Goa

ARUN SINHA

BIBLIOPHILE SOUTH ASIA
in association with
PROMILLA & CO., PUBLISHERS

BIBLIOPHILE SOUTH ASIA
in association with
PROMILLA & CO., PUBLISHERS

C-127, Sarvodaya Enclave, New Delhi 110 017, India
9 Adams St., Morganville, NJ 07751, U.S.A.
URL : www.biblioasia.com

First published by Bibliophile South Asia and Promilla & Co., Publishers 2002

Copyright © Arun Sinha 2002

All rights reserved

81 85002 31 2

Typeset in ACaslon by Radius Arc, New Delhi

Printed at Rakmo Press Pvt. Ltd., New Delhi

This book is sold subject to the condition that it shall not, by way of trade or otherwise, be lent, resold, hired out, or otherwise circulated without the publisher's prior written consent in any form of binding or cover other than that in which it is published and without a similar condition including this condition being imposed on the subsequent purchaser and without limiting the rights under copyright reserved above, no part of this publication may be reproduced, stored in or introduced into a retrieval system, or transmitted in any form or by any means (electronic, mechanical, photocopying, recording or otherwise), without the prior written permission of both the copyright owner and the above-mentioned publisher of this book.

To Nagma and Ruhi

Acknowledgement

My special thanks to social scientist Nandkumar Kamat, who has an encyclopaedic knowledge about Goa, for taking time off to vet my script and offer suggestions for improvement. I learnt important bits about Goa also from Percival Noronha, Carmo da Silva, Manohar Usgaocar and a number of other friends and well-wishers. Thanks also to Gasper D'Souza who lent his technical talent to make improvements in the formating of the manuscript. And, surely, this book would not have been possible without my wife Purnima's tremendous patience with my preoccupation.

GOA INDICA

A Critical Portrait of Postcolonial Goa

Contents

Introduction 15

1. **THE WEST INVADES** 19-35
   Albuquerque Conquers Goa 19
   The Spiritual Navy 21
   The Portuguese Apartheid 24
   Strong Native Roots 29
   Castes and Christianity 32

2. **A UNIQUE IDENTITY** 36-64
   Liberation and Lusophiles 36
   The Christian Nightmare 40
   Fight for Goan Identity 43
   Two Opinions in Congress 54
   Bandodkar Mellows Down 58
   The Opinion Poll 61

3. **FRUITS OF FREEDOM** 65-86
   The Bandodkar Charisma 65
   Goa's Village Communues 67
   Destiny of Tenants 71
   The Benign Landowners 73
   Bandodkar's Land Reforms 75
   Charisma without Vision 79
   Not Enough Rice 82

4. **PERILS OF PROGRESS**   87-113
    The Mining Boom   87
    A Better Life   89
    Progress at a Price   91
    The Hippie Invasion   93
    The Tourism Boom   96
    A Culture of Conspiracy   100
    The Domestic Tourists   103
    Rape of the Beaches   105
    Search for High-Spenders   111

5. **ROAD TO SALVATION**   114-143
    The Laity's Bread   114
    The Church and Konkani   118
    The Royal Pope   121
    A Vigilant Church   125
    The Clergy's Influence   128
    The Elusive Solidarity   133
    Ghosts of History   137

6. **AN EMPTY PITCHER**   144-169
    Goa's Uniform Civil Code   144
    Aspects of the Civil Code   148
    Scene in Rest of India   152
    Muslims and the Goa Code   158
    Goa : A Paradise for Women?   163
    The Virtual Widows   167

7. **ETHNIC FENCING**   170-208
    The Great Konkani Wall   170
    A Haunting Nightmare   173

    The Labour Paradox   **176**
    Two Meals a Day   **182**
    The Migrant Professionals   **185**
    Hostility towards Outsiders   **186**
    The Second Class Goans   **193**
    Children of Migrants   **198**
    The Goan Sovereignty   **200**
    The Rotten Apples   **203**

8. WRITINGS ON THE WALL   **209-230**
    Fading Colonial Influences   **209**
    The Invading Cultures   **212**
    The English Annexation   **214**
    Goans of a New Kind   **216**
    The Language Ghettoes   **218**
    A Multicultural State   **219**
    Migrants in the Courtyard   **223**
    The Future of Goa   **226**

A GLOSSARY OF GOAN TERMS   **231**

BIBLIOGRAPHY   **234**

INDEX   **243**

MAPS   **12-13**
    Goa Portuguesa   **12**
    Goa Indica   **13**

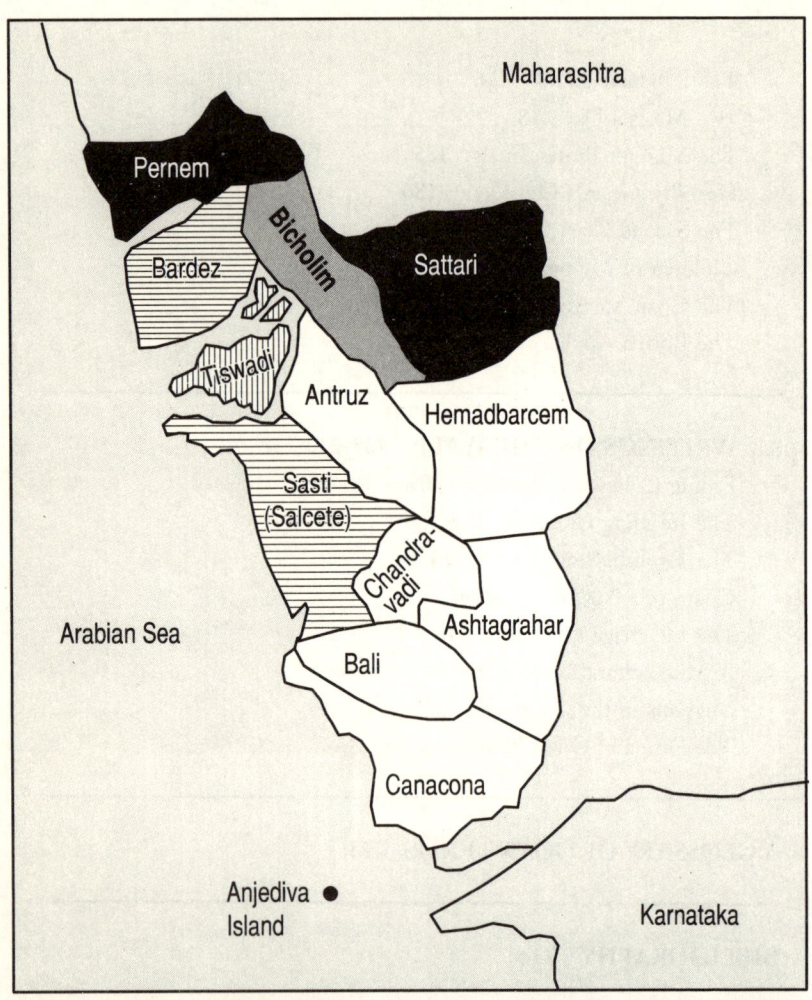

GOA INDICA

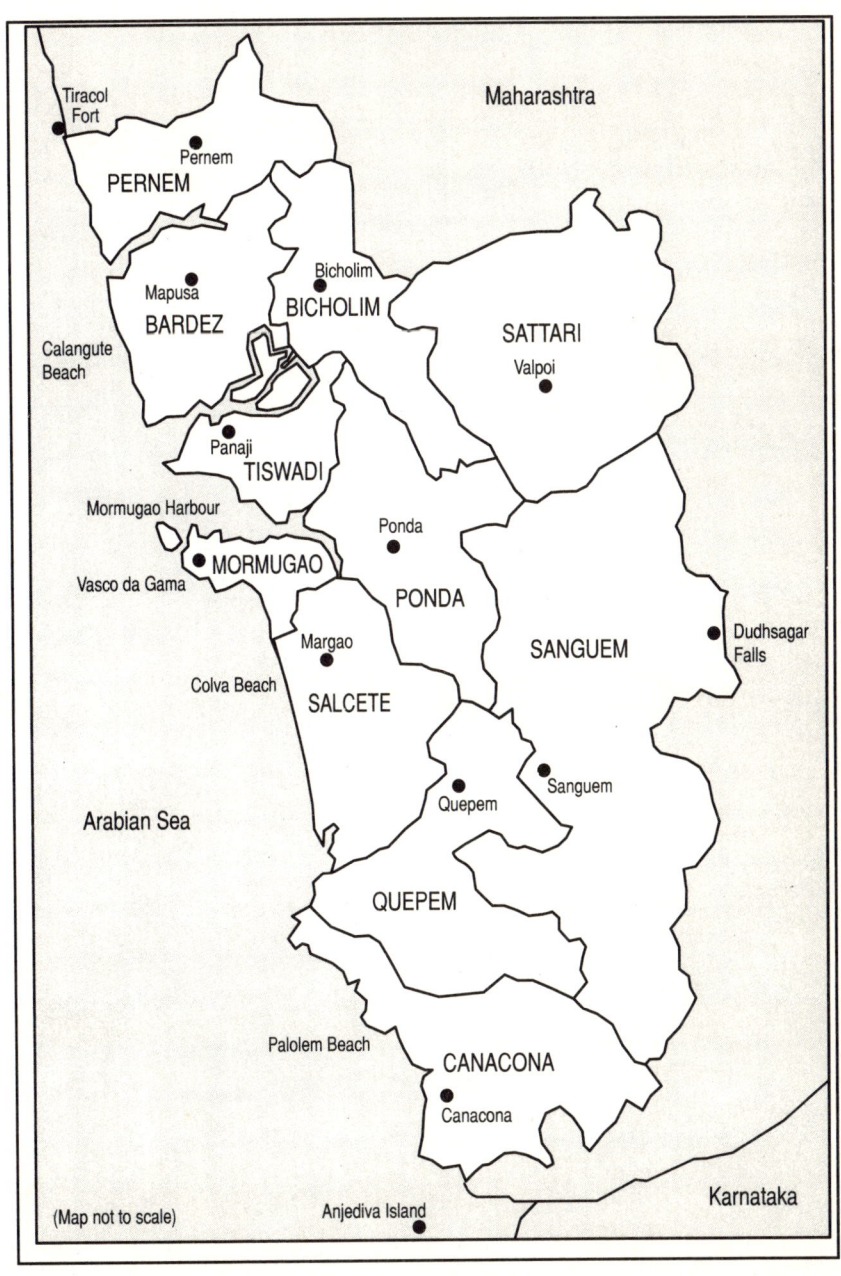

Introduction

The Portuguese conquered Goa in 1510 and soon converted a large number of Goans to Christianity. The state and the church worked in an open collaboration, suppressing the Hindu faith and penalising heresy among converts. The Hindus were not allowed to celebrate their religious festivals, not even marriages, outside the walls of their homes. And the converts were not allowed to cry at the death of a near and dear one, because that was considered a pagan and a Hindu tradition.

Protected by Britain which reigned over most of India under an old royal treaty, the Portuguese continued to rule Goa, until the Indian army marched in December 1961 to dislodge them in less than 48 hours. Salazar tried everything to get the UN to drive India out of Goa but he failed. Nevertheless, the Portuguese left behind a legacy in architecture, music, culture and attitudes that showed distinctly in Goa, especially among Christians.

This legacy was to create a problem. The Goan Hindus wanted to wipe out this legacy but the Christians wanted to preserve it. The Christians felt that it was this legacy which gave Goa a distinct identity. The Hindus asserted that the Goan identity was the pre-Portuguese Goan identity, which was no different from the larger Indian identity. A majority of Hindus supported the demand of the Maharashtrawadi Gomantak Party (MGP) for Goa's merger with Maharashtra. But the Christians and a section of Hindus wanted Goa to remain separate — for some years as a union territory under the central government and later as a state. Eventually, in 1967, the central government ordered an opinion poll in which more than 54 per cent of people voted against Goa's merger with Maharashtra.

In the following decades Goa was to develop at a fast pace as a tourist destination. Agrarian reforms by the government handed small plots of land to the tenants, which brought about a social revolution —

in terms of upward mobility of lower castes — as well as an economic transformation — in the sense that it created a land market in the state, with the hospitality industry and real estate developers seeking more and more land, especially in the coastal districts. These years also saw large-scale emigration of Goan labourers to the Persian Gulf countries for employment, which brought tremendous prosperity to the average Goan home. Today about 30 per cent of the total bank deposits in Goa, which are very high compared to other states, come from Goans working abroad.

In just four decades of independence, Goa has achieved a very high level of development. But it is usually not talked about. Economists, planners, media analysts and the average Indian influenced by them have been talking about Punjab and Kerala as the best development models. However, this view is erroneous, as a Goa government study rightly points out. Punjab is economically advanced and has one of the highest per capita incomes, but its social development (birth rate, life expectancy, literacy) is not impressive. Kerala has performed well in the social sector, but it is not economically developed and its per capita income is low. Goa is the only state which has not only one of the highest per capita incomes but also very good achievements to its credit in the social sector.

However, the progress has come at a price. There is a growing awareness among Goans that checks have to be put in place to save Goa from ecological, cultural and economic damage. Development has also brought in migrants from other states, arousing fears among Goans of a loss of control over local resources and employment opportunities. A large number of non-government organisations have sprung up in the state to put pressure on the government for making development environment- and Goan-friendly. The postcolonial church has also been playing an active role, with the clerics mobilising mass protests whenever needed.

In the coming years, Goa is most likely to encourage industries that suit both the environment as well as the Goan workers' preference for light work. Such industries could include software, IT-enabled services, biotechnology and agro-based products, apart from pharmaceuticals and hospitality which already have a significant share of the total industrial investment in the state. The focus in agriculture will shift from cereals to horticulture, animal husbandry and floriculture.

As Goa approaches the golden jubilee of its Liberation, the signs of the Portuguese legacy fading are unmistakable. However, one notable element of the colonial legacy, the Uniform Civil Code, which is unique to Goa among Indian states, has been accepted by Goan Hindus, Christians and Muslims alike and is going to stay. But most other elements of the Portuguese legacy are on their way out.

1

The West Invades

What above all needs to be noted in Portuguese India is the mentality, the outlook on life, the spiritual atmosphere. No qualified traveller passing into Goa from the Indian Union can fail to gain the impression that he is entering an entirely different land. The way the people think, feel or act is European. There may be no geographic or economic frontier, but there is indubitably a human one: Goa is a transplantation of the West onto Eastern lands, the expression of Portugal in India.

—Salazar

Albuquerque Conquers Goa

Of all the European powers which colonised India, the Portuguese stayed the longest: to be exact, 451 years, while the French ruled for 281 years and the British for 182. The Portuguese, like the French who followed them, conquered a few tiny territories and froze there, while the adventurous British, who were the last to arrive, subjugated the whole of India, leaving out those parts. Like ants to an elephant, the Portuguese and the French kept themselves out of the British way, posing no threat to them at all, and the British, by way of merciful reward, allowed them to hold on to their little possessions for as long as they wanted — the Portuguese their Goa, Daman and Diu on the West Coast and the French their Pondicherry, Karaikal, Yanam on the East Coast and Mahe on the West Coast. For both the Portuguese and the French, these tiny dots on the coastal fringes of India served, for the better part of their rule, more as symbols of national glory than as thriving maritime ports for capturing which they had ventured so far from home and slain and sacrificed thousands of lives in their wars with the Indian princes.

Where they stagnated, however, they deranged things. Ants to the British they might have been, but they were elephants in their own territories. Particularly the Portuguese, who could trample upon the Goanese, Damanese and Diuese without the slightest fear of overthrow by a popular uprising, because a royal Anglo-Portuguese alliance enjoined the British to protect them. And before the Goans could know, the men, who had arrived on the Indian coast looking for spices, had thrown everything in disorder. The upheaval was most irreversible in *Velha Conquistas* or the Old Conquests which the Portuguese occupied from 1510 to 1961. Made up of three districts by the sea — Tiswadi, Bardez and Ilhas, which constitute about one-fifth of today's Goa — the Old Conquests suffered the most savage tyrannies of the Inquisition. In the British and French Indias, missionaries entered after the traders and soldiers had established the colony; but in Portuguese India they came along with them on the battle ships. In the British and French Indias the missionaries did not grow beyond a point as they did not receive the state patronage they wanted. In Portuguese Goa, the conversions were massive and the Jesuits as well as the Dominican and Franciscan friars acquired a near-absolute power, because the man in the throne in Lisbon was not only the king but also the pope of Portugal.

When the Portuguese king issued the proclamation instituting the Inquisition in 1536 the express mandate to the missionaries was to cleanse Goa (then composed only of the Old Conquests) of all heresy. Only those who worshipped Christ could reside in Goa; Hindus who resisted conversion would be driven out of the land. Already, there were hardly any Muslims left in the territory: Afonso Albuquerque, the Portuguese general who captured Goa from the sultan of Bijapur, Adil Shah, killed all his 6,000 Muslim male soldiers and subjects without losing any time following his triumph.

Herding the Muslim women together on to the public square, Albuquerque had had them baptized in a mass ceremony and then, assuming the mantle of their fathers (whom he had killed) he gifted away the marriageable ones to the scum from the streets of Lisbon he had brought along on his fleet as sailors, soldiers, masons, bakers, cobblers, carpenters and helpers. These baptized brides were to become the first recipients of Portuguese culture in Goa. Their captivity ensured by the dual power of their upstart husbands and Albuquerque's army that backed them, they learnt how to cook Portuguese dishes and sing Portuguese songs.

Thus much before the Inquisition began, Albuquerque had legitimized the use of force in decimating local cultures. And much like the

Inquisition was later to do, he combined savagery with snares. Those who married native women were to be given a package of gifts: a plot of land, a job and financial assistance. And yet when you look at what the Inquisition did to the Goans the excesses of Afonso Albuquerque pale into insignificance. For more than 150 years the Inquisition subjected the natives to barbaric assaults, persecuting and executing heretics with the sanction of the pope-king. The Hindus were driven into a situation where they had to choose one of the two options: conversion or exile — and both options chilled them.

Soon, thousands of them were to run away to lands, which today form parts of the states of Karnataka, Maharashtra and Kerala, where their progeny, with bitter ethnic memories, still live. Many of those who stayed back, because they were deeply attached to their ancestral land or were lacking in courage to face an unknown world, gave themselves up to the satans in soutane.

The Spiritual Navy

In the forefront of the Inquisition was the Society of Jesus, the order of the Jesuits, whose vicar general, Miguel Vaz, who was not even a cleric but a layman, instigated the Portuguese king in 1546 to issue a proclamation against idolatory, banning the celebration of all Hindu festivals and ordering all Brahmans to leave Goa. Vaz unleashed a savage campaign to destroy Hindu temples and shrines and to build churches and chapels upon their ruins. So indiscriminate was his destruction that Hindus from several villages fled with their temple deities to hamlets outside the borders of the Old Conquests: as a result even now the largest concentration of Hindu temples in Goa can be found in Marcela and Ponda that lie on the outskirts of the former Old Conquests. These outlying villages later formed a part of the Portuguese New Conquests, *Nova Conquistas*, but by that time the Inquisition had been abolished and the subjects were granted liberty to follow their religious faith without any interference by the church or the state.

The pope-king's regime not only razed to the ground the temples of Hindus; it also suppressed their festivals and customs. Since time immemorial the Hindus had celebrated their weddings outdoors, with the bridegroom's procession arriving at the bride's house in style, to be received with good-humoured, fun-poking songs sung in chorus by the bride's aunts and sisters. A lot of the other ceremonies were performed outdoors too, around a sacred tree, at the temple, at a well. The feasting was done outdoors. But the Inquisition banned all that, directing the Hindus to celebrate their weddings inside their houses, behind closed doors.

Outraged by the absurdity of the proclamation, Hindu families sometimes used to move temporarily out of the Old Conquests to the neighbouring territories of British India and return only after they had celebrated their weddings with all the traditional ceremonies. When the regime came to know of this, the office of the Inquisition issued a fresh warning to the Hindus but it was of no avail. The Hindus, fettered and beleaguered, had learnt how to survive. Elephant God Ganesh was their favourite god; every family used to have His idol ritually installed at home during the Ganapati festival, which were days when they would not eat fish or meat. Away from the eyes of the Inquisition, the Hindus concealed the images of Ganesh in chests which would be opened during the Ganapati festival every year. And then, once the festival was over, Ganesh went into the chest again, to emerge the next year.

Yet the penalties for the defiance of the Inquisition were so severe that Hindus performed the ceremonies with a fear constantly dogging their mind that someone might go and report it to the tyrants. Many of their relatives, friends, neighbours and acquaintances (as well as personal enemies) had surrendered to the terror of the Inquisition, and they could not be sure whose door these sniffer dogs of the *firangi* (alien; here Portuguese) might lead their masters to. Of course, the renegades were afraid of each other themselves, because many of them, although they attended mass in the church, followed Hindu beliefs secretly in their homes.

Even on the flimsiest of grounds the officers of the Inquisition drove the Hindus into prison. And from there usually they were taken to the College of St. Paul, that turned out batches of priests every year for the triumphant church, where they were forced to eat pork or beef in the Brothers' plates. For Hindus with a sense of ritual purity as no other religious community in the world ever had, eating beef or pork was a great sacrilege, more so beef since they worshipped the cow as mother; and to have eaten it from a Christian kitchen in a Christian plate made it, sacramentally, an even more unexpiable sin. The crooked Jesuits knew very well that their prisoners, now defiled, would not be accepted in the Hindu society as they had become unworthy of a caste rank. Polluted and socially exiled, they were left with no choice but to embrace the faith of their persecutors.

Likewise, the clerics picked up orphans from Hindu joint families — children whose both parents had died — and placed them under the care of "virtuous men who would teach them good manners." The pope-king's regime justified it on the ground that the orphans were treated like slaves in the homes of their relatives who also deprived them of their inheritance. All of it was nothing but a philanthropic façade, for once the clerics had succeeded in taking away the child, they knew they had added one more number to the Christian population in Goa.

They usually placed the orphan with a Christian family or in a church home where he was taught Christian doctrines and prayers. Officially, the clerics assured the child's relatives when they were taking him away that they would not baptize him, that he, once he attained the age of discretion, would have the liberty to choose his faith, but they knew it for certain that having lived under the care of Christians, having eaten and mingled with them for several years, he would not but opt to be a Christian, because he would cease to be a Hindu. The relatives would not take him back into the family.

The Inquisition also used the caste divisions in Hindu society to its good advantage. Everyone who was a victim of discrimination in the Hindu order was welcome to Christianity which claimed to believe in equal treatment to all: the downtrodden communities, the orphans, the women. Hindu women had no right to inheritance of their father's or husband's property. The pope-king's regime issued a decree giving this right to the women who agreed to join Christianity. If the father or husband refused to give her the share, the state would seize his property and give one half of it to the woman and the other half to the king.

For the widows, the state allurement was bigger. Hindu widows had to live a life of renunciation: they had to shave their head and were prohibited to wear jewellery, cosmetics, flowers in the hair, bangles or good dress. In some of the extremely orthodox, high caste families, widows were even forced to become a *sati* — burn themselves alive on the funeral pyre of their husbands. The state banned *sati* and issued a decree encouraging Hindu widows to marry. Anybody obstructing a Hindu widow's marriage would forfeit all his properties and the same would be divided equally between the widow and the king.

In short, the Inquisition's message to the terrorized folk was: Christianity was good, Hinduism was evil. Hinduism had social inequities, Christianity had none; Hinduism reduced widows to second-class members of the family or burnt them alive, Christianity helped them marry and live life with honour; Hinduism turned orphans into servants, Christianity raised them with love; Hinduism gave no property rights to women; Christianity made them enjoy these rights equal with men; Hinduism kept women behind doors; Christianity encouraged them to socialize. To the disadvantaged and discriminated Goans all this made Christianity look supernal, and there is evidence that in many cases the temptations worked.

The Portuguese Apartheid

However, this was a very small part of the story. Mass conversions took place not because the evangelists of the Inquisition had any miraculous talents to convince the Goans of the ethical superiority of Christianity over Hinduism but because they had the full backing of the state. The state's proclamations and decrees, enforced with a ruthless penal mechanism aided by a network of eavesdroppers and spies, gave no room at all to Hinduism in the cultural space of Goa.

And it was not just cultural suppression. The state subjected the Hindus to economic and political suppression too. No Hindus were allowed to hold a public office. In the *comunidades* (known until the Portuguese came as *gaocaris*, which were essentially a commune of village founders, managing its properties, cultivation and other affairs from ancient times in Goa) Hindu officials (founders' progeny) were forced to relinquish offices in favour of the members converted to Christianity. In the *comunidade* registers the names of the Christian members were to be written first, then of the Hindu members. If the Christian members constituted a majority in a *comunidade* the Hindu members were barred from attending its meetings. Any sale or lease of the *comunidade* rice-fields or palm-groves had to go to the Christian bidders who alone could participate in the auctions. No Hindu could ride a horse or travel in a palanquin.

This was the Portuguese apartheid in its infernal glory: if you were a Christian you had all the privileges; if you were not you had none. There was no other alternative but to fall prey to the predators in cassocks if a Hindu wished to avoid dispossession, disentitlement and disenfranchisement. The king of Portugal had successfully used the church as his secondary warhead, the primary warhead being his royal navy. The royal navy would win him territories and the church their residents. The Inquisition had a religious character in Portugal, but in the colonies it acquired a political character with the church, serving as the king's spiritual navy, zealotly engaging in the consolidation of the empire.

So crucial a role did the clergy play in the king's achievement and enjoyment of imperial glory that he bestowed the provincial council of the Goa church with powers to take decisions that would be binding on the colony's civil authorities. The king maintained direct communication with the ecclesiastical and civil authorities in Goa, which gave the archbishop a status in the power structure next only to the viceroy. When the viceroy died, the archbishop officiated as viceroy till his successor arrived.

The dilemma — conversion or exile — into which the Inquisition had pushed the Hindus — defied easy resolution. For the members of a village-rooted, agricultural community leaving their ancestral land would just be unthinkable. Generations had cultivated the lands, nurtured the coconut groves, built the irrigation systems and enjoyed the produce of the land, the catch of the sea, the monsoon and the breeze. Ancestors had lived in the homes they were living in; generations had been cremated in the burning ground of the village. Every brick of the house, every clod of earth in the fields, every plant in the grove, every tree in the woods around the village preserved intimate memories from which it was impossible to turn away. And even if they did, the world away was unknown and swampy. Starting life from a scratch in unfamiliar lands sounded too frightening a thought. To make it worse, the neighbouring states were not free from strife and suffering. Maharajas, rajas, sultans and their ambitious satraps were waging wars against one another. But then for many, even these odds, which seemed insurmountable, had to be gone through, for here in the land of their ancestors they could no longer live as free, proud and ritually pure men.

The Inquisition was working on the assumption that the natives would be too tradition-bound and scared to leave their village; but many of them had proven it wrong. Even today the descendants of the Goans who fled their ancestral lands can be found living in close-knit communities in parts of neighbouring states where they rebuilt their temples with their revered deities. When the exodus from the Old Conquests started, village after village was left without a soul. The depopulation reached such alarming proportions that not enough men were left to cultivate the lands; and craftsmen — blacksmiths, carpenters, tailors and shoemakers — were also in short supply.

This threw the state into an economic crisis: the revenue from the lands declined, food had to be imported to meet the shortfall in agricultural production. The church, which had become a very big landlord with seizure of the fields and groves of the heretics and of the estates of the liquidated temples and mosques, failed to get enough produce for their clergy and laity from their new possessions due to the labour shortage.

Not all joined the exodus, though. The orphans, slaves, prisoners, prostitutes, widows and vagrants, who were snared into the task of rebuilding the Kingdom of God, of course remained. Then there were Brahman and Kshatriya families who changed their faith to maintain their high status in the colonial regime. Some of the Brahman and Kshatriya families also fled to other lands leaving behind one of their sons who agreed to be baptized so that the family could retain its right to its ancestral land and other privileges. They reckoned that the Portuguese would not survive very long in the islands; they would soon be defeated and driven back home. Then they would return to their ancestral lands. They saw allowing one of the family members to be converted as a passing sacrifice, though the orthodox Hindus, whose entire families fled, viewed it as a surrender to a grossly polluting faith. The largest number of Goans who stayed behind came from the lower Hindu castes, because conversion opened for them the doors to upward mobility.

The Portuguese have left behind no census or aggregate statistics on the baptisms in the Old Conquests. Most of the Inquisition records were ultimately destroyed, and the information that is available from clergymen's accounts sometimes looks too self-eulogistic and elephantine to be believed. In one account the population of the islands of

Goa is put at 48,000; in another the number of baptisms in just one year is put at 20,000.

The absence of authentic figures notwithstanding, there is no denying the truth that 'christianization' took place on a colossal scale. In just a few decades after the Portuguese took over, Goa was transformed from a Hindu-majority state into a Christian-majority state. The gigantic scale of 'christianization' was also evident from the fact that even after the Portuguese annexed Antruz, Pernem, Sattari and other hinterland Hindu territories (the New Conquests) 250-280 years later, in the eighteenth and nineteenth centuries, the Christians continued to be in majority in Goa. In the official census of 1851, which combined both the Old and the New Conquests, the Christians numbered 232,189 or 64.5 per cent of the total population and the Hindus just 128,824 or 35.5 per cent.

Conversion did not just mean a change in the way the Goans worshipped their god; it forced them to change their way of living. The converts were allowed no social relationships or intercourse with the Hindus: no inter-religious marriages, no exchange of invitations at weddings or any social occasion with them, no visits even for last respects to a former close relation on deathbed or on the pyre at the cremation ground; no child deliveries with the help of Hindu midwives; no dealings with Hindu craftsmen; no visits to the temples housing their ancient family deities. A segregated, Lusitanized and terrorized new population of Christians, the pope-king envisaged, would be forced to depend more and more on him, thus providing stability to his empire. And his calculation proved right. There were other reasons of course why the Portuguese survived so long in Goa — e.g., its isolation from mainland India by the Sahyadris, its lack of attraction for other European colonial powers, the protection the mighty British empire provided under a treaty, low costs of maintaining the colony — but the most important reason was the creation of a loyal population through a religious divide.

Christians were forced to intermingle only with Christians; they met at the mass and went out in church processions; they celebrated the Carnival as the Portuguese did for three days, abstaining from liquor and meat during the Lent; learnt to sing at the choirs and participated in parish feasts. Instead of having the naming ceremonies and feasts at the birth of a child at home, which were banned by the Inquisition, they went for baptism and christening to the church. According to the rules of the Inquisition, Christians were not permitted to cry at the death of a dear one like the Hindus did; so the converts, when someone died in their home, just sat or stood by the body glumly, not allowing the pope-king's spies the faintest scent of a Hindu-style outpouring of grief even when the coffin was lowered at the cemetery.

The converts were not allowed to wear traditional Goan dresses: men found in *dhoti* and turban or women in *sari* and *choli* were made to pay a fine. Outside their home, the men must be seen — in the government offices, in the streets, at the ferry wharfs, at the social gatherings, like weddings, receptions and funerals — unfailingly in suits or trousers and the women in western garments. Over generations, the embarrassment of the converts gave way to snobbery in their progeny, and there was a race among Christians to 'look like them.' Having retained their estates with conversion, some of the families, capitalising on their loyalty, came to acquire enough wealth to build a mansion for themselves, an integral part of which was a grand reception hall decorated with chandeliers, carved furniture and exotic curios, where they held parties and get-togethers in the western fashion.

The more the native Christians were westernised, the wider the chasm between them and the non-converted natives became; and this richly suited the colonial state which remained in its core white supremacist. The colonial state wouldn't stop making this chasm unbridgeable. By a proclamation the king granted the converts rights and privileges at par with the citizens of Portugal.

Nevertheless, the converts did not give up all the Hindu practices. Much like their ancestors they believed in idol worship, and had discovered a comforting continuity in the sculptures of Jesus, Mary and the saints in ivory, bronze, wood or stone. They could pray before them in the churches as well as at their homes, just as the Hindus worshipped their gods in the temples as well as at their homes. In the mansions of the rich converts the family shrines resembled the *devakudd*, god's home, of the Hindu houses. Lamps were lit and incense was burnt in the Christian rituals just as in the Hindu rituals. Often, the converts came to church carrying oil to fill in the altar lamps.

In the times of illness or at the launch of a venture or at sacred ceremonies, the converts, like the Hindus, used blessed water for recovery, success or sorrow-free future. For centuries in several villages of

Goa, peasants had followed a harvest-blessing custom. Before they started harvesting rice they would cut a few paddy sheaves and take them in a procession to the village temple to be blessed by the Brahman priests. Only after the priests had blessed the sheaves, which was considered as their revered deity's sanction did the peasants go ahead with their harvest and enjoyment of the yield. As villages turned Christian, the converts carried on this tradition along with them. They started arriving in a procession with sheaves of rice, not uncommonly with a band, at the parish church, leaving the priests no option but to place the sheaves on the altar-steps for Christ's blessing.

However, if someone thought that the continuity of such local traditions among the converts held out any hope for their return to the Hindu fold he was mistaken. The converts, in spite of the bitter awareness of the circumstances under which they had been compelled to switch their religion, had changed irreversibly. If they clung to some of the old values it was only to mitigate the acuteness of their alienation from the soil. Even as Christians they spoke of the great traditions, great literature and great culture of their ancient land. This was not to glorify Hinduism from which they had broken away but to give their collective self a greater respectability vis-à-vis the cultural arrogance of the colonisers.

Before the close of the sixteenth century thus a new kind of Goan was born: a Christian who followed some of the Hindu customs in modified forms; a Christian who took pride in the ancient heritage but refused to relate to Hinduism; someone who became a 'Black Portuguese' in the Hindu eyes but remained a *Canarin*, a native, in the Portuguese eyes; a man who belonged neither here nor there — a man who had become a stranger in his own land.

Strong Native Roots

In Latin America, Portuguese colonialism had not produced strangers. It had produced mestizos and mulattos. Latin America's native culture was decimated and wholly replaced with the Iberian culture. It could happen because the native culture was too primitive and weak to offer resistance. In Brazil, which the Portuguese discovered before Goa, they met wandering or settled tribes who did not know the use of metal and survived on wild plants and practised cannibalism by way of custom. They did not have any religion and their men and women moved about naked without any sensibility or shame — "just like Adam and Eve in the Garden of Eden before the Fall," as one of the Portuguese explorers noted in a letter to the king.

India of those times was not a country of naked savages. The Portuguese preferred to make Goa the capital of their Eastern Empire not because it was a *tabula rasa*, but because it was an important cosmopolitan and commercial centre. For centuries before the Portuguese arrived, Indians and Arabs had traded textiles, horses, gems and spices through this port. Goa's society was composed of village communities engaged in agriculture, fishing and allied activities. These communities shared the village land and other resources in the well-organised system called *gaocari*. For centuries the *gaocari* had administered the villages. Although the first settlers came from different parts of India, and in different times, they related themselves culturally with the mainstream Hindu India.

Not only were they economically advanced but they also had a high level of moral and philosophical sophistication. One of the most remarkable examples of this was available in the manner in which the Hindus conducted their sea trade. The Hindus had forbidden themselves sea travel because it involved interaction with foreigners and therefore invited ritual pollution. But that did not mean they would not do business. Balancing their principles of faith with their pursuit of prosperity, the Hindu traders exported their goods in ships operated by Muslim sailors.

It was the developed native culture that never let the converts completely erase their past. There was a gravitational pull holding them: whenever they went off up, the earth pulled them back. No wonder miscegenation never took place but on a very marginal scale in Goa. The original Hindu pride of being the most superior race in the world continued to influence the psyche of the converts, especially those belonging to higher castes.

Miscegenation remained peripheral despite the fact that all classes of Portuguese — soldiers, sailors, civil officials and workers — came to Goa without any women in their ships. Even the viceroys did not bring their wives here. During the first two hundred years of Portuguese regime, only two viceroys came with their wives. According to C R Boxer, an authority on Portuguese colonial history, a ship carrying 800 men out of Portugal might have none to a dozen women on board. Several factors restricted the emigration of Portuguese women to the East: a long voyage, danger of contracting malaria and other mortal diseases, inadequate salaries of the colonial servants and lack of encouragement by the kings.

The kings sanctioned an interesting scheme, though: by way of fulfilling their charitable obligations they would send young and marriageable girls from the orphanages in Lisbon and Oporto to Goa to find husbands on the promise of a crown job. However the number of such girls was too small to make any social impact: 5-15 in a year. Besides, not all of them succeeded in finding husbands, since most of the Portuguese males in the colony, even though they happened to be rogues, vagrants and destitutes from the streets of Lisbon, found the crown jobs offered as a dowry too low-ranked and low-paid to be worth accepting as a bargain for marrying a girl without any family background or guarantee of virginity.

Naturally, the near-absence of white women drove the Portuguese soldiers and civilians to seek legitimate and illegitimate relationships with local women. And the women who fell easy prey to them were slaves, temple prostitutes, nautch girls, widows, orphans and catches from Java, Japan, China, Molucca and other parts of Portuguese Eastern Empire. Not that women from the families of the Goan converts did not marry the whites, but their number remained small. But miscegenation usually involved women who were uprooted from their families and were ready to be taken by anybody who would provide them food and shelter. Soon after conquering Goa, Albuquerque had forced his female prisoners of war to marry his soldiers and civilians and with these couples sprang out the Eurasian stream in Goa. In the later times, the colonial state would not play the authoritarian role its first governor had played in forcing miscegenation. Nevertheless, it would foster miscegenation by legal sanctions for slave trade, seraglios, prostitution, polygamy, widow remarriage and adoption of orphans.

Despite the state-sponsored licentiousness, to which European travellers to Goa in the 16th and 17th centuries, like Linschoten, Pyrard and Manucci drew a pointed attention, the Eurasians, who were later called by a more honourable name, *descendentes*, remained negligible in number. They numbered 2,240 in 1866 and only 336 in 1950. An official Portuguese publication in 1951, exactly ten years before the

Liberation, put their number at less than one-thousandths of the total population of Goa.

The converts resisted giving up their languages as much as they resisted giving up their ethnicity. Before the Portuguese conquest the Goans were using two Prakrit languages, Konkani and Marathi. The Portuguese imposed restrictions on the use of these languages and at one time even made Portuguese compulsory for all, but they did not succeed: Portuguese never became the language of the masses in Goa. Even at the peak of colonialism, a very small number of Goans spoke Portuguese at home, and they included landlords, merchants and army and civilian officers of the government — in sharp contrast to the Latin American colonies where it became the principal medium of communication or at least a creole version of it. The two Prakrit languages of Goa never became creolized. Of course, quite a few Portuguese words crept into them due to the long interaction but these form the normal part of exchange between two languages at meeting points and do not suggest mixed speeches.

Castes and Christianity

Apart from ethnicity and languages there was one more area in which the converts offered strong resistance: the caste system. Although Christianity believed in the equality of all followers, segregation in the pews was a common sight in the churches of Goa. The converts with higher caste Hindu ancestry refused to mingle with those from the lower castes. When committees were to be formed to organise feasts in the church, or opportunities opened for higher education, government jobs or trade concessions, it would be the higher caste converts who would grab them all. Even in the parishes and the hierarchy of the church in Goa the 'high caste' priests dominated the decision-making, taking the lion's share of the good placements and perquisites.

The only difference between the Hindus and Christians was that while the former had multiplicity of castes, the latter were divided between three distinct castes. The *Bamonns* or the Brahmans were at the top, followed by the *Chardos* or the Kshatriyas and the *Sudirs* or the low castes. The principles of stratification among Christians however remained the same. The *Bamonns* considered the *Chardos* inferior to them and they both considered the *Sudirs* inferior to them. Both the *Bamonns* and *Chardos* avoided social interaction with the *Sudirs:* they did not go to weddings in their families; and even if those few who made an exception for some servant or maid or a resident of the village, they did not touch any food or water. Inter-dining was considered tantamount to losing of caste.

Marriages between *Bamonns* or *Chardos* and *Sudirs* were unthinkable. But at the same time for several years following Liberation, inter-marriage between *Bamonns* and *Chardos* was also rare. The matrimonial columns in the local newspapers still mention the caste of the bridegroom or bride wanted: a Roman Catholic (Brahman) boy looking for ... . R.C. (Kshatriya) family wants ... . The church has not been able to stop this practice. In the recent years, the caste wall has suffered erosion due to the assaults of the cosmopolitan culture, but the gulf between them and the *Sudirs* still remains unbridged.

However, the strong survival of the ancient native culture notwithstanding, the Christian converts did change under the colonial influence in many ways. Their lifestyle, their manners, their food habits acquired Portuguese traits. Like the Portuguese, they began to snooze in the afternoon: everything came to a halt during the long siesta. Dinners began to be served with drinks in their homes and liquor became an institution in Goa. Christian weddings would be unthinkable without drinks, though the Hindus won't allow it. Like the Portuguese they met, the Christians became convivial, casual, fun-loving and adventurous: and leisure became an obsession. *Sussegad,* or the Portuguese philosophy — *be contented with small profits* — became an inalienable part of the Goan character, its near end being moderate ambition and its far end being hedonistic torpidity.

At the parish schools the converts learned to sing and play western religious music. The elite Christians abandoned local forms of architecture and built houses in European style; so much so that certain parts of Goa were transformed veritably into streets of a small town in Portugal. Soon the other classes followed. The architecture, music and character traits influenced by the Portuguese formed a major attraction for the hippies who invaded Goa in the early seventies and opened it to international and domestic tourism. A British architect James Richards in his book, titled *Goa* wrote: These traits provided to the flower children the "exotic strangeness of Asia" with the "reassuring familiarity" of Europe.

Richards is one in the long line of authors who have observed that it was the presence of the Portuguese influences that provided Goa its unique identity, an identity different from the Indian identity. In the post-Liberation years, when the Hindu resurgence threatened to merge Goa with Maharashtra, the Christians trumpeted the distinct identity of Goa, asking the central government in New Delhi to protect and preserve it.

And notably, the man who first propounded the myth of the unique identity of Goa was Salazar. Faced with the imminence of loss of the Pearl of the Orient, the Portuguese dictator advanced the theory: "Geographically, Goa might be a part of India, but from the social, religious and cultural points of view she is Europe." This would be evident to anybody, he asserted, who entered Goa after travelling to India: the difference in the manners, way of life and general conditions was unmistakable. Goa represented Christian civilisation, he said; she had become indistinguishable from Portugal; she had integrated herself into Portuguese sovereignty. And, therefore, he observed, with a note of caution to the world, "We have a moral responsibility to safeguard Christianity and Christians in Goa."

Eager to throw the Portuguese out of Goa, Jawaharlal Nehru blasted Salazar's distinct identity theory. Goa, said Nehru, was not only an integral part of India geographically but also in terms of its culture, languages and economy. Portugal had conquered and held the territory under its illegitimate occupation for over 450 years, inflicted cruelties upon the people and was still committing excesses under Salazar's dictatorship. Goa was India, Nehru said, and she must integrate with her Motherland! India had become independent in 1947 but Salazar refused to free Goa, insisting on its Portuguese identity at the United Nations and other international forums. For fourteen years after India became independent Nehru tried the path of dialogue to persuade Salazar to quit Goa. With Salazar adamant, Nehru gave orders to the Indian army to drive the Portuguese out of Goa.

In what was to become one of the most poignant ironies in Goan political history, soon after Liberation, Nehru turned into a most powerful advocate of Goa's distinct identity. Nehru did not exactly use Salazar's words, but he based his observation on the dictator's logic, which held that during the 450 years of their rule the Portuguese had brought irreversible changes in Goa's culture, arts, architecture and way of life which must be protected and preserved. Nehru's political ideology of keeping India together had secularism and multiculturalism as its two main pillars and this more than assuaged the fears among the Goan Christians of a Hindu politico-cultural backlash.

2

A Unique Identity

We have made it clear that we want to maintain its separate identity, separate individuality, call it what you will, because in the course of more than four hundred years Goa had had a separate identity and the course of history had imparted it one. We have no intention of changing that or suppressing that identity.

—Nehru

Liberation and Lusophiles

On December 18, 1961 when the Indian troops stormed into Goa, the Portuguese army tried to stop them by blowing up bridges and laying landmines at ferry crossings and on the approach routes: vainly, as it turned out, because the Indian soldiers not only managed to cross the rivers by throwing Bailey bridges, rowing in boats or swimming across, but two of their cavalry squadrons arrived the same afternoon at Betim, bang opposite Panaji across the Mandovi river, only short of an order to take over the capital. The soldiers entered Goa through several routes and along all of these Goans turned out in large numbers to welcome them, offering them whatever they needed: knowledge of local topography, trucks, jeeps, boats, intelligence on Portuguese troop movements. The Indian army marched into Panaji the next morning, and within a few hours took over Governor-General Vassalo da Silva's secretariat and residence, the Treasury, the Military Camp, the Customs House, the police headquarters, the high court and all other government buildings. Those of Salazar's soldiers and sailors who had not already fled Goa surrendered without a fight. The Governor-General, leaving behind instructions to destroy all the files at his residence, rushed toward Vasco da Gama with the intention of flying away in a waiting plane to Portugal but was ambushed on the way and taken prisoner. The Goans went crazy with joy, bursting firecrackers, tearing up the sky with the slogans, *Bharat Mata Ki Jai* (Victory to Mother

India!), *Nehru Zindabad* (Long Live Nehru!) and *Jai Hind* (Victory to India!), holding rallies, distributing sweets.

The Liberation came as the culmination of a long struggle in which both Christians and Hindus had participated. However, there was a small population of Christians who had sold their hearts out to Portugal and were not happy. That December, therefore, Christmas was not celebrated in some Christian homes. It was partly confusion, partly the hope that the Portuguese would return to Goa before long. Salazar built up pressure on the United Nations to drive India out of Goa, alleging that it had committed an 'act of aggression.' When he did not get any response, he tried to blackmail the UN by threatening that he would not give up the African colonies, for which negotiations were going on, unless the UN retrieved Goa for him.

And in this effort Salazar was not alone. He had his stooges from among the Goan immigrants claiming to represent the people of Goa at international forums. One of the stooges demanded 'end of Indian occupation;' another issued a threat that the 'Goan people will resort to extreme means if India does not vacate;' and the third one demanded UN sanction for a 'right to self-determination' for Goans. Although the petitions from Salazar and his stooges never made any breakthrough, they kept the hopes for Portugal's comeback among the Goan Lusophiles alive, many of whom had not withdrawn their children from the Portuguese-medium schools as others had done.

The Liberation dismantled the Portuguese system to replace it with an Indian system, which meant a radical swing, bringing in its trail a whole lot of problems Goans did not know how to cope with. Prices soared, incomes dipped, jobs were lost, rules changed and in the absence of qualified Goans, Indians from other states came to occupy key posts in the government. Most Goans saw these as problems of transition, but not the Lusophiles, who declared it a catastrophe. Much dust was raised when Abel Colaco, whom Nehru got nominated as a member of the National Parliament from the liberated territory, portrayed Goa as 'one of the black spots' of India. But Colaco and all the Lusophiles whose hearts he had gladdened with his 'true picture of Indian Apocalypse' would not budge from their position, which was that Indians had brought anarchy and that the Portuguese must come back because they alone knew the art of administration.

And they pointed at 'tell-tale evidence:' the new Indian administration had come like the monsoon, promising good crops but also bringing dark skies, puddles and maladies. It brought people happiness such as only freedom can give, but it also gave them a thousand things to complain about. The top non-Goan officials, trained in the British system as they were, did not know anything at all of the Portuguese system of administration, laws or jurisprudence; and the officers of the Portuguese colonial government, who were retained in the new administration knew nothing of the British system.

The differences between the British and the Portuguese systems were historical, vast and unbridgeable. Under the Portuguese system the executive services were separate from the judicial services; under the British system they formed a part of the judicial services. In the Portuguese system, revenue was separated from administration; in the British system revenue was a part of administration. Penal laws were different in the two systems, and so were the civil and taxation laws. The Portuguese judiciary was subordinated to the executive — in other words, no action of the government could be challenged in a court of law; in the British system, the judiciary was independent and empowered to review the decisions of the executive according to the existing laws.

The retained judges and officers not only knew very little of the British laws and administrative procedures but they also knew very little of English, which had replaced Portuguese in the courts and offices overnight. How would the judges interpret the laws when they could not even read them! Not just the legislations but also the case laws, that is the past judgments of the high courts and the Supreme Court of India, to which they must refer in their orders were also available only in English. No better was the position of the lawyers. In the topsy-turvy situation, arguments and judgments were delayed.

In the government offices the scene was equally pathetic. The officers who had come from other states knew only English and the colonial officers knew only Portuguese. They could not explain things to each other. Suddenly, the language which had been used in the administration for 450 years was banished and declared 'unspeakable' in government offices. English had become the queen of communication. And Nehru's bureaucrats made it worse by wearing an arrogant attitude — *follow us quietly, we are your liberators* — and behaving in a manner as though they alone knew what was the best for Goans. A terrible alienation gripped the retained colonial officers owing to the combined impact of the arrogance of Nehru's bureaucrats and their inability to write or speak their language. In some the feelings got so severe they emigrated to Portugal, accepting Salazar's open invitation to the public servants of his Goa administration to come to the mother country with full protection of salaries and tenures. Some of the judges too, finding themselves too old to start learning a new language and system, left Goa for good to settle in Portugal.

Not just the officers and judges, even the Goan youth, having studied in the Portuguese medium, faced a bleak future with the switchover to English. New recruitments in the government, commercial banks and private companies required the candidates to be proficient in English. There was anger among the local youth as they saw applicants from other states taking over jobs in their land. To make things worse, Nehru's officers declared some of the departments existing under the Portuguese government surplus and fired their employees, adding to the unemployment. The Portuguese economy had been import-oriented; Nehru's officers imposed heavy restrictions on imports, causing a fall in the income of importers and, consequently, a shrink in the number of jobs available with them. A slowdown affected Goa's iron ore export, its main export, causing loss of jobs in mining.

In its last years the Portuguese administration had given its officers and staff a substantial pay hike, making their salaries look handsome compared to those of the government servants in India. Instead of paying the same level of salaries to the officers brought from the other states, the Nehru administration reduced the salaries of the colonial employees to their level in order to establish a parity! As if to rub salt on their wounds, the Nehru administration imposed taxes on salaries: there was no tax on salaries or personal incomes under the Portuguese regime. On top of that, owing to the sudden influx of people, essential commodities became scarce; the prices of cereals, potatoes, milk and fish sharply rose.

While the Lusophiles found in every trouble the people faced a good reason to reminisce the Portuguese rule in glowing terms, the Goans in general lamented the cavalier and insensitive manner in which the Nehru administration handled the transition. Heavens would not have fallen, they said, if the administration had allowed a few 'unnecessary' colonial departments to continue functioning for some more time; the government might have become poorer by a paltry sum paying a few more employees', salaries but it would have earned public goodwill. And couldn't they have waited to introduce the parity of salaries and taxes or the British system of administration and justice? By forcing the transition thoughtlessly, by refusing to give Goans time to adjust, the Nehru administration had caused embitterment among the people who had so eagerly waited for Goa to join the motherland.

Remarkably though, the Lusophiles did not get the support of the discontented Goan masses to whip up sentiments against everything Indian. The reason was that the Lusophiles were from among the elite Christians who had enjoyed a monopoly of privileges under the Portuguese regime. The historical embitterment of the Goan masses with them was greater than their embitterment with Nehru's administrators mishandling the transition. Failing there, the Lusophiles tried to win over the masses with an apocalyptic cry: *Goa is in danger*. The Hindus rejected the call; they said the Lusophiles had no credentials to speak for the entire Goa since throughout the colonial rule they had spoken only for Christian Goa; consciously and shamelessly, they had projected Christian Goa as the *real* Goa, as if the Hindus did not exist.

The Christian Nightmare

Soon the Lusophiles' dream of ruling Goa again with the return of Salazar began to fade. With the Hindus rejecting a solidarity call against 'Aggressor India,' they settled down to build a fortress in Goa for their respectable survival, a sort of protected island for themselves, with materials picked up from the Indo-Portuguese encounter. They revised their warcry: now they said — *Protect Goa's Unique Identity*. And the Lusophiles, who had failed to provoke fears of submergence of Goa by the vastness of India among Hindus, succeeded in provoking fears among Christians with this warcry.

Although it was true that the Portuguese culture had left its most lasting impress upon the Lusophiles, the large mass of converts, by following the Portuguese brand of Christianity and lifestyle, had also imbibed some Latin peculiarities. Much like the elite, the mass also found its belongingness in the institutions, cuisines and symbols the

Portuguese had left behind: the churches, the Body of Saint Xavier, *Mando*, *sorpotel*, the Carnival, the balustraded balconies, dances, liquor. It was this common belongingness that helped the Lusophiles build up a Christian solidarity against the 'Indian threat' to their 'unique identity' and they demanded to the Indian government to provide protection to it. Nehru, a great believer in multireligious and multicultural India, gave his commitment to protect this identity.

Resurgent Hinduism rejected the construct of a unique identity. Throughout the colonial rule, the Hindus said, the Christian elite had misrepresented the identity of Goa and they were out to do it again. The Christians, they said, would talk of *sorpotel*, minced pork curry, as the 'most favourite Goan dish' when in reality it was the most favourite Goan Christian dish, totally ignoring the fact that Hindus would not touch pig meat in any form. The Christians talked of the 'inevitable Mando' at the Goan weddings when it was only sung and danced at Goan Christian weddings. The real Goan identity was not the Christian identity, the Hindus said: the real Goan identity was Indian identity. Goa had existed as a part of India before the Portuguese came. The large mass of Goans were culturally no different from other Indians. Whatever features existed due to the colonial experience were 'foreign influences.' They must be rejected and weeded out, said the Hindus.

The Christians were banking on Nehru. He intervened in their favour. At a public meeting in Panaji during his very first visit to Goa in May 1963, he said:

> "Goa has a distinct personality and we have recognised it. It will be a pity to destroy that individuality and we have decided to maintain it. With the influx of time, a change might come. But it will be gradual and will be made by Goans themselves. We have decided to preserve the separate identity of Goa in the Union of India and we hold to it firmly .... Irrespective of what had happened in the past, people belonging to the two religions have to live in peace and in a spirit of good-neighbourliness. That had been the way of India since centuries. Emperor Asoka honoured all religions and his empire spread in the north and south. All religions had thrived in India because India tolerated them and even today the same tradition is followed by the secular state in the country which was brought into being sixteen years ago."

At a public meeting the following day at Margao, the 'capital of Christian Goa,' Nehru said: "The individuality of Goa must be maintained, at least for the present.... Diversity brings richness and beauty. India is like a beautiful carpet with different designs, each having its own character, making an attractive whole." At Panaji the next morning he told the press: "There is a considerable section in Goa which is afraid of being submerged by another individuality. Goa should be given a chance to preserve its individuality." When a reporter asked him to elaborate on his concept of Goa's 'individuality,' he said: "Each part of the country has certain distinctive features. Kashmir or Bihar have their own individuality. There are certain common features which are obvious and there are certain distinctive features that are also obvious. I am interested in the distinctive features wherever I go. Because of its long association with Portugal, Goa has developed certain distinctive features. The rest of India had also developed distinctive features owing to its long association with the British."

Could you please mention some of the distinctive features of Goa's individuality? another reporter asked. Nehru said:

"It is really more felt than described. You do feel that an Andhra is different from a Rajput. You do feel that a Negro is different from a European. You do feel that a Brazilian is not the same as a New Yorker. In that way, even though the Marathas from Sawantwadi, Satara and Kolhapur come from the same stock as the Goans, they (the Goans) are apparently different now, particularly due to their association with the Portuguese. I do not merely mean difference in religion so far as the Christians are concerned. But their whole mode of life is influenced. Song and dance and language have been influenced. They are Europeanized, their architecture, social customs, forms of greeting have been influenced. But all this need not lead to conflict. There can be and has been unity in diversity and Goans will be as much Indians as the Marathas or Bengalis, despite the impact of the Portuguese on their culture. We only need to have the necessary accommodating and sympathetic attitude to see all this."

The liberalism, the broad-mindedness, the spirit of reconciliation which Nehru stood for was missing among the Goan Hindus. To them those seeking protection for a unique identity were the same people who had enjoyed all the privileges in an apartheid regime based on religion. They just could not bring themselves to forgive the collaborators and servants of the Portuguese who had banished their ancestors and decimated Hindu culture and temples in their homeland. Many of those in the forefront of protection-seekers were those who, if not outright traitors, had tried in whatever way they could to undermine the freedom movement.

Fight for Goan Identity

When Dayanand Bandodkar, a mineowner from a lower social community, launched the campaign for Goa's merger with Maharashtra in the months after Liberation the Hindus came out in large numbers to support him. The Hindus feared that the Christians would continue to dominate the social and political life even in liberated Goa; and with Nehru's constant assurance to the 'traitors' to protect the territory's distinctive Indo-Portuguese identity who could be in doubt! The only way to prevent this happening — and also the only way to punish the tormentors and traitors for their sins — was to make Goa a part of Maharashtra where they would become a neglible religious minority — a small, strange, subdued school of fish in an ocean of Hindus.

The size of the crowd went on increasing at Bandodkar's meetings, taking the sleep out of the Christians' eyes. The religious divide was so clear that Hindus who spoke in favour of Goa's separate political status were treated as camp followers of Christians. And the number of Hindus who spoke in favour of separate status could be counted on fingers. The Christians knew it was their war and they must fight it with all the strength that religious solidarity gave them and fight it with the determination to win, because losing it would mean pulverization under the Hindu steamroller, a reduction of the Goan Christian population to an invisible dot in the politico-cultural map of Maharashtra.

Their fate remained in the hands of Nehru. And Nehru didn't disappoint them. Disagreeing with the campaigners for merger with Maharashtra, he declared that it was too early to decide on the political status of Goa; the Liberation had just come, things will take time to settle down, the people will take time to make up their mind. Until the Goans have decided the central government will continue to administer Goa as a Union Territory through a lieutenant governor, he said. There would be a legislative assembly of 30 members who will be directly elected by the people on the basis of adult franchise. The party winning the majority will elect a leader who will become the chief minister and nominate his cabinet. All the funds for the Union Territory would flow from the central government.

The Christians, the herd of sheep, heaved a sigh of relief. The pack of wolves called *Maharashtrawadis* had been driven away. Nehru was giving Goans a chance to rule themselves. Dayanand Bandodkar had formed the Maharashtrawadi Gomantak Party — the nomenclature told all the story; it was a party which wanted a Gomantak, a Goa merged with Maharashtra — which earned popularity among Hindus in a short time. Alarmed at the prospect of the MGP coming to power and passing a legislation in the Assembly recommending merger, the Christians set up the United Goans Party, urging upon all Goans to fight for the separate political status of Goa.

Although the Christians banked on Nehru they did not fully trust him. He had promised the Goans would have the right to decide their future political status at a later date but what was the guarantee that he would fulfil the promise? Quite a few of the members of Nehru's cabinet as well as officials of the Goa Pradesh Congress Committee supported merger. Who knows which way Nehru might tilt in the future? The Indian Prime Minister's promise did not even specify when the Goans would be given a chance to determine their political status, or who would be eligible to vote in the referendum. Would also the migrants from other states be allowed to vote? They were all Hindus and could tilt the balance, making the vote in favour of merger overwhelming.

Haunted, the Christians decided to wait no longer; they wanted Nehru to make Goa a separate state straightaway. They told him this was the only way he could guarantee the protection of the unique identity he had always promised. The Union Territory status had only given Goans (read Christians) an anxious reprieve, a low mud wall their predators could easily demolish and cross over any time.

Let it be said that Nehru was politically more inclined to see Goa as a separate state. He responded thus: "There should be no clamour for Goa's merger with this state or that. Goa should develop as it likes within the framework of India, particularly because Goa was a rich country and it had all the makings of being a self-supporting state. If the Goans brought about economic development and raised their living standards, there was no reason why Goa should not function as a separate unit of federal India."

Nehru had given a simple formula for Goa: distinct personality equal to separate status. But the Hindus contested it.

One of the leading ideologues of merger was a Hindu partisan scholar from Maharashtra called A K Priolkar. According to him, Goa's 'distinct personality' in Nehru's image was made up only of the Portuguese cultural influences. These influences existed only among the Christians. The Hindus remained untouched by them. Priolkar argued:

> "Nehru's conception of the distinct identity of Goa probably rests on the impression that Goa which was liberated in 1961 was a distinct geographical unit which had remained unaltered in its extent and dimensions since its conquest by Albuquerque in 1510. This impression is completely at variance with the facts of history. What Albuquerque conquered in 1510 was an island named Goa and a few contiguous islands. The Portuguese dominions in the area were extended in 1543 by the addition of the present administrative divisions of Bardez and Salcete. Salcete was recently divided into two separate administrative divisions, known as Salcete and Mormugao. It is customary to describe these three divisions acquired in the sixteenth century as Old Conquests *(Velhas Conquistas)*. It was not until two centuries later that the remaining part of the territory comprised within the present geographical limits of Goa came under the Portuguese rule. The southern part of Goa, which comprises the four divisions of Ponda, Sanguem, Quepem and Canacona came under the Portuguese rule in 1763. The northern part, comprising the divisions of Bicholim, Sattari and Pernem were ceded to the Portuguese by the Chief of Sawantwadi in 1788, in recognition of their assistance in his quarrel with the Chief of Kolhapur. These seven divisions acquired in the 18th century were known as the New Conquests *(Nova Conq-uistas)*. It will thus be seen that the territory at present known as Goa was brought together by accidents of history. There is no special fea-

ture shared by the entire territory which could be considered as lending it an individuality distinct from that of contiguous territories outside Goa .... The idea of a distinct identity of Goa on which Nehru's policies rest is thus based on ignorance of facts of history."

And Priolkar was right to some extent. The Old Conquests were largely Christian and Lusitanized; the New Conquests had remained overwhelmingly Hindu and traditionally Indian. If Nehru had spoken of a distinct minority culture, perhaps he would have been more right. But for political reasons he did not want to describe the Goan Christians as a minority. He wanted them to feel important and privileged. This was the way to reduce the chances of separatism taking roots in the territory. Nehru had learnt his lessons from the events leading to the Partition and from the separatist troubles in Kashmir and Nagaland. At the international level, Portugal was still at work, trying its best to force India to vacate Goa. America and Britain were supporting Portugal. As a matter of policy Nehru had decided to keep the recently liberated 'foreign pockets' — Goa, Daman, Diu and Pondicherry — under the central government as Union Territories. Having suffered a long isolation from the Mother Country, Nehru felt, these pockets would take some time before they were integrated with India.

By defining the distinct personality of Goa entirely on the basis of Portuguese influences, Nehru had certainly erred. He had excluded from this personality the characteristics Goa had developed in the centuries before the Portuguese arrived. Due to Goa's long isolation, and also due to the fact that most records were written in Portuguese, not much was known of the territory's ancient and medieval history. Even Nehru, who had written *Discovery of India*, an intelligent account of India's history for the common man, remained unaware of the institutions the Goans had built and the cultural traits they had acquired in the centuries preceding the Portuguese.

Had Nehru been aware of them and had he used his knowledge to formulate his political strategy for Goa, the campaign for merger would have petered out much before it actually did. All he needed to do was tell the Goans that the distinct personality that he was talking about was made up not only of the Portuguese influences but also of the features developed in Goa before the coming of the Portuguese. The days immediately following Liberation were emotionally charged: a wiser, culturally inclusive speech by Nehru would have assured the Hindus that he was talking as much of them as of the Christians when he referred to Goa's distinct personality. He would have beaten the Maharashtrawadis hollow, for even they never emphasized the specifically native Goan features when they talked of pre-Portuguese Goa. Ideologues like Priolkar just wanted to prove that Goa was an extension of Maharashtra; so among people everywhere in Goa, excluding the Christians of course, they found similarities of cultural traits and practices, language and customs, religion and world views with the Maharashtrians.

"Many of those who talk about the personality and individuality of Goa and its people," wrote a prominent Goan intellectual Pedro Correia Afonso in an article in *The Navhind Times* on December 29, 1963, "give hardly a thought to the basic features that go into the making of that personality. Cut off from the past by 450 years of colonial domination many are now unable to recall anything beyond a century or two of our history. We have forgotten that before the *conquista dores* we had in our *gaocari* an organisation of society which, based on mutual service, aimed first of all at the welfare of the community. The hierarchy of caste and custom was there of course but we may boldly say that the whole organisation anticipated the welfare state we now mean to attain."

If *gaocari* took care of the community lands, crops, temples, profit distribution and jobs, the *mand* — a sacred place earmarked in the village for celebrating festivals and staging cultural performances — preserved, promoted and developed arts and culture in the territory. It was left to the next generation of postcolonial Goan intellectuals, both Hindu and Christian, to broaden the definition of distinct personality Nehru had given. They traced *gaocari* and *mand* back to five centuries before the arrival of the Portuguese. And they discovered other specifically Goan features of social and religious life. But in the early '60s the polarisation was sharp (and Nehru's definition had accentuated it); the Christians clung to the Indo-Portuguese identity and the Hindus talked of a pan-Indian identity; there was no group or organisation championing the native or ethnic Goan identity.

Ironically in this polarisation, it was the Christian campaign for 'a separate identity, a separate state' which carried the seeds of an ethnic Goan ideology. The Christians were the ones fighting 'Maharashtrian expansionism.' They were also fighting 'Kannadiga expansionism,' as Karnataka too, like Maharashtra, was advancing its claim on Goa on historical, geographical and cultural grounds. Many of Goa's ancient dynasties had their roots in Karnataka, the Kannadigas said, and the Goan culture had distinct influences of Karnataka. A prominent political leader of Karnataka, Veerendra Patil even justified Goa's merger with Karnataka on the economic ground: "Goa has all its trade channels through Karnataka and is also dependent upon it for its iron and steel supplies, so it cannot but choose to merge with Karnataka."

However, the call for Goa's merger with Karnataka did not enthuse Goan Hindus who considered themselves culturally closer to 'Aryan' Maharashtrians than to 'Dravidian' Kannadigas — and the Maharashtrians, who were demanding some parts of Karnataka too, took full advantage of this attitude. In the run-up to the first elections to the free Goa's legislative assembly in 1963, the Maharashtrian lobbyists finally managed to push Karnataka out of the race. The election manifesto of the Goa Pradesh Congress Committee put the final seal: *The future of Goa, and whether it should be integrated into the neighbouring state of Maharashtra will be decided by the people of Goa.* An objective election manifesto would have included all the three questions — a separate statehood or merger with Maharashtra or merger with Karnataka — when it mentioned 'future of Goa.'

But by pressurizing the Goa Congress to include the mention of merger with Maharashtra as the only option outside separate statehood, the Maharashtrians had won their first battle: Karnátaka had been totally eliminated from consideration. This manipulation was a compromise between the Nehru line and the Chavan line — Y B Chavan was Nehru's defence minister and the tallest leader from Maharashtra championing merger — and was an indication of the intense conflict in the Congress party over the issue. Nehru wanted the assurance on the political choice to the Goans in the manifesto, so that Christians did not feel their options were closed. As long as that assurance was there he did not mind inclusion of the option of merger in it. However, for Chavan, the Maharashtrians and the Maharashtrawadis the mention of the merger option in the Goa Congress manifesto was a proof of their growing power. Their next step, they decided, would be to ensure that a majority of Goans voted for merger when the vote was taken.

The Christians hated the very mention of merger. Representative of the sentiment was a letter Alberto Lobo, a Christian resident of Margao, wrote to *The Navhind Times* on April 19, 1963:

> "There was once a young lady, lovely, highly cultured and endowed with all imaginable natural female graces. In the immediate neighbourhood lived a rich young man who coveted her hand and vowed neither to rest himself nor to give her peace until she married him. She, on her part, respected him in a good neighbourly fashion for his wealth, but beyond that she saw no attraction in him. His friends and her well-wishers thought she was a fool to spurn his advances. In vain they tried to convince her. Then one wise man got the idea to prepare a balance sheet of the rich suitor's assets and material wealth full of concrete facts and figures and to compare it with her possessions. Her advisers suggested to her that by marrying him she would have financial stability and social security which is all that mattered in this insecure world of ours. It took much convincing, (and) at last she consented to marry him. It did not take her a few hours of married life to realize that she had made a very serious mistake, for the bridgegroom began to treat her just as another of his acquisitions. For, had he not bought her with his wealth? Too late she realized she had sacrificed her culture, freedom and ideals by falling for financial security and material wealth by contracting a loveless marriage. I am sure if financial security and material wealth were our sole criterion for bartering our soul and our freedom for a probably prosperous and happy Goa as a part of Maharashtra, it would be worldly wise to do so."

Frank Moraes, the editor of *Indian Express*, one of the most respected journalists of Goan origin, attacked both Maharashtra and Karnataka for their chauvinistic, 'covetous eyes' on his motherland. "Goa," he observed, "is not a carcass to be parcelled out among such hovering vultures as Karnataka or Maharashtra. Goa is certainly not interested in being merged with either, but on the precedent of

Pondicherry with its French traditions would like to remain a Union Territory until such time as it can assimilate itself with the rest of India."

A turning point in the campaign against merger came when the Saraswat Brahmans joined the Christians. The Saraswats had traditionally been the elite of the Goan Hindu community and were well-established in business and professions. Being small and endogamic, they were a close-knit caste and vigorously protected and promoted each other's interests against the claimants from the other castes. Although 'kings' among Brahmans in Goa, the Saraswats were considered inferior in the caste hierarchy by the Chitpavan Brahmans, who were at the top of the scale in Maharashtra. Dogmatic vegetarians, the Chitpavans looked upon the Saraswats as a polluted sub-caste because they ate fish. The Saraswats knew it for sure that in the event of Goa's merger with Maharashtra they would be reduced to the status of second-class Brahmans — neglected and suppressed.

Also working upon the mind of the Saraswats was the fact that the movement for merger had become indistinguishable from the movement of the lower castes against the old order in which the elite, both Saraswats and Christians, had oligopolised the landholdings. Bandodkar had aroused passions of the agricultural tenants and labourers with his manifesto of snatching the land from the *bhatcars,* the landlords, and giving it to them; of removing the Saraswats and Christians from the jobs in the government and recruiting their sons to them; of pushing the *patrao,* the master, aside and bringing the poor on the centrestage. One of the many threads of the Saraswat web of nightmare was that if Goa merged into Maharashtra they would be sandwiched between the Chitpavans from the top and the anti-Saraswat masses from below.

Much of the ideological leadership of the separate identity camp was provided by the Saraswats. They started a Marathi newspaper called *Rashtramat* to refute the arguments made in support of merger in the first Marathi newspaper of Goa called *Gomantak.* Although the Saraswats stood for making Konkani the language of administration, instruction and literature in Goa they decided to publish their propaganda daily in Marathi, because their target readership was the Goan Hindu population who had traditionally studied in the Marathi-medium schools and accessed information only through Marathi newspapers. Had they published *Rashtramat* in Konkani nobody would have read it. The editorials, commentaries and columns carried in *Gomantak* and *Rashtramat,* mutually hostile, bitchy, toxic, spiteful and sometimes downright malignant, were to form the mainstream of the polemical literature on the merger issue.

If a writer in *Gomantak* pleaded that Goa must merge with Maharashtra because it was too small to be economically viable, less than half the size of Wardha, the smallest district of Maharashtra, the next day a columnist of *Rashtramat* would argue that despite its smallness Goa could become self-sufficient and viable. If a Maharashtrawadi wrote a letter to *Gomantak* asking the *Rashtramat* columnist how, he, the columnist, would in his next column observe that a full assessment of Goa's natural resources had still not been made, nor of its potential for economic development. Economic viability of a region, he would go on, depended on how it exploited its natural and other resources. And there was no reason to doubt the Goans' intelligence to make optimum utilisation of resources to make his motherland self-dependent.

When the Maharashtrawadis advocated merger on the ground that Goa would develop by leaps and bounds as a part of Maharashtra since Maharashtra had been "geographically, historically and culturally" related to the Konkan region that incorporated Goa, their opponents drew their attention to the Konkan region in the large state, seriously lamenting that its government had not done anything to eliminate poverty in the region. The region comprised three districts, Thana, Kolaba and Ratnagiri, which had traditionally been suppliers of labour to Mumbai. About 40 per cent of the labour engaged in the Mumbai docks, they said, came from these districts, Ratnagiri topping the list. And close to 45 per cent of labour employed in the Mumbai textile industry came from the same districts, Ratnagiri again beating others.

An anti-merger writer Arvind P Bhatikar commented: "The Konkan region, with both its agriculture and industry bed-ridden and too weak to stand on their legs, cries for government help to support, feed and revitalise them, so that they can bring home the economic destitutes (from Mumbai) and feed them. Has the government of Maharashtra heard these heart-rending cries? If it has, has it done anything, or is it doing anything to alleviate the sorrows of Konkan? If it has not delivered the goods, why not? Are the reasons for its inability inevitably rooted in the economic system? And if they are, will they be inevitable in case of Goa too?"

While the Maharashtrawadis and the separate identity camp were engaged in an intense polemical battle, the Nehru administration, having put off the vote on Goa's political status to an indefinite date, set about implementing policies for its agricultural and industrial development. The priority was not merger or separate statehood, decided Nehru; the priority was the economic development of the territory. "Britain, despite her colonial system, had brought some benefits to India, such as introduction of science and technology," he observed. "But the same could not be said of Portugal. Portugal was a backward country in a rich Europe and as such could not bring to Goa what she herself did not have."

Goa Portuguesa carried about itself several myths, unconnected, yet repeated over and over again — Golden Goa, the Rome of the East, the Pearl of the Orient — but the reality was that it was stagnant and sickly, frozen in time like an old and discarded clock. The Portuguese had built very few roads and no bridge over any of Goa's two main rivers, the Mandovi and the Zuari. Nehru declared he wanted Goa, neglected by the Portuguese and held back by them for 14 years from joining independent India, to grow faster. He started off by laying the foundation stone of the first ever bridge on the Mandovi that would connect North Goa with the capital and beyond, southwards toward the Zuari river where the bridge would come later. Nehru's lieutenant governor announced that the Mandovi bridge would to be completed within four years. "We," he said with pride, "will do in four years what the Portuguese had not done in four hundred years." The rest of India had already been through two five year plans, Nehru noted. Goa must "catch up;" and the surest way to do it was by enjoying assured special attention and funds from the Centre.

If Goa immediately became a separate state, warned Lal Bahadur Shastri, who was to become India's prime minister after Nehru's death in May 1964, it would be "left to its own resources and (its) economic development would be delayed by a century." He wanted Goans not to "waste their time and energy over questions such as merger or separate state, but to devote themselves to developing the territory and making it prosperous." They were going to have an elected Assembly of their own and they could make their own laws through their representatives, and their own plans for development.

But the exhortations of Nehru and his colleagues had no effect on the Maharashtrawadi Gomantak Party (MGP) or the United Goans Party (UGP). The war between the two continued unabated.

The MGP refused to accept that there was anything like a Goan identity. Goans were essentially Maharashtrians, Bandodkar argued, as they shared the same history, geography and culture. This was gross misrepresentation, of course: the Goans shared nothing of these with the Maharashtrians. But Bandodkar went on: Even their language was the same!

It was true that during the colonial rule, the Goan Hindus went to the Marathi-medium schools and the Christians to the Portuguese-medium schools: there were no Konkani-medium schools then. It was also true that Goan Hindus used Marathi as a medium of cultural expression: they read or wrote literature, treatises and gave or heard discourses only in Marathi. However, there was no denying the truth that Konkani was the mother tongue of all the Goans, of Hindus and Christians alike. As the language had been suppressed by the Portuguese, there was no recent literature in Konkani, but there were hundreds of works that formed its literary heritage, which the Maharashtrawadis unconvincingly denied. Konkani, pronouced the MGP's intellectual spearhead A K Priolkar, was a only a dialect of Marathi. Konkani was used only by the Saraswats, he argued, not convincingly. There was no standard Konkani, he screamed; there was no Konkani literature and there was no common script for it. Goan Hindus wrote Konkani in the Devanagri script, the Goan Christians in the Roman script, he said.

Outraged, the UGP insisted that Konkani was central to the Goan identity. This thesis represented a dramatic retreat of the Christian elite from the stance which had pegged the Goan identity to the Indo-Portuguese heritage. In the colonial times the Christian elite used Portuguese in the official business as well as in private correspondence and conversations: they looked upon Konkani as the 'language of the servants.' However, with the Hindu resurgence threatening to gobble them up, the Christian elite had given up their snobbery and turned overnight into champions of Konkani. Konkani had been the mother tongue of Goans for centuries, they said, and it had produced great literature.

The reality was that Jack Sequeira, the big landlord who was leading the UGP, or the other lights of the Christian elite, were not aware of any heritage in Konkani language until those fountainheads of wisdom, the Saraswats published a 'Bibliography of Konkani literature' listing over 400 publications in Konkani in the past three centuries or more. They claimed that the first book in Konkani was printed as early as 1632. The bibliography listed books written in Devanagri, Roman and Kannada scripts; and its preface said the list was incomplete.

Yet the MGP insisted that Marathi, and not Konkani, was the mother tongue of Goans and Chhatrapati Shivaji, the hero of Maharashtrians, was their hero too, but this propaganda had no historical substance. Soon the MGP came out with a brush and a pail of black paint: the men fighting for a separate statehood, they said, were Goans who had extra-territorial loyalties, a bunch of Black Portuguese whose ultimate aim was to turn Goa into *Pedaco de Portugal*, a piece of Portugal, again. But, they warned, the traitors would never be victorious against the overwhelming majority of Goans who were 'rediscovering' their 'immediate kinship' with the Marathas and integral kinship with all Indians.

Two Opinions in Congress

Meanwhile, the religious polarisation caused by the MGP-UGP war had driven the Congress into a dilemma. The political strategy of the Nehru administration was to keep Goa under its direct control until such time the transition from the Portuguese to Indian rule had taken place smoothly. The Goans, who had lived in isolation for 450 years, needed time to politically and emotionally integrate themselves to the Indian Union, particularly the Christians who felt threatened by the Hindu backlash. Besides, the central government didn't want to take chances with the Portuguese agents creating trouble in Goa.

But quite a few of the senior local Congress officials favoured merger, an immediate merger — not because the winds in most Assembly constituencies seemed to be blowing that way, but because they really believed in it — and they were guided, tipped and backed by some of the party's national leaders from Maharashtra. But Nehru and most of the party's national leaders wanted Goa to remain a Union Territory for some time. Lal Bahadur Shastri wanted Goa to remain a Union Territory for at least five years. Not that Nehru or most of his colleagues were totally opposed to merger. Their approach was that whether it was merger or separate statehood, the decision must be left in the hands of the Goans. No political status should be imposed on Goa against Goans' will. Let them decide their own future. The time was not yet ripe for a referendum due to the problems of integration, but that was the right course.

Implicit in the commitment of the Nehru administration to the self-determination proposal was the idea that the central government was giving Goans a chance to run their own affairs for five or more years, and if they proved their ability to administer the territory themselves they could easily qualify for separate statehood. "For the present," said a senior Congress leader S K Patil, "that is for some years — maybe five years, maybe twenty-five years — the question of merger is not going to be raised. It may never be raised if Goa's government makes satisfactory progress in every field and raises its own resources for itself and does not depend upon the central government for financing them for ever, except in the normal way in which all state governments are given a share of the all-India taxation proceeds. In one word, the Goans have been given the opportunity to shape and mould their future. They have to prove their mettle and they can well be a full-fledged state. It is a challenge to them to raise themselves fully to their stature and their opportunities and get it."

Manifestly, Nehru and his colleagues were looking at the next few years in the life of Goa as an experiment in self-governance. They thought this would take care of the interests of both the Indian State and the Indian National Congress. Elections to the Assembly were approaching, and there was no other party better placed, they concluded, to win a majority and rule the Union Territory than the Congress, because this was the party that had driven away the Portuguese and won the Goans freedom; this was the party whose government at the Centre had launched development projects to end the stagnation left behind by the Portuguese; this was the party (and here was the hope for all the Christian votes) that had promised the preservation and protection of the Indo-Portuguese heritage and culture. The eagerness to grab the Christian vote toward the end grew so intense that Nehru outrightly rejected moves to establish an electoral alliance between the Congress and the MGP to beat the UGP. Nehru said the MGP represented a parochial cause, mass hysteria, revivalism and illiberalism. Such a party was unfit to be an ally of the Congress which was committed to secularism, multiculturalism and nationalism.

Nehru's commitment to multiculturalism and a future referendum notwithstanding, some of his partymen never lost an opportunity to create the impression that Goa was destined for merger with Maharashtra. Again and again they returned to the small size of the territory to poohpooh the idea of its viability. These were the fellows who were in the forefront of the moves to set up an alliance between the MGP and the Congress.

Maharashtra's revenue minister Vasantrao Naik, who later took over as the state's chief minister, said: "*Prima facie*, so small a territory cannot aspire to be a full-fledged state. Even granting that the Centre will give a generous share of income tax and customs revenues that Goa's trade, industry and port may contribute to the central chest, I am afraid Goa will not be able to raise the rest of the revenue from taxation for running the state." D K Khanvilkar, deputy labour minister of Maharashtra, said, "A small autonomous state of Goa cannot be successful in the long run. It is in the best interest of Goa to merge with Maharashtra." And he assured: "Goa won't be neglected."

Then there was Chavan in Nehru's cabinet. "I feel thrilled," he said at an election meeting, "when I hear the slogan of my pro-merger friends." He went on: "I have formed a very clear impression that, by and large, the Goans do not want a separate state. They want to merge with Maharashtra. The slogans I have been hearing all over Goa and the talks that I am having with people ceaselessly have led me to conclude that this is their desire, and I am glad to note that the direction and the process of it has been unmistakably indicated in the manifesto prepared for the Goa Pradesh Congress Committee on the eve of the election. If I was not certain of this, I would not have come here to recommend the Congress candidates to the voters of Goa."

Chavan said the campaign for a separate state had drawn the support mostly of Christians: "The Christians are welcome to follow Christianity and adopt western ways of life, western music, western dress and even western food if they like it. Quite a few Hindus and Muslims have also adopted them in India. That is a matter of individual convenience. But they do not need a separate state for preserving it. They can preserve all this not only as a Union Territory but even as a part of Maharashtra." Most of the times during electioneering, however, Chavan was not so soft on the UGP. The men behind the 'facade' of the separate statehood campaign, he said, were men with 'extra-territorial loyalties' and "I warn them to be on their guard."

Are you not aware, a journalist asked him, that the UGP wants a separate state inside the Indian Union and not a separate nation?

Chavan replied: "Yes, I am aware of that and I know the implications of that position, because I cannot be blind to recent history. Among the United Goans are people who but yesterday thought of a Goa state on the lines of Kashmir, Ceylon or Burma. In order to remain a constitutional and legal organisation they have got to say that they want to remain a unit of the Indian Union. But in sentiment they want an aloofness from India. This feeling of separatism and the wish to maintain it denote a dangerous trend. Such atmosphere breeds fifth columnist tendencies. This is a legacy of the Portuguese rule of centuries. The legacy has to be liquidated and not given opportunities to flourish.... I am informed that the padres are conducting the election propaganda on behalf of the United Goans. They are asking their congregations to vote for the UGP."

Nehru proposed it, Chavan disposed it. The Christians were alarmed at Chavan's diatribe. In the religious polarisation, the Christians had rallied behind the UGP. However, Nehru had succeeded in gaining their sympathy with his strong commitment to Goans' separate identity and their right to decide their political future. But with Chavan's malevolent insinuations, the Christians who were thinking of voting for the Congress party were alienated. The UGP took almost the entire Christian vote, which was evident from their sweep of the ballot in the Old Conquests. Most of the constituencies in the Hindu-majority New Conquests went to the MGP. Nehru's Congress failed to win a single seat. Of the 30 seats, the MGP took 14 and the UGP 12. Three seats were won by independents supported by the MGP, which gave the party a comfortable majority. Of the total vote, the MGP got 42 per cent, the UGP 30 per cent. The Congress came in third with 17 per cent.

Nehru was stunned by the outcome. In none of the states or Union territories the party of India's freedom had suffered such an ignominous defeat. It was at this moment of his bewilderment that Nehru made his famous observation, *Ajeeb hain ye Goa ke log* — Goans are a mysterious race, indeed — which was to become the favourite repartee of the Goan intelligentsia in moods of jocular self-derision. Nehru's was a discreet outrage at the betrayal by the Christians on whose support he had banked because he had provided them security against Hindu backlash and promised to protect their unique identity and give them an opportunity to determine their political status at a future date. In spite of all this he had done for them they had favoured the UGP!

Nehru's barb was, however, not only directed at the Christians. He was expecting the Hindus to vote for the Congress too, because he had liberated Goa and financed projects on an unprecedented scale for its development. The projects were expected to expand the scope for employment which should have enthused the Hindus, since they had been deprived of employment under the Portuguese regime in which the Christians got the preference. As well as the Christians who went to the UGP the Hindus who clung to the MGP were also an enigma to him.

Nehru's fulminations, facts showed, were not justified. If the Goans irrespective of faith had been alienated from the Congress, the fault lay with the party. In the first two years of Liberation, the two crucial years before the election, the Congress had sent out confusing signals to the Goan voter. With an alarming frequency, the party spoke in two conflicting voices: one advocated merger, the other a unique identity. And the average Goan voter was not able to decide what kind of future political status to expect from a Congress rule. To add to the ambiguity, the party set no date for a referendum, asking the Goans not to think of it but to think of development. In other words, the Congress message to the Goans was: *do not think of political status until you have improved your economic status*. It made the matter look too prolonged. Goa was in the midst of a communal battle for domination. Both Hindus and Christians thought their political fate — and with it, the fate of their religion, culture and future generations — was being decided in the first election. Whoever wins this election wins.

Bandodkar Mellows Down

Immediately after victory, Bandodkar pressed for merger. He argued that the election had been fought, virtually like a referendum, on the single issue of merger and the party's triumph proved that the majority of Goans had endorsed it. Seeing a golden opportunity, Chavan patted him, calling upon Nehru to accept the verdict as a vote for merger. In turn, it emboldened Bandodkar to demand that the Parliament lose no time and pass a legislation bringing about the merger, since people had waited for too long and had lost patience with the Centre's procrastination games.

But Nehru would not buy the Bandodkar-Chavan formulation. He announced that he would stick to his pledge of maintaining Goa's Union Territory for a while. "Merger of Goa with any neighbouring state is not desirable at present," he said. "We should wait for some time before people take a final decision." The campaigners for merger were free to canvass support for their cause during the period; it was up to them to win over the hearts of the opponents of the proposal.

Now, at heart, Bandodkar was a Congressman. He had been with the Congress until he decided to found the MGP. He had trememdous respect for Nehru and other senior Congressmen. Chavan patronised him; many senior Congressmen in Maharashtra and Goa backed him. "Both the Congress and the MGP want merger," Chavan often said. "The only difference is that we are patient and they are in a hurry." After the victory Bandodkar observed, "I do not feel it is a defeat of the Congress, the organisation we all love .... The success of the MGP is the success of Congress ideals: it is the success of the people who had remained oppressed for centuries and who are awakening, thanks to the untiring efforts of our beloved Prime Minister."

Owing to his deep Congress links, Bandodkar decided against a line of confrontation with the central government on the merger issue. Bandodkar before the elections and Bandodkar after the elections turned out to be two different persons. Before the elections he had given the impression that the first thing in the new Assembly the MGP would pass a resolution favouring merger. But after the elections, he had temporized and mellowed; no more did he seem in a hurry to push the merger legislation through. And he covered up his temporizing in these words: "I had founded the MGP with the single aim of securing the merger and I will dissolve it the moment this aim is fulfilled. But that moment is still far. If the merger were to take place tomorrow I will be happy. But it will not happen so easily." Also in these words: "Our party will not press for the merger for some time. We do not want to impose merger on anybody." The MGP would concentrate, he said, on creating the necessary atmosphere, on preparing the proper ground, before it introduced the merger resolution in the Assembly.

Expectations ran high when Bandodkar had his first meeting as chief minister with Nehru after the election. But they were belied. Nehru had obviously prevailed over Bandodkar. After the meeting,

Bandodkar told an eager gathering of newsmen that he would not press for 'immediate merger' as this was not possible due to 'certain difficulties.' He would refuse to elaborate on the 'certain difficulties.' When they asked him what stood in the way of his party fulfilling its promise of passing a resolution in the Assembly in favour of merger, he said passing such a resolution would be meaningless, since the ultimate power lay in the hands of the Centre which alone could introduce an appropriate legislation in the Parliament. "For the time being, we have decided to canvass our case with the members of the Parliament," he said. He refused to put a time limit for the merger. "All I can say is that if and when Goa merges it will merge with no other state but Maharashtra."

Bandodkar's decision not to press for immediate merger in deference to Nehru's wishes brought disappointment to the ranks of the MGP. Bandodkar had a hard time explaining to them that merger will come, that it was only a question of time. Soon it became apparent that Bandodkar would not be able to restrain the tide: if he stopped the party workers pressing on he might be pushed by the wayside. The challenge before Bandodkar was to devise a strategy by which he retained his charismatic leadership without precipitating things with the Centre.

He found the way. Since Nehru wanted him to wait for some more time for the referendum he would wait for it. But meanwhile he would go on preparing the people for the referendum, because he did not want to lose it. So in the following months, the MGP would make a relentless assertion of its commitment to merger. All the forums were used by it to propagate the cause. Whether it was a debate in the Assembly, a literary conference, a public meeting or a seminar, the MGP men harped on merger and merger alone, assuring the voters that they had not forgotten the mandate they had given them and they would soon bring it to fruition.

And they demonstrated their commitment by a variety of measures: the Bandodkar administration would follow an unwritten rule to recruit non-Brahman Hindus rather than Christians and Saraswats to government posts; the MGP men in the government and outside promoted Marathi over Konkani at all forums: their statements in the Assembly, public speeches and press releases were all in Marathi; the

Marathi-medium schools received generous state patronage. A prominent advocate of separate identity for Goa, Sarto Esteves regretted:

"The record of the first elected government in the legislative Assembly is one of dismal failure — failure to understand the high dignity of the Assembly and to build up democratic traditions ... . Probably to please and pamper their friends from the other side of the border, the ministers insist on delivering budget speeches, answering questions and replying to debates in some sort of Marathi, knowing well that neither the legislators nor the people in Goa understand anything of that language. The result is a glorious confusion ... . A minister reads out a ready-made speech in Marathi but is unable to go very far in answering supplementaries in (that) language. One minister speaks in Marathi but his next colleague at the very next second switches over to Konkani. One member asks a question in Konkani and the minister concerned pretends not to understand it and replies in English. One minister speaks in English and the next moment an opposition member is booed and shouted down by the treasury benches because he retaliates by asking a question in Portuguese, for, according to some members, both the languages are foreign and if one foreign language can be used in the Assembly, so can be the other!"

The Opinion Poll

Nehru, on being informed by the Congressmen of the consternation the MGP's aggressive campaign had caused among the Christians, made a smart, artful move: he convened a meeting of the central parliamentary board of the Congress party and persuaded it to pass a resolution, which said: "For the coming 10 years Goa will continue as a Union Territory. There should be no change in the present status. After that the views of the people of Goa will be ascertained in regard to the question of merger and the final decision will be taken in accordance with their wishes."

Shocked beyond belief, the MGP men threatened a public agitation for the scrapping of the central parliamentary board resolution. The Congressmen in Maharashtra promised to join them. Chavan insisted that the majority of Goans had already given their verdict in favour of merger; so where was the need for a plebiscite? That too after ten long years from now when many things could change!

A few weeks after the Congress central parliamentary board passed the resolution Nehru died. He had done his last bit to provide central government patronage for the cause of a separate political status for Goa. Shastri, who succeeded him as prime minister, had supported the board resolution and remained committed to it during the one and a half years of his reign. Also vigorously supporting the resolution was S K Patil who had been among the first senior Congressmen to suggest a 'plebiscite' after ten years in Goa to decide its future status.

Finding the Shastri administration unresponsive, the MGP passed a private member's resolution in the Assembly seeking merger. In protest, the UGP members abstained from voting. The resolution contained seven arguments why Goa should be merged with Maharashtra: one, the first elections were fought on 'definite issues' and the party which won the majority of seats fought them on the 'definite and specific issue' of merger. Two, the Union Territory status involved 'very huge' and 'totally wasteful' expenditure on the 'paraphernalia of a topheavy administration.' Three, the nation had accepted linguistic basis for the formation of states, and Goa was 'predominantly populated by people with their mother tongue as Marathi or its dialect Konkani.' Four, the territory had had geographical, cultural and historical links with the territories now forming parts of the Maharashtra state. Five, the delay in the implementation of the promise held out by the victorious party was giving rise to a 'sense of discontentment' among the people. Six, the delay had caused 'frittering away' of the energies of the people and preventing them from 'concentrating on the development activities.' Seven, merger with Maharashtra would complete the process of the integration of the former colony with the mother country.

Quickly following this, the Maharashtra Assembly passed its own resolution, moved by none else than the chief minister Vasantrao Naik, demanding merger of Goa with the state. The resolution emphasized on the strong ties between the Goans and Maharashtrians and made a solemn promise:

"The House hereby assures every section of the people of Goa, irrespective of their caste or creed, that Goa will have a special claim on the state of Maharashtra, that the economic betterment of the people of Goa will be the special concern of this state, and that the religious, social, educational and cultural heritage and aspirations of every section of the people of Goa will be fully safeguarded and respected by this state in the best of its traditions, and further that in order to preserve, promote and cherish these objectives, the state of Maharashtra will take all such steps as are necessary for their fulfilment."

Not to be left behind, the Karnataka legislative Assembly also passed a resolution a few days later, opposing the resolution of the Maharashtra Assembly, saying it amounted to "a negation of the policy laid down by the late Prime Minister Jawaharlal Nehru that the people of Goa should have the right of self-determination as to its future." Emphasizing that "every consideration bearing on the history, culture, language, geography and economy of Goa would support its merger with Karnataka rather than Maharashtra," the resolution nevertheless pleaded for implementation of the Nehru policy on self-determination.

Karnataka's claim remained formal. But the Congressmen in Maharashtra led by Chavan set up such a powerful agitation in collaboration with the MGP that the central government had to take some steps to calm down their feelings or the situation could have gone out of hand. Religious polarisation could have led to religious violence. It looked unwise for the central government to stick to the Congress parliamentary board resolution that spoke of a plebiscite ten years later. A meeting of the central parliamentary board was convened to reconsider the resolution. And after assessing the situation, the board passed a revised resolution calling upon the central government to hold an opinion poll on the political status of Goa 'as soon as possible.' The central government saw no point in postponing the referendum; a date was set for it. And on January 16, 1967 for the first time in any territory of independent India would a referendum be held to determine its political status.

During the one month of campaigning before the Opinion Poll, the MGP focussed primarily on the cultural inseparability of the Goans and Maharashtrians, joined by the zealous Congress leaders from Maharasthra. "Bhavani, the chief goddess of Maharashtra, eagerly waits to rejoin Shanta Durga, the chief goddess of Goa," the MGP campaigners roared from the podiums at mass meetings. By way of strategy, the MGP almost wholly concentrated on the Hindu electorate, which was 19 per cent more than the Christian electorate, trusting that it would be more than enough to guarantee the democratic endorsement the party needed for merger.

However, the MGP dream was to come crashing down. The Opinion Poll had asked the people to vote for merger or against it. And only 43.50 per cent of them had voted for merger; 54.20 per cent of them had voted against it. The Christians and Saraswats had gone en bloc against merger. But — and this came as a great shock to Bandodkar and his Congress patrons — a significant number of non-Saraswat Hindus had also voted against merger. This was evident from the fact that, in the predominantly Hindu constituencies in the New Conquests, the number of voters who opposed the merger in the 1967 Opinion Poll was much larger than the number of those who had voted for the UGP in the religiously-divided first election to the Assembly in 1963. Looked at in another way, it was also evident from the fact that while the UGP got 34.70 per cent of the total vote in the state in 1963, the anti-merger camp got 54.20 per cent of the total vote in 1967.

3
Fruits of Freedom

In the villages particularly, the labourer since Liberation has become a dictator. In the name of freedom he does what he likes, and what is worse, gets away with it. He demands higher wages and in return works less ... . While the Portuguese have departed, the labourer continues with his drink and afternoon nap, and if pulled up, he talks of Swaraj ... as though freedom connoted licence.

—editorial in *The Navhind Times*, February 27, 1963

The Bandodkar Charisma

The Christians had triumphed over the *Maharashtrawadi* Hindus with the backing of *Goawadi* Hindus and this gave the MGP leaders a creepy, indignant feeling but something that had been done in the Opinion Poll could not be undone — even if the margin of triumph was less than five per cent, meaning that with a little more effort the verdict could have swung in favour of merger. Bandodkar and the MGP workers, having done their best and lost, reconciled, respecting the public opinion, to the separate status of Goa. Bandodkar turned his attention to the promises he had made to the people, especially the poor.

Bandodkar's meteoric rise had much to do with the release of the pent-up anger of the poor against the *Bamonn*. This anger was mainly directed against the Hindu Saraswat Brahmans but the *Bamonn* included the Christian Saraswat Brahmans too, since their character had 'remained unchanged' even after their change of faith: both the communities were seen as acquisitive, guileful, manipulative and untrustworthy. Bandodkar exploited the 'social villain' image of the *Bamonn* fully to build up his political support.

The poor identified with Bandodkar not only because his social status was low, but also because he was a mineowner and had plenty of money. In the common people's eyes Bandodkar epitomised triumph over the ossification of caste ranks. If his social status established an immediate relation between him and the poor, his economic status earned respect from them. He mingled easily with the ordinary folk, behaving like a fellow country-dweller, speaking their lingo. Not only earthy and accessible, he was also liberal with his money — his own money which he earned from his mines — never disappointing the needy at any hours of the day or night who knocked at his door for help.

Seeing Bandodkar, *one of us*, rise to a wealthy status was miracle enough for the poor. When they found that he had not changed at all, that instead of assuming the trappings of a parvenu, he remembered his past and displayed a monumental contempt for money they worshipped him with even more devotion. Bandodkar, who never missed an opportunity to tell the crowds who used to come to his meetings that he had plunged into politics only to end the *Bamonn raj,* presented himself as a model benevolent aristocrat in sharp contrast to the accumulative Saraswats.

But if the poor had been aroused it was not only due to Bandodkar's charisma. The Liberation had raised the expectations of the people sky-high. Bandodkar's charisma and popular upsurge for fruits of freedom worked to consolidate each other. In his book, *Aspects of the Agricultural Activity in Goa, Daman and Diu,* J C Almeida, who had served as an officer in the colonial government, observed that on the Liberation Day "in the twinkling of an eye the light was turned into darkness and the darkness into light." Almeida blamed the self-styled 'social workers' for it who had stirred up the passions of the lower classes of the population. His allusion was to Bandodkar who used to often describe himself as a social worker. "I am not a politician and I would go back to social work as soon as my mission is fulfilled," Bandodkar used to say.

Almeida's post-Liberation despondency, which represented the mood of the elite, mistakenly portrayed the poor as innocent persons and the 'social workers' as villains. According to him, the agricultural tenants and labourers of Goa had been illiterate and lazy until they came under the influence of 'unscruplous leadership' who promised them 'heaven and earth.' It was only then that they started flooding the government with petitions, saying that "the cultivator in Goa lived a harassed life, when, in reality, the truth was quite a different one." The hubris of the poor was hitting the elite right on the nose.

Freedom was threatening the old order. In Portuguese Goa, agriculture was not a full-time activity. The 58 per cent of all inhabitants whose main occupation was agriculture also earned incomes from other occupations. Agriculture in Portuguese Goa was not pursued for profit but for growing enough rice and coconuts for the family. As much as 87 per cent of the rice-fields were cropped only once a year. Plantations of coconuts and cashewnuts were done without a method or any care: they grew on the slopes of hills amid minor forests or in open pastures, without irrigation or application of any cultivation or manuring skills. The Portuguese never seriously engaged themselves with the task of providing incentives, like new techniques or credit, to the farmers. Government investment in irrigation was virtually non-existent; Goan peasants drew water from their old village tanks, wells or the monsoon. Productivity was low, and land was divided into small fragments.

The Portuguese never even once during their 450 years of rule considered promoting self-sufficiency in food. Goa was condemned for ever to be a net importer of foodgrains. In the years immediately preceding the Liberation, the colony was importing 30,000 tonnes of rice annually. Fresh vegetables and fruits were also in short supply, which was made up with the import of canned vegetables and fruits. Goa did not produce sufficient quantity of fresh milk, and again the deficit was met with the import of milk powder and condensed milk. In the second half of the 1950s, agricultural production fell to the lowest levels in the colony due to the imposition of the Economic Blockade by India, which closed the channels of export of commodities like coconuts and arecanuts to the mainland, and the shortage of field labour caused by the heavy demand for labour from the iron ore mines which were witnessing a postwar boom.

Goa's Village Communes

How can agriculture be developed on modern lines in Goa? How can it be made more productive and efficient? How can Goa be made self-sufficient in food? These were the questions that afflicted the minds of Nehru and his colleagues first before they troubled Bandodkar. Nehru was a socialist without any ideological gods, but a socialist anyway, so he would always search for a solution, if he was faced with a problem, concerning 'equitable distribution of wealth.' If agriculture stagnated and India had to import foodgrains, the answer lay in land reforms: take away the land from the big landlord who does not pay attention to his land and redistribute it in parcels among the tenants and landless labourers who will pay all their attention to them. Direct involvement of the owner with the land will bring all-round improvements in land and inputs. The result will be higher productivity; and, the achievement of the goal — end of dependence on other countries for food.

Nehru's picture of agrarian inequality was essentially drawn from the experiences of the *zamindari* system prevalent during the British rule in the eastern and northern provinces of India which had allowed the *zamindars*, the landlords, to enjoy ownership of lands in perpetuity in lieu of a fixed rent for over 150 years. Denouncing *zamindari* as the principle obstacle to agricultural progress, Nehru prevailed over the concerned states to pass a legislation absolishing it. Accompanying this were also legislations providing for a ceiling on agricultural landholdings, distribution of surplus land seized from the landlords to the landless, security of tenure to the actual cultivator and so on. With the extension of Indian administration to Goa following the Liberation, the entire package of Nehru's land reform measures was sought to be enforced in Goa.

Nehru did not know anything about the peculiarities of the agrarian system prevalent in Goa; nor did his colleagues or bureaucrats. A blind application of the national land reforms policy could create obstacles in the path of agricultural progress, rather than removing them. The Portuguese had never fixed land rents in perpetuity with the landlords *(bhatcars)* as the British had done with the *zamindars*. Huge estates did not exist in Goa, and the *bhatcars* never held the absolute power of life and death over the tenant or labourer the *zamindars* did. Although during the most part of Portuguese rule Goa had been a flourishing market for slaves, there was no bonded labour in the villages.

The most unique institution in Goa's agrarian system was *gaocari*. At the time of Liberation, the *gaocaris (comunidades)* owned more than half of the paddy lands in Goa's coastal belt. All the male descendants of the founders aged twelve and above naturally inherited the membership of the *gaocari*. The *gaocari* was a kind of commune; all the village's land was not vested in the *gaocari*. The male founders owned private lands. And collectively as members of the *gaocari* they owned the rest of the village land. For the purpose of developing and exploiting its lands, the *gaocari* invited bids from among the *gaocars* or the *cuntocars*, the new settlers in the village who had no right in the *gaocari*. Over the years families from lower castes were provided homestead in the villages and used as a constant supply of labour by the *gaocars* and *gaocaris*. The income earned by the *gaocari* was mainly spent on community works; a part was distributed as share of profit, called *jono*, among the *gaocars*.

At the time of Liberation, according to Almeida, the average *gaocari* or *comunidade* was distributing 16 per cent of its earnings as *jono* or dividend among its members. The other items of expenditure were: 22 per cent on administrative expenses, 19 per cent on land tax and quit-rent, 16 per cent on ordinary and extraordinary services, 6 per cent on religious and social works, 2 per cent on amortization of loans and payment of interests and 19 per cent on miscellaneous heads.

In the ancient times, the *gaocaris* functioned like village republics which could run their affairs without a king. They paid no tax or revenue to any ruler. Authority was concentrated in the oligarchy of male descendants of the village founders. They even exercised civil and criminal powers. They organised village defence and were also responsible for the construction and maintenance of irrigation and flood protection works as well as public education.

In the centuries before the arrival of the Portuguese frequent wars were fought between Hindu and Muslim kings in the Deccan and the *gaocaris* were forced to contribute to the military expenses of one or the other ruler. After they ran out of their surpluses they sought loans from the new settlers, the *cuntocars*, as well as well-to-do *gaocars*. In exchange for the loans the *cuntocars* and *gaocars* were issued non-transferable shares by the *gaocari*. These shares entitled the *cuntocars* to a division of income of the *gaocari* but did not give them any right of participation in the administration of the institution.

Soon after their conquest, the Portuguese imposed their administration on the *gaocaris*. They passed a legislation entitling their local officials to overrule the decisions of the *gaocari* if they deemed it necessary. This was the first time in history that the *gaocaris* had lost their power to govern the village. And it only became from bad to worse. The Inquisition eventually crushed and mangled the *gaocaris*. Forced conversions led to depopulation of the villages, triggering off the tragic Goan diaspora in which *gaocars* found themselves scattered over several regions of India. In the disturbed situation too many disputes arose between the *gaocars* and the *cuntocars* which had to be arbitrated by the colonial authority, a phase that finally drew the curtains over the autonomy of the *gaocaris*. The Portuguese abolished several *gaocaris* and rented their villages out to individual landlords on a long lease, thus establishing total authority on the *gaocaris*.

In the villages where *gaocari* survived, the *cuntocars* fought with the *gaocars* for equality of rights. The number of new settlers having increased in the aftermath of the Inquisition the *cuntocars* began to press for the abolition of *gaocaris (comunidades)* and division of their lands between them and the *gaocars*. The Portuguese allowed not only the *cuntocars* but also outsiders to buy and sell the shares of the *comunidade*. There was soon a market in *comunidade* shares. The Portuguese had transformed village republics into oligarchic corporations.

A Land Reform Commission set up in 1963 found that the number of shareholders in the *comunidades* had risen to 30 per cent of the total membership by 1962. In the 227 *comunidades* in the eleven *concelhos*, sub-districts or talukas of Goa, there were about 36,000 *gaocars* and 15,000 shareholders. The transformation was most remarkable in the three *concelhos* of, Salcete, Mormugao and Ponda, where the shareholders far outnumbered the *gaocars*. In Salcete there were 3,000 *gaocars* and 6,300 shareholders, more than double the number; in Mormugao there were 526 *gaocars* and 1,500 shareholders, three times more; and in Ponda there were 750 *gaocars* and 1,560 shareholders, nearly double. These were gross figures for the *concelhos*; there were several *comunidades* where no *gaocars* were left; they had been entirely taken over by the shareholders.

Gaocaris — councils of male founders — had turned in several villages into associations a majority of whose members were not residents of the village. Of the total of 36,000 *gaocars* in the colony only 18,000 or 50 per cent were residing in the village; over 10,000 were living in other parts of Goa, and nearly 8,000 in places outside Goa. Among the shareholders, only 6,500 of the total of 15,000 or roughly 40 per cent were residents of the village, 8,000 were living in other parts of Goa and 480 outside Goa. The *gaocari*, thanks to the colonial intrigues, had given way to a form of absentee landlordism. And this strange and ironical form of village with founders living elsewhere was more common to the *concelhos* of Salcete, Bardez, Tiswadi and Mormugao, the Old Conquests.

Destiny of Tenants

Goa looks green because in its ascent from the seashore to the Sahyadri mountains the land is largely covered with rice-fields, cultivable fallow, tree crops and forests. In the coastal belt, that is the Old Conquests, rice was the main crop because the land was flat and suitable for ploughing, while in the uplands or the New Conquests, garden crops like cashew, coconuts and arecanuts dominated the output. Rice was also grown in the uplands but of a poor quality; the main cereals there were millets, like ragi, which people used as a substitute for rice. At the turn of 1960s, of the total land available for agricultural purposes in Goa, 34.60 per cent was given to food crops, mainly rice, 18.5 per cent to tree crops, 32.30 per cent to forests and 29 per cent to culturable waste. The ownership of the agricultural land was divided thus: private owners 54 per cent, government 32 per cent, *comunidades* 11 per cent, Hindu temples 3 per cent, Christian religious associations 0.3 per cent and municipalities and other institutions the rest.

Although in the overall figures of ownership of agricultural land, the share of *comunidades* came to 11 per cent, in the coastal region the picture was very different. The *comunidades* owned 46 per cent of all agricultural land in Bardez, 41 per cent in Tiswadi, 37 per cent in Salcete and 31 per cent in Mormugao. The government owned no lands in Bardez, Salcete and Mormugao and a mere 2.7 per cent in Tiswadi. Considering the fact that the *comunidades* were the largest single owners with an average of 40 per cent of agricultural land in their possession in the coastal region, it was hardly surprising that their membership became a very competitive affair, leading to a phenomenal growth in the number of shareholders.

The coastal region contained most of the territory's rice-fields, both of the *khazan* and *kher* types, which were comparatively more prized. The *khazan* were salty, muddy lands located by the riversides, prone to inundation by high tides in the sea. Over the centuries the *comunidades* had maintained embankments and sluice gates for the *khazan* lands. The *kher* were alluvial tracts located inland, away from the salty waters. The *comunidades* used to auction their lands for rice cultivation or tree plantations for 3 to 6 years on a fixed amount per hectare. There were no permanent tenants, although it was normal custom with the *comunidades* to renew the leases, provided no dispute arose over the use of land or payment of rent. Even the private landowners seldom changed their tenants.

Tenancy was the dominant form of land tenure in Goa before the Liberation. In 1956, an Agricultural Mission from Lisbon visited the colony to study the agricultural problem and it found that most of the lands, whether of the *comunidades* or private owners, were not cultivated by the title-holders but leased out to tenants. The share of leased to total land was 75 per cent in Salcete, Mormugao, Sattari and Canacona, 84 per cent in Sanguem and Quepem, 88 per cent in Ponda, 90 per cent in Bardez and Bicholim, 93 per cent in Pernem and 98.5 per cent in Tiswadi. The rest of the lands were self-cultivated or tilled on 'partnership' basis.

The word 'partnership' used by the Lisbon Mission was a misnomer. It was actually a form of tenancy that was known in the rest of India as sharecropping. The landlord leased out his land to a cultivator on a fifty-fifty basis of sharing the harvest, providing him some financial assistance toward the costs of irrigation, manuring and land tax. If these lands are added to the lands mentioned as leased by the Mission, the actual incidence of tenancy rose from 75 per cent to 85 per cent in Salcete, Mormugao and Canacona, from 84 per cent to 87 per cent in Sanguem, from 84 per cent in Quepem to 88 per cent, from 88 per cent in Ponda to 90 per cent and from 98.5 per cent in Tiswadi to 99 per cent.

Apart from tenancy, there was another form of relationship between the landowners and labourers. It was called *mundcari*. The *mundcar* was a landless, homeless person who was given by the *bhatcar*, the landowner, a small plot and a loan *(mund)* to construct a dwelling in lieu of his services as a caretaker of his properties. The *mundcar* paid no rent for the plot or his dwelling; nor gave back the *mund* unless he wanted to leave and go elsewhere. His main duty was to ward off cattle and thieves from the *bhatcar's* coconut plantations and rice-fields. He was also labour-at-hand for the *bhatcar* whenever he needed any, at home or in the fields, and most of such toil would be poorly paid in cash or kind. At the time of plucking of coconuts on the *bhatcar's* properties, the *mundcar* also got a share, say, 6 to every 100 nuts plucked. Legally, the *bhatcar* owned not only the plot but also the dwelling of the *mundcar*, made usually of mud and sometimes of stone; and he could throw him out whenever he wanted.

In practice, however, the *mundcar* was seldom thrown out. Because in most cases an intimate relationship developed between him and the *bhatcar*. Many of the *bhatcars* took women in the *mundcars'* families as their concubines — these women were called *naikins* — who often even bore children to them, like the *devadasis* of the temples. However it was also true that when the need arose, like a marriage or illness in the *mundcar's* family, the *bhatcar* felt obliged to provide help.

The *mundcars* have sometimes been identified as bonded labourers, but they were not so. They were not serving the *bhatcars* generation after generation to pay off debts their forefathers had taken. They were free to leave. Had they been bonded the large-scale emigration which started in the colony at the turn of the 19th century would not have been possible. In some cases the *mundcars* were also agricultural tenants of the *bhatcar*. But not all agricultural tenants were *mundcars* and not all *mundcars* were agricultural tenants. However, it was true that the overwhelming majority of the tenants and *mundcars* came from the lower castes.

The Benign Landowners

Unlike in most parts of India, the landlord-tenant or landlord-*mundcar* relationship in Goa did not have those extremely exploitative, oppressive and violent features. The gross social and economic inequalities were involved in it of course, but the general attitude of the landowning class was benign and moderate.

A number of historical factors shaped this attitude. The first was the strong institutional presence of Christianity: it kept the Hindu landlords in perennial fear that their labourers might switch religion if they proved bloodsucking and barbarous to them. Through their benevolence and good treatment the landlords could maintain the Hindu solidarity in order to keep an aggressive Christianity at bay.

The attitude of the Christian landlords, who were converts from the Brahman and Maratha castes, was partly shaped by the church which constantly preached equality among the flock. Even though the high-caste *Bamonn* and *Chardo* converts never married or socially mingled with the low caste converts, the statutes and norms of the church restrained them from subjecting the *Sudir* tenants to cruelties. Thus, both among the Hindu and converted landlords, it was the dominant Christian environment that shaped their moderate and tolerant attitude.

In this possibly the Portuguese national character also played a role. By and large the Portuguese did not make any discrimination at the social level; unlike in British India, there were no 'Indians-and-dogs-not-allowed' clubs in Goa; the two clubs that existed had both the Portuguese and natives as members. The Portuguese officials and soldiers drank, laughed and roamed around and played football with the natives. The colonial government encouraged the children from the lower castes to go to school and study with the children of the landed gentry. In public transport people of all classes sat together.

Then there was the emigration factor. Tens of thousands of Goan cultivators and labourers had left their native villages to take up work as cabin crew, stewards and cooks on the British ships, as domestic maids, nurses and governesses in Mumbai, Kolkata, Bangalore and other cities of India, and as lower-ranked officials and skilled labour in the colonies of British and Portuguese Africa. The sole aim of the immigrants was to earn good money, and how really their lot improved showed in the money orders they sent home. Until the mining boom of the 1950s brought unexpected incomes to the mineowners and workers, the people of Goa had depended on the remittances of the immigrants.

The shortage of labour due to large-scale emigration did not allow any room to the landlords to treat their tenants and labourers brutally. On the contrary, the landlords had to be over-indulgent, like giving the labourer more than one peg of coconut *feni* that was customary offer at the end of his daily work, in order to keep him in good humour. When mining opened new avenues for employment, the shortage of labour became more acute for agriculture. Mining brought wages to the labourers the kind of which they had never dreamt of.

A *bhatcar* from Bicholim, one of the main centres of iron ore mining, recalled: "It caused us a lot of heartburn, but that was the reality and we had to face it. The *mundcar* of yesterday had become the driver of a mine truck or a loader, earning hundreds of rupees as his monthly salary where he earned less than fifty. He moved around wearing trousers of latest fashions, shoes, a Swiss watch and gold rings." The cash-rich mine workers not only enlivened the textiles and consumer goods market but they also began to influence the economics of agriculture.

The Land Reform Commission found that in the 1961 auction new bidders replaced as many as 3,500 old tenants of the *comunidades*. One of the major factors the Commission traced this phenomenon to was 'greater availability of funds with agriculturists earned in mining and other employments.' What was more, the bids had in many cases exceeded the reserve price fixed for the lease. The dispossession triggered off unrest among the old tenants, who had cultivated the lands at least for 12 years preceding, with the *comunidades* twice renewing their leases.

Responding to their petitions, the governor of liberated Goa asked them to apply for the restoration of the land they had lost to the new bidders and also reduced the ceiling of rent payable by a tenant to the *comunidade* to 50 per cent of the gross produce. The tenants were given relief on commutation of rent in kind to cash too. If a tenant wanted to commute his rent thus he had to pay only Rs 24 per *khandy* of paddy (a measure of 160 litres) instead of the previous rate of Rs 32 per *khandy*.

Bandodkar's Land Reforms

With these reliefs to the *comunidade* tenants, the land reforms in Goa had begun. The next few months saw the governor pass an order banning the eviction of tenants who were in possession of the land on July 1, 1962. This was applicable to both private and *comunidade* lands. The rent payable to a *comunidade* already reduced to 50 per cent of the gross produce or less, the governor directed the rent payable to private landowners also to be cut down by 20 per cent.

"There is no doubt," the Land Reform Commission observed, "that these measures brought a substantial measure of relief not only to the tenants of *comunidade* lands but also to tenants of private lands. The position now is that tenants all over Goa with a few exceptions have in fact been enjoying security of tenure. In the *comunidade* lands there has hardly been any displacement of tenants since 1949. In private lands, though no records are available, our enquiries reveal that, by and large, it has been customary not to change a tenant except for special default on his part by way of non-payment of rent or neglect of land."

In its recommendations, the Commission gave top priority to security of tenure, confirming the governor's cut-off date of July 1, 1962, regardless of whether the tenant leased in the land of a private landlord or a *comunidade*. However, a small landowner who had no other means of sustenance but the leased-out land was given a right of resumption of his property from the tenant. On rents the Commission warned against a sudden huge reduction, due to the fact, firstly, that the *comunidade* and private landowners may neglect the irrigation and other developmental works they had been undertaking for centuries for paucity of funds, and secondly, that the majority of private landowners being small they needed time to find additional sources of income for buying rice and coconuts that they used to get from their properties.

In its scheme of gradual rent reduction, the ceiling for *khazan*, coastal salty land, was placed at one-thirds of the gross produce, for *kher*, inland sandy land, one-fourths, and for *morod*, hillside land, one-sixths, provided the government made up for the loss of income to the *comunidade* and private landowners with a 50 per cent subsidy for agricultural development works. Desperate to save the *comunidades* from collapse, the Commission asked the government to also bear the administrative costs of running them, leaving more funds in their kitty for improving agricultural yields. The *comunidades* should be reorganised as a village co-operative society of the resident *gaocars*, many of whom were cultivators, and the tenants, retaining the non-resident *gaocars* only as honorary members. For a few years, a ceiling, based on the average of preceding four years 1958-62, should be fixed on the dividends of the *gaocars*.

When the Commission's recommendations reached into Bandodkar's hands he found them too lenient with the *comunidades* and private landowners. He fixed a flat rent of one-sixths of the gross produce for all types of lands and all types of landlords. This wrought havoc in the Goan countryside. Already in the past two or three years, the *comunidades* had seen their rent fall from 50 to 40 per cent. With a rent of 16 per cent under Bandodkar's legislation, they would just be paralysed. As though anticipating the wailings of the *comunidades*,

Bandodkar entrusted the task of maintenance and conservation of irrigation works, and of meeting of all the costs thereof, to the tenants. As far as the small landowners were concerned, the legislation gave no right of resumption to them; instead a section on 'Termination of tenancy' was incorporated, allowing a few grounds on which a landlord could terminate the tenancy but a hundred constraints were laid down on his way so that he could never possibly do it legally.

What a blind legislation it was! Tenants individually were expected to repair and conserve community irrigation works! Too poor until yesterday to feed themselves, the tenants could not have turned from land labourers to good managers of resources overnight. And then a tenant was merely a tenant after all; the land belonged to the *comunidade* and landowners. All that Bandodkar had promised him was security in his tenancy and reduction of rent to one-sixths of the gross produce. Was the tenant supposed to spend the higher income resulting from rent reduction upon the river embankments, sluice gates, tanks and wells and drainage? Why prevent him from using it to buy his children new clothes or send his adult son to Mumbai for trying his luck with a shipping company?

Bandodkar ought to have brought in his government to fill the institutional vacuum caused by the removal of *comunidades* and landowners from the responsibility of maintaining irrigation works. Or provided them with sufficient finance to carry out their traditional responsibility. In the later years the Goa government was to take up some river irrigation projects, but the damages caused by the first land reform legislation in the Union Territory to the embankments, tanks, wells and drainage systems were irremediable. The most valued heritage in terms of the land development technique of the Goan people, the *khazan* embankments were to suffer further damages when succeeding governments encouraged large farms in the backwaters for prawn culture for export purposes.

As tenants matured to overcome fatalism, Bandodkar, subsequent to the first legislation, went on introducing amendments to consolidate and improve their position vis-a-vis the landlords. One of the most important of these amendments granted the tenants the right of first purchase to the lands they were tilling. If the landlord wanted to sell his land, he had to first ask his tenant and give him sufficient time to decide on the purchase. The government would not allow the landlord to fix an arbitrary price for his land, and it would arrange for a loan for the tenant, if he didn't have money, to purchase the land.

From the security of tenure to the right of first purchase: the tenant had really benefitted under the Bandodkar regime. But it was left to Bandodkar's daughter Shashikala Kakodkar, who became chief minister following his death, to complete the task of granting full rights to the tenants. Her amendment in 1976 declared the leased lands as 'deemed to have been purchased' by the tenants, and fixed the purchase price to 'fifteen times the net average annual income of the land for the three years immediately preceding,' or, in cash value, from Rs 1,600 to Rs 4,000 per hectare depending on the type of land, whichever was lower. The tenant was given the option of paying the entire purchase price in lump sum or in ten equal instalments.

A petition before the judicial commissioner of Goa on behalf of the landlords challenged the Shashikala amendment as an unjustifiable piece of legislation, since it did not allow the owners a right of resumption and did not impose a ceiling on the area the tenants could hold. It was not uncommon for a tenant to lease in lands from several landlords, either in the same village or in different villages, and by this piece of legislation, he would become the owner of all the lands. Making the tenants big landlords went against the spirit of land reforms, said the petition. The judicial commissioner upheld the landlords' view and struck down the amendment as unconstitutional. However, the Goa government went in appeal to the Supreme Court and got the judicial commissioner's order vacated.

Some months before the Shashikala amendment, another legislation was passed; this one banned the eviction of the *mundcars* from their dwellings in the *bhatcar's* property. According to the act, the *mundcar* was 'deemed to have purchased' the dwelling or a plot of approximately 300 square metres from the landlord at market value. This legislation attacked the Goan landlord's most cherished system of feudal privileges and hence generated a lot of disputes and angry encounters in the Goan countryside. A study by a committee headed by Goa's agriculture minister Tony Fernandes in 1966 had found that there were 41,000 *mundcars* in the territory who, if their families were included, formed more than 32 per cent of the territory's population. The largest concentration of *mundcars* was in the Old Conquests. Occupation-wise, most of the *mundcars* were engaged in agricultural tenancy or labour, but there were also fishermen, goldsmiths, barbers, cartmen, priests, tailors and teachers among them.

Poor as they were, the *mundcars* did not get instant relief from the legislation. They had to struggle against the bureaucracy which refused to take up their cases with urgency. Vaman R Naik in his unpublished doctoral thesis titled *A study of agrarian relations in Goa* in 1991 observed that the government, even 15 years after the legislation, had not completed the registration of the *mundcars* which was necessary for their entitlement to the land on which their dwelling stood. Both the applications, the one for registration and the other for the purchase of the dwelling or plot, said Naik, should have been disposed of within weeks. But they had taken years.

There were other problems faced by *mundcars*, noted Naik. The legislation had been made applicable only to the private landowners and not to *comunidades*, temples, churches and mosques, thus leaving out a significant section. Though the Tony Fernandes committee had promised it, the government had failed to make provisions for interest-free, long-term loans to the *mundcars* for meeting the cost of purchase of the dwelling from the landlord. Then the *mundcars* who had been benefitted by it were finding it difficult to get 'no objection certificates' from the owners of adjoining properties for the purpose of drawing electricity lines or piped water supply. Even when the *mundcars* were ready to pay for the damages to the owners of the adjoining properties the matter was not easily resolved due to resistance of their neighbours. The government had not yet clarified, Naik said, that in case of destruction of his dwelling, the *mundcar* could reconstruct his house with the permission of the local authority.

Charisma without Vision

The principal objective of Nehru's national land reform policy, which his governor introduced in Goa and Bandodkar and his daughter pursued, had been to clear the path for agricultural progress. Had the objective been achieved? Had land reforms unleashed the productive energies of the Goan peasant? Had the land legislations increased the cultivated area, the crop yield, the intensity of cropping? A search for answers led to depressing revelations. It was true that the tenants had got the land and the *mundcars* the homestead. But that was all. The steps that were needed to enable them to unleash their productive energies were not taken. The infrastructure required for promoting modern agricultural develoment was never created. This when the land reforms had destroyed the traditional infrastructure.

Traditional irrigation, for instance — and irrigation was the most basic input — had been developed and maintained by the *gaocaris*. The Land Reforms Commission gave this picture of traditional irrigation available at the time of Liberation:

"No proper data regarding irrigated area is available. A rough estimate has put the area at 6,070 hectares. The crops most benefitted are paddy, arecanut, sugarcane and vegetables. The main sources of irrigation are storage tanks, small diversion *bhandaras* (reservoirs), *nalas* (channels), springs and wells. There are no major irrigation works. The only two government canals are Candeapar and Paroda which are diversion works on rivers having a post-monsoon flow. However, the area actually irrigated by these canals is small. We may refer to the irrigation of Vangana (rabi crop of rice) which gets its water supply from storage tanks of which there are over 400 located mostly in Salcete and Bardez. The age-old practice is to store rain water from the receding monsoon in the fields at the higher levels and then utilise the water for irrigating the low-lying areas. In the interior tract, especially in Ponda and Bicholim where rivers have a post-monsoon flow, small *kutcha* (clay) diversion works are constructed to irrigate rice fields and arecanut gardens. Well irrigation is found mostly in Pernem and Bardez and low-lying areas."

Goa received a very high annual rainfall, about 3,000 mm, but most of it was received during the monsoon months from June to September and due to lack of a proper watershed management, the rainwater made its way to the sea. And then for eight months from October to May there was drought causing low production of annual and perennial crops.

In 1986, twenty-five years after Liberation, only 8.6 per cent of the total sown area was irrigated in Goa, compared to the all-India average of 29.2 per cent. In 1993-94, about 16 per cent of the total sown area was irrigated, and by 1996 about 19 per cent. This was less than half of the target set by the mid-1990s. Little wonder the area sown more than once remained low in the state. Only 2.32 per cent of the land was sown more than once in 1986-87, a figure which rose marginally to 3.39 per cent in 1989-90 and doubled to 6.62 per cent in

1993-94. "The low net sown area implies," said Vijay Paranjpe in his study of the Selaulim irrigation project, "that the potential for development of agriculture in Goa is very high. More land could be brought under cultivation if irrigation is assured, and more scientific methods of farming implemented. Employment can be generated."

The Selaulim project, Bandodkar's most ambitious irrigation project, proved to be a disaster. The project involved construction of a large dam across the Sanguem river in southern Goa. The Central Water Commission of the government of India was asked to prepare a project report and it took six years to do it. The report, which it submitted in 1972, provided for the design of a dual-purpose dam, one that was to irrigate 14,500 hectares of land and also store 35 million gallons of water for domestic and industrial consumers daily. Bandodkar immediately sanctioned the Rs 96 million-project but the work did not start until 1976. By 1982 the project was supposed to be completed; until the late 1990s it had not been. Meanwhile the cost of the project was revised to Rs 350 million in 1981, Rs 730 million in 1985, Rs 1,530 million in 1995 and Rs 1,600 million by 2001. After paying fifteen times the original cost and taking nearly two decades from the time of sanction to partially complete the largest dam project in the state, the government was able to create an irrigation potential of only 8,224 hectares or a little over fifty per cent of the promised coverage.

But even this was *potential*. The actual use was much less. In 1987, out of a potential of 2,118 hectares the demand was only from 657 hectares. The then irrigation minister lamented that "There was plenty of water for irrigation but there were hardly any takers." He said he failed to understand why this was so when his government was offering the farmers financial assistance and subsidies on seeds, fertilisers and other inputs. The environmentalists provided answers to the minister's puzzle: first, sugarcane, which required a lot of irrigation, gave low yields in the local soil, so farmers had not gone for it. Secondly, farmers preferred to grow cash crops like cashew, coconut and mango, rather than rice which fetched them marginal profit, side by side with food crops that required less water.

The state government put out figures in early 2002, claiming that the Selaulim project had created by December 2001 an irrigation potential of 5,229 hectares out of which 2,700 hectares was utilised.

Even more monumental is the waste of resources in the Tillari irrigation project. This was a joint venture of Maharashtra and Goa across the Tillari river at Tillarwadi village in the bordering Sindhudurg district of Maharashtra. It was supposed to irrigate on its completion about 17,000 hectares in the Bicholim, Bardez and Pernem talukas of North Goa and 6,676 hectares in the Sindhudurg district of Maharashtra. Apart from sharing the cost of the project, Goa was also to make allocations for the canal branches and distributories for water inside the state. The original estimated cost of the project at 1988 rates was Rs 2,172 million, which has gone up to Rs 7,767 million at 2000 rates, of which the major share is Goa's at Rs 5,380 million. However, according to a government assessment, only 200 hectares of irrigation potential has been created and even this is not utilised.

Not Enough Rice

Traditional irrigation had been ruined with the ruin of the *comunidade*. With its land parcelled out to tenants the *comunidade's* revenue sharply declined, leaving it in no position to maintain the irrigation works. Bandodkar's answer to the problem was unrealistic: he asked the tenants to take the responsibility. The tenants were hardly in a position to take care of themselves, what to speak of community works. With the land reforms, the percentage of uneconomical, marginal holdings (below 1 hectare) to total holdings had risen from 29 in 1960-61 to 66 in 1970-71 and to 77 in 1985-86. And the percentage of small holdings (below 2 hectares) to total holdings rose from 86 per cent in 1960-61 to 90 per cent in 1985-86. The total area under small holdings rose from 15 per cent in 1960 to 44 per cent in 1990-91. In contrast, the total area under large holdings (above 2 hectares) fell from 85 per cent to 56 per cent in 1990-91.

Land was also fragmented in the reforms. The average size of operational holding, which was 2.40 hectares in 1960, declined to 1.34 hectares in 1970-71, 1.14 hectares in 1976-77, increased slightly to 1.19 hectares in 1980-81 and dropped again to 1.03 hectares in 1985-86. One of the main reasons for the falling size of the holding was the division of the tenant's property among his brothers. During the period from 1970-71 to 1985-86, the area held by wholly owned and self-operated holdings had risen from 32 to 54 per cent of the total holdings, and that held by wholly rented holdings fallen from 39 to 19 per cent. This showed that while more and more tenants had acquired land from the landlords, an increasing number of them had also been forced to partition their acquisitions among their brothers, who might or might not have been engaged in cultivation. Land had become a valued possession.

And why not! The industrialisation, the expansion of the size of the government, the execution of public works, the tourism boom required land and more land for factories, hotels, shops and housing. Thus, even before anybody had the time to think of how to undo the damages the land reforms of Nehru and Bandodkar had inflicted on Goa's agriculture, even before the tenants could be motivated to adopt modern practices and improve production, the scene had turned adverse for agriculture. Land had ceased to be a means of food production: it had become a marketable commodity. Land reforms had paved the way for industrialisation and urbanisation.

Agriculture had always given low returns in Goa, but with the neglect of the traditional irrigation and soil conservation works following land reforms, followed by the emergence of a market in land — with prices which were a hundred or more times the existing value — cultivators lost interest in agriculture. The sight of agricultural plots lying fallow became common. The booming market in land gave rise to pervasive corruption in the government. Those who had ceased to be cultivators and wanted to sell their land had to get the land use changed for it from agricultural to non-agricultural purposes. For this reason too the plot had to be left uncultivated for some years. The change of land use, popularly known as 'conversion,' involved payment of bribes from the minister right down to the last clerk. The logic behind taking a bribe was simple: if you are going to sell your plot after conversion at Rs 1,000 per square metre you must pay Rs 100 to us.

Between the year 1961 and 1971, the number of cultivators in Goa declined from 104,139 to 60,519, or by 42 per cent. By 1981 the number dropped to 58,376, and by 1991 to 56,528. In the thirty years of land reforms, thus, only 56 per cent of cultivators had survived, the rest presumably having sold their properties and moved to other professions. The trend of declining importance of agriculture was also visible in the figures of labour force. Of the total labour force, agriculture had a very high share of 58.3 per cent in 1960, which fell to 38.33 per cent in 1971 and drastically to 28.57 per cent in 1981 and to 24 per cent in 1991.

Not only in employment, agriculture's share in the net state domestic product of Goa also declined. Whereas in 1970-71, agriculture contributed 27.1 per cent of the NSDP at constant prices, in 1980-81 its share fell to 18 per cent, in 1985-86 to 15 per cent, in 1990-91 to 10.8 per cent and in 1993-94 to 9.8 per cent. Vaman Naik observed, "A declining share of agriculture in the national income is often regarded as an indicator of economic development. But such an inference is justifiable only if, though the relative share of agriculture is falling, the absolute share of this sector is rising at an appreciable rate and that too fairly continuously. In Goa, though the relative share of agriculture in the net state domestic product has been declining, the absolute share has not been growing appreciably. In fact the agricultural sector exhibits an erratic way of growth."

Agriculture often registered a negative growth. Although the net area sown increased, as did productivity, Goa continued to be highly deficit in cereals, pulses, vegetables, milk, poultry and other commodities. Between 1960 and 1995 the area cropped with rice increased from 50,300 hectares to 54,072 hectares, and its production from 53,300 tonnes to 138,000 tonnes; in terms of per hectare yield, the rise was from 1.05 tonnes to 2.55 tonnes. The area under cashew expanded from 32,500 hectares to 49,600 hectares and its production from 3,000 tonnes to 13,200 tonnes. The area under coconut grew from 18,000 hectares to 24,000 hectares and its production from 70 million nuts to 116 million nuts. Of vegetables the coverage and production had risen most dramatically: from 1,500 tonnes in 2,500 hectares to 67,000 tonnes in 7,350 hectares. In spite of this growth, the state had to import over 32,000 tonnes of rice, 40,000 tonnes of vegetables and 15,000 tonnes of pulses. The food deficit increased in the years when the crops suffered as a result of natural factors.

The problems of rainfed agriculture were compounded by degraded soils. The state agriculture department's report in 1996, titled *Advances in agriculture* said 44 per cent of the total geographical area of Goa was 'affected by various soil degradation problems induced by human intervention.' One of the reasons, said the report, was the degradation of the forests. "Forests," it pointed out, "have decreased due to widescale private encroachment and also allotment of forest lands to cultivators for agricultural purposes."

On this subject Paranjpe observed: "Prior to 1961, forests were not managed in any way and they were also not 'worked.' However the monster of 'scientific forestry' hit Goa in 1963 and the evergreen moist deciduous forests were clearfelled for 14 years. The clearfelled areas, instead of being planted with indigenous varieties, were planted with teak, acacia, auriculiformia and eucalyptus, purely for earning revenue over an area of 28,582 hectares. However, the blunder was soon realised and since 1977 this practice was officially discontinued, though barring the Western Ghat areas, clearfelling still goes on surreptitiously. This proved to be very damaging." Further damage to the soil was caused by the lack of practice of multi-cropping by the farmers. Crop rotation, like paddy-groundnut-paddy, nourished the soil and controlled pests and diseases, and so did intercropping with fruit-bearing and nitrogen-fixing trees.

The Portuguese had never nursed the illusion of making Goa agriculturally advanced. They never made investments for agricultural development. Partly it was due to their own poverty: they had to struggle hard even to find funds to meet the administrative costs of the colony year after year. Their poverty was so well-known among the people that they had woven numerous stories about it. One of them ran thus: once a group of choir singers approached the governor general of Goa for financial assistance. The governor general frankly told them: "I have no money to pay the people who cry. How do you expect me to pay those who sing?" Another story had some Christians asking the governor general to provide them transport for a long pilgrimage. "If you are truly faithful you should go walking," the governor general coolly said. In yet another story, a delegation of nuns sought an audience with the governor general to apprise him of the dilapidated state of their chapel and ask for an official grant to renovate it. As the nuns were narrating the condition of their chapel they broke into tears. Seeing them cry, the governor general also began to cry. The governor general's secretary looked baffled. After the nuns left, the secretary politely asked the governor general what had made him cry. The governor general replied, "I had to cry only once. But these poor sisters are going to cry forever since their chapel is going to fall."

But it was not just poverty: the Portuguese also let Goa stagnate by political design. With not much investment, Goa could have produced enough rice, vegetables and fish for its needs, but this potential was never tapped, since economic development would also have brought political consciousness and courage to stand up to the colonial rulers.

Portuguese Goa imported most of its cereals, vegetables, milk and other essential commodities from British India. It was this over-dependence that had encouraged Nehru to impose an Economic Blockade on Goa. Nehru had calculated that the Portuguese would fail to withstand the blockade and be forced to surrender. But, helped by Pakistan, the Portuguese filled the Goan market with canned vegetables, frozen foods, milk powder and condensed milk imported by the sea route via Karachi.

Dependence on the outside world for food and other requirements had become the destiny of Goa. Even with Liberation and Bandodkar's land reforms Goa failed to produce enough rice, vegetables and dairy. With a market emerging in land and agriculture declining as a consquence, dependence on the outside world for food increased. The number of cultivators declined by 26 per cent and the number of agricultural labourers by 19 per cent between 1991 and 2001. During the same period, the number of workers in the household industry rose by 43 per cent and that of workers in other categories by 26 per cent. In 2002, more than four decades after Liberation, the bulk of Goa's demand for rice, pulses, vegetables, milk, eggs, chicken and spices were met by imports. With globalisation, cheaper arecanuts and coconuts flooded Goa's market from other parts of Asia, threatening indigenous growers. The state government had to announce support prices to local growers of coconuts and arecanuts in view of the fall in prices.

There are overwhelming signs that the focus of agricultural development in the state will be vegetable and fruit crops, rather than rice and other cereals. Horticulture in 2001 covered about 60 per cent of the total cultivated area and this coverage was going to increase in the years to come with the state government accepting it as 'the key to rural prosperity and creation of employment.' The agricultural export from Goa was poor, amounting to 200 tonnes of cashew kernels shipped to the US and Japan. Cashew and coconut are the two main horticultural crops in the state but a lot needs to be done to cut down on their cost of production and improve their quality and yield. There is a good scope for developing cultivation of vegetables, seasonal fruits like mangoes and medicinal plants.

4
Perils of Progress

One must not lose sight of the fact that any development has a price to be paid. Dislocation and rehabilitation are an integral part of this process. One has only to ensure that development decisions are based on a strict cost-benefit analysis which should lay due emphasis on social costs.
—Prabhakar Angle, Goan economist

The Mining Boom

One of major reasons why the Portuguese managed to withstand Nehru's Economic Blockade was the sudden revolution the exploitation of the iron ore mines and allied commercial activities had brought in the economy of Goa. Both the Goan businessmen and the colonial state became flush with money, valuables and hot foreign exchange, with which they imported enough essential goods via Karachi to defeat Indian attempts to throttle them. Goa's red earth had not even given its people sufficient rice all these centuries; but now, in the form of iron ore, it was producing gold.

And they had called it a 'Red Gold Rush' when the first iron ore mines opened in the mid-1940s. Cities of Europe and Japan devastated in the Second World War required enormous amounts of iron and steel for their reconstruction. The iron ore found in Goa was of very low grade, of 62 per cent ferrous content or even less, a type which was thrown out as reject in the mines in the other parts of India or abroad, because it did not lend itself readily to conversion into value-added products, such as pig iron, sponge iron or steel. However, postwar Europe and Japan needed to keep the costs of rebuilding under control; so they found it a cheaper option to blend Goa's low-grade iron ore with the finer iron ore grades from other countries.

The cash-starved Portuguese government liberally granted leases for prospecting and working of mines, and within a short span the number of mining lease-holders zoomed to 400. The scramble among

Goan entrepreneurs for a lease was not only due to the enormous profits from iron ore export but also due to low taxes on minerals. Peasants abandoned their rice-fields to work in the pits dug up with primitive machinery on the forested hill slopes. Neither the lease-holders, who came from the landed and trading classes, nor the peasants had ever seen so much money. Overnight, the iron ore mines emerged as an alternative to emigration, offering jobs to thousands of hands that had ploughed agricultural fields or plucked coconuts. The economy of Goa had ceased to be agrarian.

With the mining boom — the production of iron ore more than doubled between 1956 and 1960 from 2.45 million tons to 5.86 million tons — scores of new businesses opened in trade, transport, and allied sectors throughout Goa, giving employment to a large number of former farm labourers. By 1960 the mines and the related businesses in trade, transport and export employed about 18 per cent of total labour, the manufacturing and construction sectors employing only 7.4 per cent. The same year the share of mining and mining-related businesses in the state income was 62.6 per cent, while manufacturing and construction contributed 8.8 per cent, agriculture 22.6 per cent and the income earned from abroad 7.3 per cent. The contribution to the state income per earner the same year in terms of rupees was: mining and mining-related businesses, Rs 6,888, manufacturing and construction, Rs 1,166, and agriculture, Rs 369.

Not only iron ore, the red earth also yielded manganese ore, bauxite and China clay. In 1947, when ore exports began, only 14 tonnes of iron ore (worth Rs 400) and 100 tonnes of manganese ore (worth Rs 4,000) were exported. In 1957, 2.7 million tonnes of iron ore valued at Rs 82 million and 130,000 tonnes of manganese ore valued at Rs 21 million were exported. In 1967, 7.2 million tonnes of iron ore worth Rs 324 million were exported: the figures for 1977 were 9.4 million tonnes worth Rs 675 million, for 1987, 9.8 million tonnes worth Rs 1,406 million, and for 1994, 140 million tonnes worth Rs 5,319 million. The manganese ore deposits being limited, its exports had dropped from the mid-fifties onwards.

Iron ore exports became the lifeline of the Mormugao port. Till today iron ore makes over 90 per cent of its export cargo. The ore was brought from the mines upland in trucks to the loading site by the bank of a river where barges waited to carry it downstream to the port. Luck smiled on the mineowners once again, since had there been no inland waterways to carry their ore to the port, they would have had to transport it in trucks to the port which would have increased the costs of production and consequently the prices of the ore, making it prohibitive to buyers. And there would have been no mining industry.

Although the mines gave direct employment to about 8,000 people, they indirectly created jobs in mining-related businesses for about 20,000 people. And the mineowners invested their profits into manufacturing, tourism and other industries, creating more jobs away from agriculture.

A Better Life

It was industrialisation that was to change the character of Goa's economy and people's life completely. Portuguese Goa was an import-oriented economy, with hardly 60 small scale industries whose products included canned food, tiles, laundry soap and matches. The investments made in these units were very low; and the employment generated by them was small and often, seasonal. Even in postcolonial Goa, industrialisation did not pick up immediately. For more than a decade the local government unsuccessfully struggled to get entrepreneurs to set up units at their first two industrial estates at Corlim and Margao, despite the package of ready sheds, roads, telecommunications, power, water and public transport available at one place. However, during the period three large industries were established in the territory: Hindustan Ciba-Geigy, producing pharmaceuticals and chemicals, Zuari Agro Industries, producing fertilisers and MRF, producing tyres.

The scene changed with the declaration of Goa as an 'industrially backward area' by the central government in 1973 and the offer of investment subsidies. By 1980, there were more than 1,300 small scale industries set up in Goa, employing 12,800 persons. By 1990, there were 3,900 of them, employing over 26,000 persons; in addition there were 41 large and medium industries, providing jobs to 8,800 people. By 2000, there were 6,000 small scale industries employing 40,000 people; in addition, there were 140 large and medium industries employing 19,000 people.

In recent years industrialisation has moved away from the coastal belt and there is a trend toward an even dispersal of units. By 2000, the state had 18 industrial estates, at least one in each taluka. The industries produced a diverse range of goods, including cement, washing machines, electrical machinery, fertilisers and pesticides, but the single largest concentration was of pharmaceutical industries.

The share of manufacturing and service sectors in the state domestic product (SDP) and employment rose while that of the primary sector comprising agriculture and mining dropped. The share of manufacturing in the net SDP rose from 8.8 per cent in 1960 to 33 per cent by 2000. Agriculture, due to small size of average holdings, lack of irrigation and poor institutional support for credit and marketing, was not considered a profitable economic activity. On top of it the labour demanded higher wages in view of the shortage of hands caused by the mining boom. So agriculture employed a lesser number of people.

By the end of 1970s agriculture employed one-thirds of the labour. By 1991 it employed only 23.94 per cent of the total labour as against 64.81 per cent all-India. By 2001, agriculture employed less than 17 per cent of the total workforce. Jobs were being created mainly in the manufacturing and service sectors which were fast expanding and also paying better wages. By 1995, large, medium and small industries were providing employment to 45,000 persons, while agriculture employed 35,000 people. In 1999-2000, the service sector contributed 60 per cent of the state domestic product, the secondary sector 25 per cent and the primary sector only 15 per cent.

Mining had first brought sunshine to the starvation-diet, sub-subsistence agricultural economy of Goa; industrialisation had metamorphosed it. Goa's net SDP increased from Rs 290 million in 1960 to Rs 14 billion in 1993-94 and Rs 31.18 billion in 1996-97. The SDP grew at the rate of 6 per cent in the 1970s and 1980s. The per capita income at current prices increased from Rs 424 in 1960 to Rs 11,658 in 1993-94, by 27 times. In 1996-97, the per capita income rose to Rs 19,719 which was the next highest among all states after Delhi. Goa's SDP had grown at the rate of 6 per cent in the 1970s and 1980s while the GDP of India registered 4 to 5 per cent growth rate (Hindu growth rate); and this, in spite of the fact that the territory had joined the Union in the middle of the Third Five Year Plan.

Goa's other socio-economic indicators were also impressive: the per capita deposits of commercial banks in the state was Rs 10,617 in

1989, five times the national average. The number of vehicles in operation per 100,000 inhabitants was 7,050 in 1986-87 in the state against 931 in India. The length of roads per 100,000 inhabitants was 596 km in 1987-88 against 104 km in India. The per capita electricity consumed in the state in 1988-89 was 413 kwh against 154 kwh in India. The number of telephones per 1,000 inhabitants in 1985-86 was 12 against 5 in India.

The quality of life had improved beyond imagination in postcolonial Goa. People were eating better, travelling faster from one part of Goa to another and, moreover, had purchasing power.

Progress at a Price

However, the progress had come at a price. Industrialisation had created imbalances. More than two-thirds of the industries were set up in the four coastal talukas of Tiswadi, Bardez, Salcete and Mormugao. These talukas, forming the Old Conquests, had had some sort of an urban infrastructure even during the colonial days; with public investments flowing in after Liberation this infrastructure had been more developed. Entrepreneurs preferred these talukas for the location of their industries for reasons of lower costs of transportation of their raw materials and finished products. Bandodkar and the chief ministers who succeeded him had, in their eagerness to bring industries to Goa, surrendered to the entrepreneurs' preference. It was only later that the state government realized that industrialisation had gone ahead in a very uneven manner, developing the already relatively more developed coastal belt, thus increasing the gap between the Old Conquests and the New Conquests.

It was not only in the location of industries that the state had succumbed to the demands of the market forces. It was also in the type of industries. Although the chief ministers often talked of plans to develop agro-based and food-processing industries they never actually went beyond demagoguery. What was happening was industrialisation from above; it had no relation with Goa's agriculture or horticulture or traditional occupations. The state produced enormous quantities of coconuts but no industry existed to add value to them. The case was no different of cashews.

Most of the industries, large or small, used Goa as a production base. They brought raw materials from the other states, produced goods in Goa and transported them to the dealers or clients in the other states. The state government had been so solicitous of industries that they allowed the entrepreneurs to deprive the state of sales tax (which went to the state where their product was marketed). It was only in 2001 that the state government began to charge a minimum compensation for the loss of sales tax.

Concerns were growing in the state about the environmental pollution caused by industries. Scores of NGOs had sprung up to put pressure on the government not to allow polluting industries to come to Goa. No doubt, sometimes the fears of pollution were exaggerated; and public protest was set up even when adequate technology was available or used for keeping pollution at a safe level in a particular line of production.

A whole lot of factors had contributed to a strong movement against industrial pollution in Goa: people's legitimate concern for the preservation of ecological balance; people's attachment to the beauty of Goa, much of which was composed of greenery; ethnic Goan interest to allow only industries for which local talents and skills were available; a kind of parochial territorial consciousness; the Christian minority's interest in safeguarding its numerical importance from the influx of people from other states; and fear among sections of the Goan Hindu elite of the 'submergence' of Goan culture by the 'invasion' of other cultures. The public protests had achieved their purpose: the state government was very circumspect and choosy about the type of industries it wanted to be set up.

If it was in their hands, the NGOs would not allow any industry to be set up in Goa. But the state government could not let them do that. After all, it was mining and industries which had brought prosperity to Goa. A substantial part of the government revenue came from industries. With the attainment of statehood in 1987, Goa had come under increasing pressure to raise its own resources for development and reduce its dependence on the central government. It would have been impossible for the state to raise its own resources without a sustained industrial growth.

In order to achieve this, the government needed not only to get entrepreneurs to set up large and medium non-polluting industries but also to help the registered small scale industries go into production and to save the established small scale industries from closure. Many of the small scale industries registered with the directorate of industries were never set up. And many of the small scale industries set up became sick.

The state government had also betrayed a lack of vision in not linking industrialisation to education. Education had expanded phenomenally in postcolonial Goa; the enrolment in schools was 232 per thousand in 1987-88 against the all-India figure of 173; the enrolment in the colleges of Goa per million population in 1985-86 was 16,000 against 4,825 in the colleges of India; the literacy rate in the state in 1991 was 75.5 per cent which rose to 82.32 per cent in 2001. The chief ministers often expressed regret that the expansion of education had produced too many degree-holders of the generalist kind and too few diploma-holders in the technical streams. They talked of establishing a relationship between education and industry, of making courses job-oriented, but nothing ever seriously materialised. As a result, jobs in the industries went to immigrants from the other states.

The Hippie Invasion

The state government did not develop tourism in a planned manner, either, which grew as a major industry in the 1970s. More than 90 per cent of tourism in Goa was confined to the beaches in the coastal talukas of Bardez, Tiswadi, Salcete and Mormugao, where over two-thirds of all Goa's industries were also located. Thus, the growth of tourism widened the gap between coastal Goa and hinterland Goa. The families in the coastal belt earned more income due to the employment of all the adult married and unmarried members, which was not the case with the families in the hinterland to whom job or petty business opportunities were not many. The gap showed in the living standards of people.

Goa's beaches had attracted European and American tourists in small numbers even during the last decades of the colonial regime. The rest of India did not know much about Goa's beaches, since the colony had been isolated and virtually closed to them. The number of Indian tourists registered an increase in the years immediately following Liberation, forcing the Goa government to start acquiring land near the beaches and elsewhere to build bungalows, huts and lodges for them. But beyond expanding accommodation the government did pretty little for the tourists. Goa's shore was made up of a series of beaches flanked by low, green headlands jutting out into the sea, and the government left them just as Nature had created them. Goans, westerners, Indians had all been charmed by Calangute's long, suavely curving beach full of white sands — they had called it the queen of beaches — and yet the government had not even given them an access to the beach. The government did not have the financial resources to take up improvement in the tourist infrastructure. One of the reasons advanced by them was that though tourism was growing the number of tourists was still small and inadequate to generate good enough income for the government to make investments in value addition.

It was the beaches that had been left idyllic, virgin and untouched by a government handicapped by lack of funds that proved a magnet to the hippies in the late sixties. Long-haired, marijuana-smoking young and alienated nirvana-seekers from Europe and America, escaping the crass materialism of the West, moved in droves from their first mystical oriental camp at Kathmandu to Goa and made the twin beaches of Calangute and Baga their home. There being no access to Calangute, the iconoclastic ascetics made their entry to it through the Baga beach, 1.5 km away. Bordered by a headland on its right, the Baga beach curved like a half-moon and then stretched itself southward to meet the Calangute beach. Close to the half-moon the hippies found plenty of space for parking the caravans in which they had travelled from Kathmandu to Goa.

Although the flower children were seeking *moksha* (liberation of the soul) they were wise enough to carry enough stocks of eatables, drinks and other daily requirements in their vehicles — not to forget the material goods their culture asked them not to touch, like cameras, wrist watches, transistor radios and tape recorders which they brought along to sell to the local people for meeting any financial emergency, just in case. The hippies, whatever revolution they might have brought elsewhere on Planet Earth, only enhanced the attachment of the people to material goods in Goa.

By the turn of the 1970s more hippies arrived. The first hippies had lodged themselves in their caravans. The new ones, pitching their tents deeper into the mystical land, lived in shacks already existing or raised by them on a villager's property for a rent. They described themselves as a commune in which nobody was related to nobody and everybody was related to everybody. There was no possessiveness and there was plenty of sex. Hundreds of them walked, bathed or lay about the Baga and Calangute beaches, naked or in skimpy clothes, by day or night as if they owned them. They carried the 'sugar,' 'acid' and 'weeds' with them which they smoked in clay-pipes or cigarettes; and the 'smack' which they injected into their veins with a syringe they called 'artillery;' and of course all the music equipment that blew their tops off and transported them away from this damned world.

Shortly, drugs would start arriving from other parts of India by the land route, or from the Far East and the Persian Gulf in ships from which smaller boats picked up the marked consignments midsea.

The hippies were not the type of tourists the government or the Goans wanted, yet they were there, insisting upon to be understood and taken in. The residents of villages close to the Baga and Calangute beaches were shocked by the sight of the multitude of naked hippies walking or dancing or lying stoned as they willed. Sometimes the hippies 'on the high' would walk in their birthday suit through the streets of a village, driving people indoors.

In those days Baga and Calangute were like any other coastal Goan village: scattered laterite or mud houses with tiled roofs amidst tall and slightly bent coconut palms on the edge of rice-fields inland and fishing boats on the beach. A few landlords from other parts of Goa had their bungalows close to the two beaches where they stayed with their families during the summer. The family spent the afternoon on the beach, with the children running wild on the sandy stretch while the elders soaked themselves with sea water on the beach, because they believed that such soaking cured several ailments, like skin diseases and arthritis. There was no electricity, and life would vanish from the village with the sunset. People went to bed early and woke up early. Today the Calangute-Baga strip stays awake, alive and aglitter with coloured bulbs on tree branches of restaurants and shops that remain open well past midnight.

Drugs, Bohemianism, defiant nudity, vagabondism: the hippies represented a highly unwelcome bunch, but they were not chased away, stoned at or harassed. In the beginning there were isolated protests by villagers but then it subsided with a rationale that the hippies were after all preaching or practising those ugly things only among themselves. Unless their pernicious philosophy or perverse activities enrolled their own sons and daughters the Goans were not worried. This was negative reasoning; but there was a positive reason too why the hippies were tolerated. They brought in a little extra income to everyone in the coastal village: the houseowner who rented out rooms to them, the farmer who sold vegetables and fruits and herbs to them, the storekeeper who sold eggs, kerosene, cooking oil and candles to them, the country bar-owner who served Indian-made foreign liquor and local brew to them and the young men who helped them peddle drugs and the policemen who, with their palms greased, promised not to take any action against them. Then there was the love and affection that developed between the hippies and the beachside villagers in the flea market. When the flower children ran short of money they sold away their little possessions, like cameras, wrist watches and radios to the local people.

The presence of nude white females on Goa's beaches made sensational news in an India ruled for centuries by law-mouthing, armed and baton-wielding white males who prided in presenting their wives in public as elegantly — and elaborately — adorned *memsahibs*. News magazines carried snapshots of them on the beaches in various forms of undress, triggering off a tourist boom. Thousands of men from other states of India started coming to Goa by air, rail and road for witnessing the spectacle of the hippies walking the Baga and Calangute beaches nude, hot on spot with their cameras. Detached from the world as they were, the hippies were least bothered what was happening around them. This transcendence, together with the spicy stories the male tourists carried back home for their friends and neighbours, augmented the flow of visitors.

In the sixties and seventies, the Goa government had not done anything to attract tourists to the beaches. It was the young white nude female who had done it for them. She had added an exotic value to Goa's tourism. Little wonder the state government did not drive the hippies out of Goa despite their drug peddling and obscenity. The hippies had proved to be like worms on the hook of its fishing line to get tourists. Soon the hippies were to lose the way to their own revolution, but they had, quite unintentionally, unleashed a revolution in the economy of Goa.

The Tourism Boom

Within four or five years of the hippie-triggered boom the twin villages, Calangute and Baga, were transformed into twin towns. As many as 80,000 Indian tourists and 4,700 foreigners came to these beaches in 1970-71 alone. And their numbers went on rising every year. Land became scarce and costlier as hotels and guest houses sprung up. Villagers added rooms to their traditional houses for hire, with the family moving into an outhouse or a smaller accommodation nearby. An official survey in 1986 found that an average of 21 per cent of the foreign tourists coming to Goa preferred a hired house to a hotel (only 6 per cent of domestic tourists preferred this kind of accommodation.) In the Bardez taluka, which included the Baga-Calangute stretch, 27 per cent of foreign tourists (and 9 per cent of domestic tourists) stayed in hired houses.

Poorer men bought motorcycles and plied them as taxis, carrying their passenger on the pillion. Bazaars grew up where there was nothing, selling curios, jewellery, swimsuits, T-shirts, beads and handicrafts. The occupational pattern of the villages was completely altered. Agriculture vanished as the rice fields and orchards passed into the hands of hotels and shops. The number of fishermen and fishing boats dwindled. Yesterday's fishermen, tenants and landowners had taken a new *avataar* as innkeepers, restaurateurs, luxury coach owners, cooks, bartenders, storekeepers, store attendants and guides.

The tourism-engineered collapse of the traditional occupational structure set off social tensions in the coastal belt. In the past in the villages — vocations, ownership of land, rights to natural resources, social ranks — everything seemed to be fixed in perpetuity. The upper castes had both the social supremacy and the economic power. The poorer castes, who were agricultural tenants, *mundcars* and fishermen owned no resources. Luck smiled on them when the hippie-triggered tourism boom coincided with Bandodkar's land reforms. Overnight they became the owners of the land they had tilled or dwelt upon, free to build a hotel or a bar or a store or an extra room upon it or to sell it to the highest bidder. The elevation in the economic status of the lower castes caused deep resentment among the upper castes, who had not only lost their lands to them but had also now to compete with them for a share of the tourism pie in the coastal belt. A whole host of new characters had emerged in the belt: travel agents, taxi unions, speculators and touts.

Upper caste families slipped down the economic scale, lower caste families climbed: so much so that the criteria of social ranking had to change. Tourism accelerated the downfall of the caste system. Yesterday whoever was upper caste was rich. Today whoever was rich was upper caste. It was tourism again which had revolutionised the world of women in the coastal belt. Conservatism had given way to public exposure of women in the families of tenants, *mundcars* and fishermen who had come into money through their tourism-related enterprise. It was not unusual for the women to even sit at the cash counters of bars. Slowly the women from the upper caste families took up front office and guest relations jobs in the hotels and other service industries. Increased presence of women in workplaces and businesses led to positive changes in the male attitude toward them.

In these fundamental economic and social changes in the coastal belt the government played no role. None of the five-year plans had taken into account the entrepreneurship of the coastal villagers in the developmnet of tourism-related services. As there was no such thinking, there were no promotional guidelines or regulations put in place with regard to the coastal villagers' enterprise. So people went on setting up or expanding their businesses at their will. A government study in 1987 recorded illegal constructions on a large scale in the form of extensions to existing houses in the Baga-Calangute stretch. Those involved said the law required clearances from too many offices of the government and they, when opportunity was knocking at their door, could not go on running from office to office, without the guarantee of how long it would take for them to get the clearances.

Calangute and Baga were not the only villages that had witnessed large scale growth of unauthorised constructions. Candolim, north of Calangute, and Arpora, Anjuna, Vagator and Arambol, south of it, also developed accommodation, restaurants, bars and stores without planning. These were the villages the hippies had moved to in the later part of the 1970s when Calangute and Baga were filled with domestic tourists. The hippies, especially the young white nude female, brought multitudes of domestic tourists in their train to these villages too, accelerating the growth of properties and businesses.

By the middle of 1980s, but for a few who stayed on, the hippies had disappeared, leaving it to the low-budget tourists who came in chartered planes from Europe looking for an affordable beach destination, to keep the 'permissive' image of Goa's beaches alive. Ignoring the 'Nudity Prohibited' boards propped on the sands by the government, the female charter tourists frolicked and sunbathed topless on the beaches. The charter females, unlike the hippies who were young, were normally middle-aged; nonetheless they did not fail to attract the Indian voyeur-tourists.

Together the hippies and the initial droves of charter tourists were to create an image of Goa which the Goans had come to resent. It was the image of a place where everything was possible, which was the ultimate land of freedom where inhibitions could be hurled away together with clothes into the sea. Today there are a number of websites run by known and unknown groups who promote Goa as a land for the ultimate hedonist experience. One the websites lures visitors thus:

"Beaches, sun, palm trees, fenny and beer ... not to mention the great variety of continental food and all the colour and friendliness of the locals!! If you're looking for a nice peaceful vacation on the beach with your girlfriend or a nice vacation with the boys to get wasted on the beaches with all that booze flowing around, Goa still is THE place to be! This is exactly what Goa is ... and will be to the run of the mill 'holidayer' !! ... This is what Goa is all about ... !! Right?! WRONG!! Goa is a haven for drugs and other forms of psychedelic and hallucinogenic substances. The parties (raves) that happen here are unique to Goa and the experience is unlike any other party destination. OK ... First things first ... we're talking about 'Trance,' a genre of music which has evolved into 'Psychedelic Goa Trance' ... It all started in the 60's actually, when all the hippies and the flower power generation discovered Goa. Drugs, nudity and music ... is all they needed and that's what they got!! It's still pretty much the same today too ... only ... the drugs have taken modern twists and the music is all electronic (ahh...! now I get it!). The evangelists of Goa Trance, if you may, were basically the Israelis who came to Goa during their post-war years. Of course, the Germans played a major role too ... most of the DJ's during the early 80's were Germans, who kicked off the electronic techno scene, which has finally evolved into Psychedelic Goa Trance. Goa is a party place for a new generation: the Techno- and Rave-heads. They come from all over the world, from Israel, New Zealand, Chile, Switzerland, Kazakhstan, Japan and from Germany to find parties on the beaches here ... ."

This was the price the Goans had paid for having shown tolerance toward the hippies and slowly developing a profitable relationship with them. The hippies had projected Goa as the mecca of spiritual liberation, as the way to lose oneself, as one centre in the East where one found the ultimate happiness. Goans had allowed them all their indulgences. After their departure, the Goa Techno and Goa Trance crowds and charter tourists had taken liberties with Goan tolerance. It was hurting their self-respect. Not only individual self-respect but also community self-respect. Because the tourists from other parts of India, who came generally from a conservative background, superimposed the doped image of hippies on the Goan male and the libertine image of the white woman on the Goan woman. They saw too many Goan women working, freely moving or talking with males seemingly not their fathers or brothers in the beach belt, which, since such liberalism did not exist in their native places, made them think these women must not mind flirtation or a fling.

A Culture of Conspiracy

When the state government promoted a commercialised Carnival as a tourist attraction, the Goans protested. Carnival during the Portuguese time was celebrated as a village-level festival before Lent among the Christians of Goa, with people singing songs and hurling *cocotes,* balloons filled with white powder, often talcum powder, at each other and winding it up with a folksy skit mimicking and satirizing everybody, not excluding the landlords.

The tourists' Carnival was a spectacle in the street, with innovatively designed floats sponsored by businesses parading through the main cities. Every float had its own musicians and dancers dressed in shiny, flamboyant costumes. If the government's intention was to show the world a slice of Goa's cosmopolitan culture, the purpose was defeated by the competitiveness among the clubs and groups organising the floats. In order to draw attention, some of them paraded young women in short and skimpy clothes, the photographs of whom, when they were published in the outstation papers, increased the tourist flow to Goa.

Goans saw the danger inherent in the commercialisation of the Carnival: the domestic tourists would refuse to distinguish between the hippie girls, the charter women and the float girls. They put pressure on the government to prohibit indecent costumes on the floats. When the Carnival came out in the street with sanitized floats the following years the size of the tourist crowd that was increasing every year dwindled. That brought home the cruel realisation to the Goans how much dependent Goa's tourism had become on its permissive image. The other Indians were just not ready to accept Goans as normal people, as people who cared as much for moral character, public decency, individual dignity and social norms. This image had been reinforced by travel writers and journalists who projected Goa as a land of fun and fiesta.

Tourism was responsible not only for gross misrepresentation of Goa's culture but also for the degradation of its moral and physical environment. It had given the state problems it had not known before: drug addiction, alcoholism, male prostitution, violence as a means of settling disputes, criminality, total surrender to materialist culture, putting of self above community. Added to these were the crises faced by the physical environment: the gases from too many buses, taxis and motorcycles which polluted the air, the plastic bags, liquor bottles and other rejects that littered the beaches, the high decibel music at the hotels and open air concerts which caused noise pollution, the garbage bins which overflowed in the streets. Agitated by these crises some of the citizens' groups had pelted the charter tourists with rotten eggs and tomatoes at the Dabolim airport. The negative features of tourism far outnumbered the positive features, they said.

However this view was not shared by the beachside villagers. Having been condemned to the bottom ranks of the society for generations, most of them saw in tourism a tremendous scope for their upward mobility, and they were least concerned if it came at some costs to the environment. But for the income from tourism they would not have ever dreamt of buying a television, refrigerator or motorcycle, or to give their children all the good things the elite's children enjoyed. Their heart was not gnawed at by ethical questions. If tourists wanted drinks they must have more bars — if that promoted alcoholism it was not their concern; if selling a bit of a brown sugar brought good money they must take the risk (there were risks in every business); if that sucked some of the local boys into addiction on the way why should the good money the others got without being addicted be condemned for that? And why blame all those local boys who were 'servicing' the middle-aged European female tourists for the spread of AIDS in Goa if a few of the silly fellows did not use any protection?

There was a culture of conspiracy at work in the beach belt: the policemen would normally not know all that was going on. The officers of the state Anti-Narcotics Bureau found it hard to gather intelligence on drug peddlars or retailers. Even if they managed to catch somebody witnesses would not come forward to give evidence or clues against him. Even those who were not involved in drug retailing or flesh trade preferred not to talk about these activities to the police or the media, more out of sympathy for those who were involved than out of the fear of any mafia. Tourism was the Wealth Bringer in the beach belt, and nobody dared to upset this God with moral screams. If the police were let in to poke their nose in everything the God might emigrate to a more hospitable environment. After all, tourists came for entertainment, pleasure during leisure; if we were taking their money we should be ready to offer them outlets for their fancies.

There was another good reason why the tourists, especially the foreign tourists, had to be allowed their indulgences. Goa did not have high quality infrastructure or tourist services to offer: the food in the hotels was terrible and costly, the cuisines unauthentic, the restaurant music ludicrous, the power supply irregular, the sanitation poor, the room tariffs exorbitant. If on top of that the bad hosts demanded that the tourists follow a strict moral code during their stay, that would be the end of it. They will never look toward Goa. Poor quality services must be made up with services that were not easily available to the foreign tourists elsewhere. What was pollution of moral environment to some was elixir to the beachside villagers. Silence on indulgences was consciously promoted as a secret investment in tourism.

And tourism grew phenomenally, throwing up opportunities to every family in the beachside villages in the business of providing food, entertainment and accommodation to visitors. In 1970, 84,700 tourists came to Goa; in 1980, the figure rose to 366,824 or four times. By 1990, the number rose to 862,443 or ten times, and by 2,000 to 1436,034 or seventeen times. In other words, the population of Goa during the tourist season, that is from the month of October to February, almost doubled. If you took into consideration the fact that the majority of tourists spent their days in the beach belt the beachside villagers had a huge floating market to exploit.

The number of foreigners, who wouldn't go anywhere but to the beach, also went on rising. In 1970 they formed only 5.5 per cent of total tourist arrivals. This share rose to 9.3 per cent in 1980, 11.84 per cent in 1990, 14.28 per cent in 2000. Although the share of domestic tourists had been going down, in terms of sheer numbers they were overwhelming. Besides, unlike in the past when most tourists came from Maharashtra and Karnataka, they came from other parts of the country too. A survey by the state town and country planning department in 1986-87 of the profile of the tourists in the Calangute area found that the bulk of them, 63 per cent, came from North India, 22 per cent from South India and 15 per cent from the North-eastern states. The survey also found that 75 per cent of foreign tourists were from Europe, followed by 13.4 per cent from Asia, 11 per cent from North America, 0.4 per cent from South America and 0.2 per cent from Africa.

The Domestic Tourists

Preferences of the domestic and foreign tourists varied. The foreign tourist came to Goa mainly for the beach and the sunshine. Even though he stayed longer than the domestic tourist, nine days against five days, he stuck to the beach, bathing and tanning himself on the sands or a deck-bed. The hospitality, beauty and warmth of the physical environment in winter months became even more attractive with the relatively cheaper costs of air travel, accommodation, transport and food. In the winter of 1998 at an incredibly low price of 149 pound sterlings per head British tourists flew Gatwick-Goa-Gatwick on a seven day stay with breakfast.

The beach did not form the central appeal of the domestic tourists. Even though all domestic tourists flocked to the beaches, they went there more to pay homage to the beauty and bountifulness of Nature than to bathe or tan themselves. The bulk of domestic tourists — usually whole families — just loved standing on the frothy edge of the sea and let themselves be teased by the rolling waves, sometimes expressing their enjoyment with a cackle or a shriek. The brave ones went farther into knee-deep water and played chase-me-if-you-can games with the attacking waves. Children were left to play or make castles in the sands, or sometimes taken closer to the sea for the whole family to have fun with the little fellows screaming their guts out watching those surging waves. There were domestic tourists who swam on the beaches like the foreign tourists but their number was very small. Coming from landlocked districts as the majority of domestic tourists were, they could not relate to the sea. They spent a few hours on the beach to enjoy their game with the waves, the cool breeze and the sights for a few hours and went away.

Nonetheless, the domestic tourists came to Goa because of its fame for its natural beauty. The cities and towns in which they lived were densely populated, had very little greenery, were dotted with squatter colonies and littered with squalor. They felt the difference as soon as they set their foot in Goa: the greenery, which dominated the Goan landscape with forests, coconut plantations, fruit-bearing trees and rice-fields, overwhelmed them. Every house in the village had coconut trees and one or more jackfruit, breadfruit and mango trees towering around them. Adding to this distinctiveness of the Goan landscape was the strangeness of the Indo-Portuguese architecture and the high density of foreign tourist population — in 2000, more than 10 per cent of India-bound foreign tourists came to Goa — that gave the domestic tourist the feeling of having landed in a very un-Indialike country. By the turn of the 21st century, three decades after the hippies had provoked perverse tourism, the semi-nude white female had ceased to be an attraction to the domestic tourists. Yet the 'foreign,' uninhibited and hedonist image of Goa persisted.

However, it was not just the foreignness which was attracting domestic tourists to Goa. There were other factors at work too. A study titled *Tourism and the environment case studies on Goa, India and the Maldives*, by the Economic Development Institute (EDI) of the World Bank in 1998 listed the following factors for the rise in domestic tourism: Increased disposable income of the middle class, increased urbanisation and stress of living in cities and towns, increased ownership of cars, improved employment benefits, such as leave travel concession, development of inexpensive mass transport, greater advertising targeted at domestic tourists both by the central and state governments as well as the tourist industry, and development of time-sharing of holiday accommodations.

Over 90 per cent of domestic tourists came by road and rail and stayed in small hotels, whereas the bulk of foreign tourists came by air and were lodged in starred hotels or hired houses. The six months covering autumn, winter and spring, October to March, witnessed the arrival of 65 per cent of all the year's foreign tourists and only 55 per cent of domestic tourists. According to the *Report on Study of Tourism*

Industry in Goa, done by Kirloskar Consultants Ltd. in 1994, the average domestic tourist stayed for 5 days and spent a total of US$110, while the foreign tourist stayed for 9 days and spent US$590. The bulk of domestic tourists belonged to middle and lower-middle classes, and of the foreign tourists to labour classes.

Rape of the Beaches

The Regional Plan 2001 A.D. of Goa envisaged that by the end of the century about 1.12 million tourists would visit Goa. However, by 1996, the tourist traffic had already reached 1.15 million. The Regional Plan forecast the number of foreign tourists by the end of century to be 120,000 whereas by 1996 this figure reached almost double that size to 237,214. In July 1987 the tourism department released a Master Plan for tourism development in Goa which projected a target growth rate of domestic tourists of 10 per cent during 1986-91, 8 per cent during 1991-96 and 5 per cent during 1996-2001. The actual growth rate turned out to be 2 per cent during 1986-91, 19 per cent during 1991-96 and 4.5 per cent during 1996-97.

The Master Plan projected a growth rate of foreign tourists of 15 per cent for 1986-91, 12 per cent for 1991-96 and 8 per cent for 1996-2001. The actual growth rate during 1986-91 was negative by 19.75 per cent, but even if we exclude the particularly bad year of 1991 in this case and took 1990 for consideration, the growth rate came to 7 per cent or half the projected figure. During 1991-96, the growth rate rose astronomically by 219 per cent. And during 1996-97, it grew by 10.3 per cent.

With the market growth beating all projections, questions have arisen about the holding capacity of the land, or the optimum level upto which, the resources of Goa can be exploited without damaging the harmony of the ecology and the evolutionary human experience. In the tourism department's Master Plan the concept of holding capacity was accorded a central focus. "This concept is to try and establish in quantitative, absolute and empirical terms the number of visitors and the degree of development that can be (allowed) without any permanent damage to the resources," the Master Plan said.

Development, it is sad to see, has taken place without very little regard for preservation. Everybody has been busy making a fast buck — developers and hoteliers, bureaucrats and licensing officers, and lawmakers and village councillors. The government never really exercised any control over the volume of tourism or the extent of development that was taking place. Relaxations were made in most of the cases of construction. The beautiful beaches, the main asset, were left to the mercy of the marauding market forces.

However, corrupt and rule-bending politicians and bureaucrats and the predatory builders were not alone responsible for the rape of the beach belt. The local residents too gave priority to their economic and social elevation at the cost of the ecological balance which their ancestors had maintained. The whole culture of the beach belt was commercialised. The fisherman whose hut fell in the way of the development of an apartment block or hotel project demanded a very high price for his property; the *mundcar*, over the roof of whose hut a holiday home project drew its electrical wires from the pole would not let this without a good compensation; the sarpanch would not issue licences to anybody without graft.

Unplanned growth had ruined the sand dunes. For centuries the sand dunes, 10 to 20 metres high, had provided a natural defence against the tidal waves and sea erosion. With wild vegetation growing upon them, the sand dunes collected the sand that was blown landward by the wind and dispersed it with the wind blowing seaward on the beach to replenish the vacuum left there by the sand carried away by the sea, thus playing a major role in protecting the coastline. The sand dunes also served as a habitat for a number of organisms, including turtles. With neither the government nor the local people stopping them, the real estate developers bulldozed the sand dunes or flattened them to the shape of a plateau to make way for concrete constructions. The ones that escaped the rapacity of the developers were illegally quarried by sand suppliers to the builders.

The Master Plan wanted the government to declare sand dunes as 'no development zones' to prohibit construction and sand extraction; otherwise the coastal area would be exposed to erosion and other irreparable environmental damages. The government took no steps. Sand extraction continued unchecked. The EDI study had this to say on the subject: "The ceaseless mining of sand and sand dunes has effectively razed gentle slopes of sand which stop the tides from rushing further onto the shore. The consequent tidal ingress has reduced the area of beach at different places, such as Miramar in Panaji, the

Baga-Calangute-Candolim-Sinquerim stretch and Anjuna in Bardez, and (Colva, Betalbatim, Varca, Cavelossim and Mobor) in Salcete and Mormugao on the north and central coasts of Goa."

The beaches were not only shrinking but they were also getting polluted. Multitudes of tourists littered the beaches with oil, grease, plastics and other pollutants which affected the coastal marine environment. Several organisms became extinct due to these pollutants invading their habitats. Fish catch along the coast declined. By a government order in 2000 use of non-biodegradable plastic bags was prohibited throughout Goa. They were replaced with bags made of degradable materials.

That saved the beaches from one pollutant, but there was no endeavour on the part of the state government or the panchayat to set up a system for cosntant cleaning of the beaches. The onus of keeping the beaches clean was placed on the tourists who showed little interest, and on the shack owners who did not even observe minimum rules of hygiene while cooking food or washing dishes. And there was no law to punish the polluter. All that the government did was put up boards asking people to keep the beaches clean. There was nobody to see whether the people were following the instruction or not. On some of the beaches tourists, especially foreigners, freely rode motorcycles, even jeeps, yet no policeman or official ever caught them.

For want of state or community vigilance the beaches acquired a repulsive face. The traditional architectural styles gave way to commercial monstrosities for more and more saleable and renting space. The houses in the beachside villages stood close to each other, separated by narrow, winding lanes, of only good enough width for walking or herding your cattle through: when the tourism boom came and everybody wanted a share in the pie, these houses or vacant plots between them were developed for a lodge, restaurant, bar or a store without any attention to aesthetics or standards. The erections and extensions left very little space for movement of vehicles or pedestrians or sewage. The cottage industries of Goan hospitality spilled out on the roads. The tourism Master Plan, realizing the threat, recommended control on site planning and density of construction. "The landscaping," said the Master Planners, "should respect the natural order in the area and enhance the diversity of plant and wildlife in the coastal belt. The form and configuration (of buildings) should ensure the continuity of feeling of openness from the settlement of the sea-land interface and be within the scale of the natural environment." These words of the Master Planners ignored, as their other warnings were, the beach fronts could not be saved from turning into concrete slums.

The Regional Development Plan of Goa for 2001 A.D, prepared in October 1988, keeping in view the degradation caused to the beach areas, set some guidelines for the development of tourism. One of these guidelines called for a strategy for selective development of the coastline. Not all the sandy beaches should be open to tourism, the Plan said, because "it is not advisable from the standpoint of conservation of resources both natural and man-made. Instead, beach-head development at certain selected centres should be encouraged." However, as the EDI study found, the coastal zone management plans submitted by the Goa government in 1995 and 1996 for approval by the central government contradicted the Regional Plan's restrictive guidelines and recommended "tourism-related development" for almost the entire length of the coastline.

The contradiction revealed a process in which the desire for economic gains overrode the commitment to ecological preservation. This was true of the government which saw tourism as an earner of foreign exchange, a significant employer and a good sectoral contributor to state domestic product; and this was true of the market forces, from the five-star hotelier down to the beach shack owner, who saw a good income in it; and this was also true of the political parties which saw support-building opportunities in it. Lawmakers elected from the coastal districts actively promoted development of service industries in their constituencies as this helped them build an image of a benefactor for themselves. Every year an increasing number of residents approached them for their recommendation for licences for a beach shack or other businesses and they never failed to oblige them.

The coastal zone regulations had been undermined by the market forces and the politicians too. Back in November 1981 prime minister Indira Gandhi wrote to all the chief ministers, drawing their attention to the 'degradation and misutilisation' of the beaches. She asked them to do two things immediately: Ban development within a distance of 500 metres from the line of maximum high tide; and start planting suitable trees on the beaches that had been made vulnerable by development. "Beaches," said Indira, "must be kept free from all kinds of artificial development. Pollution from industrial and town wastes must also be avoided totally. Please give thought to this matter and ensure that our lovely coastline and its beaches remain unsullied." The states banned all development within 500 metres of the high tide line — but only in principle. When it came to enforcing the ban, most states flouted it. The Prime Minister's Office did not chase the chief ministers, and the concerned ministries of the central government also did not put a regulatory mechanism in place to enforce the ban. When the Union ministry of environment started receiving complaints of violation of the ban by the states they were shocked but they could do little to undo or stop it, since the responsibility for enforcement had been entrusted with the states.

The Goa government, issuing its own guidelines on coastal development, diluted Indira Gandhi's ban, providing for construction within 500 metres of the high tide line if there were grounds to justify it. The state had given the the hospitality industry enough room for manoeuvres. The 1980s promised to be a high growth decade for tourism in Goa, and nobody wanted to see it stunted by heavy restrictions on beachside development. In 1982, the Goa government issued an order that constructions between 90 metres and 500 metres from the high tide line would have to seek approval of a new body called the Ecological Development Council. By this order the Goa government meant to achieve two ends: one, to fix 90 metres from the high tide line as the no-development zone instead of Indira Gandhi's 500 metres; and two, to allow development selectively between 90 and 500 metres with its blessings.

Ecoforum in its 1993 book, *Fish, Curry and Rice*, observed that the ecological development council of Goa kept the central department of environment in the dark about several constructions on the beaches of Goa. Although the department of environment was a member of the ecological council as the guardian of all beaches in the country and the final authority for clearance of projects on the coastline, the state government went ahead with its approvals of beach development on its own. Ecoforum lamented: "The small department (of environment) was unable to keep track of what was taking place on the country's beaches. But it stubbornly resisted efforts to relax the 500-metre no-construction policy .... The department's annual report for 1984-85 explicitly states: 'The department has received several proposals for relaxation of the (PM's 500 metre) directive. Those concerned have been advised to abide by the directive and come up with detailed justification for such cases where relaxation is sought.'"

Taking advantage of the inability of the department of enviroment to regulate development on the beaches, the ecological development council gave a clearance in the early eighties to a large Indian hotel chain to develop a five-star resort in a 100,000 sq metre area on the Sinquerim beach in North Goa within 90 metres of high tide line, thus violating its own rules. Construction of another five-star resort started mysteriously on the Majorda beach in South Goa even without the ecological development council's clearance. Several smaller buildings also came up the beach front, with or without the approval of the panchayats.

Rajiv Gandhi, who succeeded Indira, reduced the "no development zone" from 500 metres to 200 metres from the high tide line in 1985 with a view to developing beach resorts for attracting high-spending domestic and foreign tourists. Goa's star hotel projects took full advantage of the relaxation, extending themselves closer to the beaches, so much so that they virtually usurped them, closing the access of local residents or tourists other than their guests to them. Not satisfied with that, the hotels demanded reduction of the "no development zone" from 200 metres to 90 metres. But the department of environment rejected it. From time to time, the department issued directives tightening the restrictions on coastal development within the 200 metre zone.

Undeniably, tourism had proved a boon to Goa. The EDI study observed that tourism provided 13.7 per cent of the net state domestic product, 7 per cent of employment and 7 per cent of tax revenues. The Regional Plan 2001 A.D. placed direct and indirect contributions of tourism to the net state domestic product at 16.75 per cent. In the beachside villages, tourism encouraged new talents in small business, improved family incomes, provided avenues for productive investment of emigrants' savings and offered an alternative to emigration to the younger generations. Right from fishermen in Calangute to the toddy-tappers in Arambol, they all profited from room-renting, vehicle-hiring or wine-selling.

However there is a limit to the number of people who can survive on tourism. In their craze for a share of the tourism pie everybody became a taxi owner, a restaurateur, a hotelier or a shopkeeper. Today they all do not get customers because they are too many in the trade. A lot of youths who took bank loans to buy a car to run as a taxi are finding it difficult to get passengers. More often than not they have to wait for hours at the taxi stand or outside the hotels before they can hope to get a passenger.

In the recent years violent clashes between the owners of taxis and coaches have almost become a routine every tourist season. The tourists staying at the five-star hotels find it cheaper and more enjoyable to go sightseeing in coaches, especially when they are in a large group. But the taxi owners don't like it; they have sometimes put up a road blockade of their vehicles to stop the coaches from proceeding and demand that the passengers be offloaded and put in their taxis in smaller groups. The owners of car-taxis have also fought with the owners of jeep-taxis who carry passengers to a fixed destination at much cheaper rates.

Even in accommodation there are too many hotels, lodging houses and room-hirers competing. At the turn of the 1990s, even the builders, in order to overcome recession, entered the scene with their "rent-back accommodation." They built apartment block after apartment block and sold the flats to non-resident buyers who were willing to rent them back to them for a fixed annual payment. After having got back all the flats on rent the builders used their apartment blocks like hotels without having to pay the public exchequer the taxes and cesses that registered hotels had to.

The availability of a huge number of apartment blocks led to a price war in the beach belt, depressing the rent to a few hundred rupees a night in ten years since they started to be built. The charter operators and travel agents based in Europe had never had it so good. They became hard bargainers and were willing to pay only the lowest price, because in that lay the prospect of motivating a large number of tourists.

Search for High-Spenders

The tragedy in the beach belt at the turn of the 21st century was haunting: rising tourist arrivals and falling local prices. If it went on longer, the tourism-related businesses were doomed. Studies had found that about 55 per cent of expenditure by domestic and foreign tourists was made on accommodation, 20 per cent on shopping and over 10 per cent on transport. With cheaper prices, an increasing number of working class Europeans would be attracted toward Goa and their preponderance would keep the foreign individual tourists (called FITs in trade parlance) away. The working class tourists had little to spend on food, transport and shopping.

Although the state government often talked of schemes to attract the high-spending foreign tourists they failed to make any headway for a number of reasons. One, the state would have to start by discouraging charter tourism, by reducing the number of charters or by raising the local prices, because without changing the class identity of the tourist profile, it could not start attracting the high class tourists. But this would be a hazardous strategy; it would mean a drop in the occupancy of hotels, apartments and houses and may force the weaker players out of the market. It will reduce employment. The cottage industries of the hospitality sector, owned by the residents in the beachside villages, will suffer a drop in income or closure, and all this might create popular unrest.

The second reason why the state should give up its dream of attracting the high-spenders is its inability to provide top class services to them. The roads of Goa are in a poor condition; the beaches are dirty; cesspools breeding malaria mosquitoes are abound; garbage spills over on to the streets in congested cities. The state does not offer even an enclave where high-spenders can enjoy all of their stay. There is no golf course. Owing to protest by local villagers the state government has been highly reluctant to support a Japanese Holiday Village project in Pernem, providing for cottages, a golf course and other facilities, to attract upmarket tourists from Japan.

In short, the low-budget foreign and domestic tourists are Goa's destiny. This is perhaps the best way to provide income not only to the cottage industries set up by the residents of the beachside villages but also to the star hotels, big restaurants and crafts emporia set up by the outsiders (and Goans). With a determined effort, the state government can reach the benefits of tourism to the other parts of Goa as well. There has been a constant complaint from the Goans living in the hinterland that tourism benefits have gone only to the coastal people.

The government must set up 'backward linkages' between tourism and the hinterland. The hinterland can be linked to the tourist industry by supplying vegetables, milk, eggs, poultry, butter and other items which are required in bulk by the hotels and restaurants in the beach belt. It would have provided a solid market support to the agriculture, horticulture and dairy sectors in Goa. In the absence of backward linkages, the hotels and restaurants have been getting their supplies from other states. The government can further break the spatial monopoly in tourism of the beach belt by promoting tours of Hindu shrines, trekking, horse-riding, cross-country walks and jungle tours which are possible in the interior highlands and the mountaineous regions of Goa.

Since the state government has failed to take these balancing steps, the conflict between beach tourism and the rest of Goa is growing. A majority of Goans feel hostile toward the tourists, both foreign and Indian, since they think that these people come and not only give them no benefits but also make a heavy demand on their limited resources of drinking water, electricity, land and roadways, curtailing their availability to them; and raise the prices of essential items. The agitation of the NGOs against the five-star hotels has been on the same grounds and the logic is quite appealing to the heart of the hinterland Goans.

5
Road to Salvation

Liberation was a timely blessing for Christianity in Goa. It provided the best possible set-up to evolve a spirituality that was integrated with struggles of existence, to grow as citizens of heaven but fully involved in the building of the city on earth. It was a challenge to cast off the old mould into which Christianity had been frozen. And stop living as crippled children. It was a challenge to rise and walk.

—Teotonio R de Souza, Goan historian

The Laity's Bread

The January 1-15, 2000 issue of the *Renovacao* (Renewal) the mouthpiece of the Goa archdiocese of the Roman Catholic Church, carried the text of a statement issued by eight prominent Goan writers and artists asking the ministry of information and broadcasting to restrain Doordarshan from presenting a live telecast of road shows and beach parties in Goa as a part of the Millenium New Year celebrations. The statement said: "The telecast is a direct attack on our cultural ethos .... We all know what the so-called New Year Nights constitute. There is free flow of liquor, display of vulgarity, ear-splitting techno music .... We would like to unequivocally convey our strong feelings (against) these covert plans to portray Goa as the Land of Booze and *Masti* ...." The *Renovacao* did not add any editorial comments to the statement, but the very fact that it published the full text of it was proof that the church sympathized with the cause espoused in it. What perhaps made it even more remarkable was that all the signatories were Hindus. The church obviously wanted to convey the message that not only the Christians but even the Hindus were opposed to the commercialisation of tourism.

The postcolonial church was in desperate need all the time to discover good reasons for Christian-Hindu solidarity: it was its new rationale for existing in a Hindu environment. And they did find several good reasons: 'misrepresentation' of local culture by tourism was one of them. The Christians and Hindus could together fight the lascivious cloven hoofs of the marketing business. Since the early 1980s the church had directly or indirectly patronised several NGOs which fought the battle against tourism on its behalf. As a matter of fact, in postcolonial Goa the church made its presence felt through the NGOs. Outwardly these NGOs did not seem to have any support of the church, run by a few individuals as they were, but the church was morally and in other ways behind them. These organisations could bring out thousands of lay Christians on the street if they wanted to demonstrate mass support to any of the issues they had taken up: and this could not be possible without the direct and indirect participation of the members of the clergy. An apparently quiet populace, and here we largely mean Christian populace, could, on an unexpected day, surprise and shock the ministers with noisy and vigorous street demonstrations, forcing them to concede their demand keeping the next elections in view.

Fighting against tourism the church ran into a problem, though. The Old Conquests, from where most of its flock came, had been the biggest beneficiary of tourism. Virtually, tourism had come like a second Inquisition, forcing people to convert under the terror of being wiped out by the march of the new faith. Almost all Christians in the coastal belt had converted and were earning a good income from tourism. They were all in favour of the expansion of tourism. The church and the NGOs campaigned against expansion of tourism. But the coastal Christians did not relent. The church realized what it was up against when some of the NGOs supported by it organised protest demonstrations against foreign charter tourists at the airport and elsewhere. The protests petered out for want of public support.

However, the church would not withdraw itself into the confines of altars and pews following this fiasco. It had a greater aim before it: one or two damp squibs would not shove it away from its path. The church in colonial times had been a powerful institution; and, the high priests thought, it must remain so even in the postcolonial times. In the years following Liberation, the church constantly searched for opportunities to demonstrate its power. It was as a part of this exploration that the church found that though the Christians for economic reasons backed expansion of tourism, they were ready to lend their support to an agitation against the extremities of the business — the profligate, sinful inventions of it.

The commercialised Carnival was one such perversion. Although in the traditional Goan environment they could not have assumed the hyper-sensuality of the Rio de Janeiro Carnival, Goa's floats, by parading young women dancing to band music in dresses remarkable for high hemlines and low necklines, tried to take something of the Brazilians' marketing techniques. What was more alarming to the church was that almost all the young women used as bait on the fishing line of Carnival promoters were from Christian families. The church began to demand that the government ban the Carnival parades, decrying that they portrayed a wrong image of Goan women. In the forefront was the church's Diocesan Centre for Social Action which set up a propaganda campaign against the Carnival parades in the media and the parishes. The NGOs, whose agitation against mass tourism had been a fiasco, joined the agitation. After three years of campaigning, the church and the NGOs backed by it succeeded in forcing the government to withdraw its patronage to corporate-sponsored Carnival floats. The decision was as good as a ban on the floats. If corporate sponsorship was not allowed who had the money to construct a float! For five years there were no Carnival parades.

Then, with the central tourism ministry insisting that Carnival was important for tourism promotion in Goa, the sponsored parades made their appearance again in the main cities of the Old Conquests in 1993. The ministry even gave the state government a special fund to organise the parades. Fearing resistance by the church, the state government set up an advisory-cum-screening committee headed by a Christian minister with a mandate to keep vulgarity out of the floats. In order to doubly assure the archbishop and his brother priests the government also gave the parades an august and virtuous theme: *National Integration*. All the participants were told to design and present their floats depicting the same theme. There was no room for the organisers of floats to exhibit indecency, thought the government, when they were exhibiting patriotism! And when the first parade came out in the streets of Panaji, the government was happy to find no trace of obscenity on the floats. But the church and its favourite NGOs opposed even this sanitized, unembarrassing form of parade. They wanted no Carnival at all on the streets. For centuries Goan Christians had celebrated Carnival among themselves in the local communities, they said, complaining that by giving patronage to a commercialised Carnival, the government was misrepresenting the Christian culture.

Unsuccessful with a government that thought it had kept the obscenity out and couldn't do more, the church and its favourite NGOs released statements in the media asking the people to boycott the parades. There was no impact of their call on the inaugural parade in Panaji, neither on the sponsors nor on the participant clubs and associations, nor on the spectators who filled the spaces behind the barricades on the either side of the street. The residents of Vasco da Gama and Mapusa, too, did not heed the call.

But in Margao — the central city of the Salcete taluka, home to mutinous Christianity — the mood turned bellicose. The day before the Carnival parade was scheduled to be taken out, a large number of slogan-shouting Christians paraded through the streets of the city under the leadership of the director of the Diocesan Centre for Social Action, Monsignor Albert Luis. Accompanying him were two Christian MLAs, who always sang militant Salcete tunes, officials of the church's favourite NGOs and a good number of priests and nuns. When the demonstrators began to march toward the Lohia Maidan, Margao's most famous public ground from where the Carnival was to start the next day, the police blocked their way.

The demonstrators hurled stones at the police and tried to break through their cordon. The police began a lathi charge, wounding several of them, including Luis. Incensed, the demonstrators damaged a few government vehicles and set a few others on fire. The following afternoon Christian mobs barricaded all the entry routes to Margao city, preventing the floats from joining the parade. As a result, out of the fifty floats scheduled for participation, only two managed to enter the city.

The Salcete mutiny, however, failed to sustain itself. The government organised Carnival parades the next year, but there was no resistance, not even in Margao. Now both the things seemed to have fallen into a pattern: the government organised the float parades every year and the church voiced its concern over the commercialisation of Carnival from time to time. Neither disturbed the other. There was a growing realisation in the church that perhaps it was not within their powers to stop commercialisation in all walks of life. They had opposed the vulgarity on the floats, and they felt satisfied they had succeeded in expelling it. They could not go beyond that as there was this additional problem too: a lot many Christians took part in the parades as designers, float-makers, dressmakers, musicians, dancers, comperes and clowns; and they would not support any agitation that would take away their bread (or the icing from the cake). When the church wanted obscenity out of the floats they went along with it. But when the church asked for a ban on the parades, they did not support it, because it amounted to throwing the baby with the bathwater. The reality then was that although the church condemned the parades as misrepresentation of a Christian festival, the street show held every February in the four major cities had received the indelible stamp of a Christian festival by the mere fact of the overwhelming participation of Christians in the parades. The church had succumbed to the realities: it was following its flock; it had to be where the Christians were.

The Church and Konkani

The colonial church had tried to be where the rulers were. Free Goa's church tried to be where the laity was. The strategies of the church in the two eras looked poles apart but its ambition remained the same: to stay as an influential force. The postcolonial church played its first major role in the anti-merger movement. Christians were going through a nightmare of being reduced to a negligible minority in a vast Maharashtra and of being lost in an avalanche of Hindu backlash. The church began to sing the chorus of its flock: *We want a separate political status for Goa*; and gave full backing to the United Goans Party (UGP). The priests gave political speeches from the pulpits to the laity and marched in the streets with them. They addressed public meetings with UGP leaders. So involved in the campaign against merger the priests were that they often worked together with the Saraswat Brahmans who were the most vociferous opponents of merger among the Hindus. They sometimes joined meetings convened by the Saraswats in the temple premises, and ate and stayed overnight there.

It was in the course of their joint campaign against merger that both the church and the flock came to realize the indispensability of a Christian-Hindu solidarity for the protection of Goa's separate identity. Despite their full turnout, the Christians would not have won the

Opinion Poll without Hindu support. In the Bicholim taluka, where the Christians constituted only 6 per cent of the population, about 30 per cent of vote went against merger. In the Ponda taluka, where the Christians formed 10 per cent of the population, over 28 per cent people voted against merger. In the Old Conquests generally the vote cast against merger was much higher than the size of the Christian electorate.

With victory in the Opinion Poll, the Christians had thwarted Maharashtrian expansionism but they still nursed fears that it might be undone at a future date. They wanted an impregnable home to themselves; and the surest way to build one was to have a separate state and a separate language. The Maharashtrawadi Gomantak Party, that had ruled Goa since the first elections, was vigorously promoting Marathi, the language of Maharashtrian expansionism, and if the Christians let it go unchecked, the expansionists could enter and occupy Goa through the backdoor. During the colonial rule, primary schooling had been available in Portuguese and Marathi, and the Christians had gone to Portuguese schools and the Hindus to Marathi schools. After the Liberation, the Christians switched over to English schools; so knowledge of Marathi among them remained non-existent. The MGP's aggressive campaign to promote Marathi as the language of administration and education, therefore, aroused fears among the Christians that they would become foreigners in their own land. In order to avoid this fate, they began to promote Konkani.

Following the flock, the church threw its weight behind the Konkani movement, swearing to build a stronger Christian-Hindu solidarity to defeat the *Marathiwadis*. And, indeed, this solidarity was strengthened with the participation of a large number of non-Brahmans in the language movement. The Saraswats who were in league with the church since the beginning of the anti-merger campaign continued to be with them. Shenoi Goembab, who was to be later regarded as the Father of the Konkani Movement, addressed his first gathering at the Rachol Seminary. Yet the Konkani movement was not a linguistic but a political movement. The Christians were using it just to ensure a separate status for Goa. Their game was exposed when they refused to send their children to Konkani-medium schools. The church, which ran a number of schools, agreed to follow a government directive to change the medium of instruction in them from English to Konkani, but when they met with strong resistance from the flock, they backtracked.

The Christians had fought so fanatically for making Konkani the official language of Goa but when it became the official language by a legislation they would not fight for the enforcement of it. There was a great obstacle in the way, of course: there was no common script for Konkani. After their conversion the Christians had adopted the Roman script for Konkani under the Portuguese influence. Even after Liberation they had stuck to reading and writing Konkani in the Roman script. The Hindus used the Devanagri script. When the question of making Konkani the official language came the inevitable question followed — in which script? And although the Christians formed the majority of Konkani agitators and could have forced the Roman script into the legislation, they preferred to step aside and let Devanagri have the honour. Actually, more than the Christian masses, it was their leaders who let this happen, because they saw a danger of Hindus, who had come along with them during the anti-merger movement, moving away from them. The church backed the move, since it wanted the Christian-Hindu solidarity to strengthen, not to weaken.

Once again it had been proven that the Konkani movement was a political and not a linguistic movement. The church and the Christian leaders knew that the Christian masses would never allow Devanagri Konkani to actually become the state language, because they would not understand a word of it, because for them it would be as good as a foreign language. In the general perception of Christians Roman Konkani alone was Konkani; anything written in Devanagri was Marathi — *Kokanno,* language of the Hindus.

If the government tomorrow declared that it would write all its files in Devanagri Konkani, that it would issue all its notifications, circulars and notices in the same language and that it would not entertain replies or representations from the members of the public in any other language, the Christians would organise themselves into a rebellion. The converse was also, nonetheless, true: if by an amendment Roman Konkani was made the state language, the Hindus would rise in revolt. Konkani would therefore never be able to become the state language in practice: in theory it can enjoy that status for eternity. The mother tongue of Goans had become a victim of the Portuguese apartheid. During the colonial times, Christians and Hindus had been forced to have mutually exclusive cultures, mutually exclusive lives, mutually exclusive languages, mutually exclusive scripts. Free Goa had to live with the segregationist legacy.

The Hindus in the Konkani movement believed that the Christians would one day accept the Devanagri script. They may be overoptimistic in this, though it was a fact that younger generations of Goans, Hindus or Christians, have to learn the Devanagri script for the language subjects in Hindi and Konkani in schools. Even the church schools impart education in Devanagri Konkani. Thus, although a majority of Christians continued to prefer the Roman script for reading and writing, the number of Christians at home with the Devanagri script will go on rising in the future.

The Opinion Poll had thwarted Maharashtrian expansionism, the legislation making Konkani the official language had blocked its entry by the backdoor, but Goa could not feel secure without a separate political status. The church and Christian political leaders built up a campaign for grant of statehood to Goa with the Hindus, a campaign which forced the territory's politicians to lobby with the central government with all their legal might. Fulfilling the implicit promise his maternal grandfather had made in 1963, Rajiv Gandhi as prime minister granted Goa a separate statehood in 1987.

Exactly here, as soon as the separate statehood was granted, curtains fell on the the Christian-Hindu solidarity. The common objective achieved, the walls of Portuguese apartheid went up again. The church returned to nurse its Christian constituency, taking up big and small issues that agitated the Christians: *Ramponkars*, traditional fishermen, versus the trawlers, the influx from other states, the threats the Hindu communalism posed to secularism. The Goan Hindus, with historical memories of the Inquisition rankling in their minds, could never bring themselves to trust the church, leave aside coalescing with them for ever. Even the section of Hindus, Brahmans as well as non-Brahmans, who had fought shoulder to shoulder with them from anti-merger days to statehood had entertained within their hearts a deep hostility toward them. That is why, as soon as statehood came, they terminated their alliance with the church.

The Royal Pope

The church had indeed played a sinful role in history. It landed as a handmaiden of imperialism, to produce Christians loyal to the

Portuguese crown. Those were the times when the Pope had no means to send his missionaries out in the world. But the Portuguese had the navy and they were discovering new worlds. The Pope wanted more faithfuls; the Portuguese wanted loyal natives. The Pope and the Portuguese king struck a deal: the Pope would by a proclamation grant the king the right to become the patron (in other words, the pope) of all the churches set up in the lands he conquered. By virtue of this bestowal, the Portuguese king exercised all powers over ecclesiastical appointments in Goa. Should the Pope intend to recommend a cleric to Goa, he had to first send him to Portugal where the king's advisors put him under scrutiny for an indefinite period in order to be sure of his abilities and, above all, his loyalty to the Portuguese crown. If he passed their severe tests he was made to sign allegiance to the king before they gave him the licence to work in Goa. Even during his work in Goa he was kept under watch, and if he was any time found wanting in his allegiance to the king he was repatriated without any reference to the Pope.

For almost four hundred years since he conquered Goa the Portuguese king acted like a half-emperor, half-pope. Not just the privilege of clerical appointments, the king even appropriated to himself the right to examine all the Papal Bulls, allowing their enforcement in his conquered lands only if he found nothing detrimental to Portugal's interests in them. Until Goa was declared a diocese by the Pope in 1534, the vicar-generals were appointed by the king and were answerable to him. Even the bishops appointed after 1534 (or the archbishops after 1557 when Goa became an archdiocese) served their ecclesiastical mission under the king's patronage. The Portuguese kings knew that their soldiers could conquer territories but it was only by creating a large Christian population in them that they could consolidate and perpetuate their empire.

The state and the church complemented and interpenetrated each other. In the official hierarchy, the archbishop was placed next to the viceroy. If the viceroy died or was transferred to another colony or to Portugal, the archbishop took charge of the administration and held it until the new man took over. Of the state council, which advised the viceroy on legal and administrative matters, the archbishop was an important member. Among the other members were the local heads of the religious orders — the Dominicans, Augustinians, Franciscans and the Jesuits — and together with the archbishop they exercised an enormous influence on the viceroy's decision-making. An example: in 1704, they made the viceroy impose a *'xenddi* tax' upon the Hindu population, a tax which every Hindu wearing *xenddi*, a long braid of hair on his head, had to pay. And most Hindus, by way of custom, wore a *xenddi*. This was a satanic ploy to make Hindus feel like foreigners in their own country, to convey an unmistakable message to them that: convert and conform or face perpetual harassment. During the forty years since the instituting of the Inquisition the ecclesiastics held five provincial councils in Goa, passing resolutions seeking the king's sanction for more and more severe measures to increase the conversion tally. The king never disappointed them.

So much the king relied on the church that whenever he needed to send an emissary to the Mughul emperor or the Maratha king, he preferred an ecclesiastic to any of his civil officers. He had granted the church the privilege of policing the religious orders: the jurisdiction of the civil administration in this area was taken away. If a member of a religious order was found to have broken the law the civil officials could not arrest, imprison or prosecute him: they had to send him to the authorities of the order. Each one of the orders had its own court and prison. All the activities of the church were funded by the king. Not only did the royal treasury pay the salaries of the archbishop (the next highest paid man after the viceroy), the vicar-general and the other ecclesiastics but it also gave grants to the churches. A large share of the income of the state every year was in fact set apart for the church. Over and above the grants, the church also often received from the state the revenue rights to the estates of the demolished Hindu temples on the plea of raising more funds.

Slowly the state became poorer and the church richer. Misusing the royal patronage, the ecclesiastical houses came to own enormous agricultural properties and businesses. An idea of how prosperous they became can be had from a letter some Portuguese civilians of Goa wrote about the Jesuits to the king in 1603: "If this State of India is lost it will be solely because of the Society of Jesus ... . They are absolute masters of a great part of this island. Most of it they have bought, and at this rate there will be no house or palm grove left which they will not acquire within ten years from now. The Portuguese settlers are finding themselves impoverished, because they have no lands to invest in, and whatever capital they had they have lost it in the sea. The income which the Fathers derive from their properties in Salcete alone would suffice to maintain all the Religious houses that we have here."

Inebriated by their evangelizing success and gargantuan wealth, the Jesuits carved a state within a state, alienating not only the civilians but also the officers of the king. In 1759, the Portuguese crown banned the Society of Jesus, arrested Jesuits on charges of corruption and conspiracy against state and sent them to prison. In 1835 the other religious orders, the Franciscans, the Dominicans and the Augustinians, whose ecclesiastics too had accumulated undreamt-of riches, were also banned. With this, the era of state-church collaboration came to an end. The church had gone out of hand: the state had reasserted itself. The Portuguese king who for three and a half centuries had interchangeably acted as king and pope would now try to be more a king than a pope. In the Vatican, the Pope was disturbed. The Portuguese king did not have the resources for the evangelization in his empire; he had banned the religious orders that were vigorously engaged in the task; and now he did not have the inclination to fill the gap. This, the Pope decided, would stop Christianity from growing in the discovered worlds. In 1886, he created a separate church hierarchy to undertake evangelization in India and other lands, excluding the Portuguese colonies, thus bringing to an end the status of the Portuguese king as the absolute patron of the church in the newly conquered lands. By way of compensating the loss to the Portuguese king the Pope awarded a grand honorific title of 'Patriarch of East Indies' to the archbishop of Goa, a title which the region's pastor still carries.

After Portugal became a republic in 1910, the state began to withdraw whatever patronage the church enjoyed. The stress was on the separation of the institutions of religion from the institutions of governance. But soon after Salazar took over power, the state began to extend patronage to the church again. Lacking in resources for raising a strong army that could contain liberation movements in the colonies, the Portuguese dictator came to rely more and more on the church, the secret police, the censored media, the Lusophiles and his American friends. The church resumed its propaganda that to be a good Catholic was to be loyal to Portugal. The man who served as the archbishop-patriarch of the East Indies from 1942 to 1953 issued no less than 60 circulars during his tenure to the priests of the archdiocese, asking them to make the Goan Christians sever all their links with the rest of India as their salvation lay only with the Portuguese. Some archbishop-patriarchs even led processions of Christians to the Tomb of St. Francis Xavier at Old Goa for seeking his blessings for the victory of the Portuguese over the Indian expansionists.

And the church did not confine itself to religious propaganda. It also promoted a political counter-revolutionary group called the Catholic Action Movement, with its nerve centre in Lisbon, to curb the activities of the freedom fighters. The members of this group worked in close collaboration with Salazar's secret police, keeping a watch on the movements of traitors (bad Catholics), reporting them to the authorities and getting them sent to jail. You did not have to be an active freedom fighter to deserve the traitor tag. Even if you merely argued with the 'Actionists' that someone could be a good Christian without being loyal to a colonial power you invited the police knock at your door. You could find yourself in a boat rowing toward a Portugal prison in a few days! The venomous, authoritarian sermons and homilies of the clergymen in the parishes did not leave any scope at all for reason and debate. Either you were with Salazar or you were fit for the worst. Many of the 'bad Catholics' had to leave Goa to escape arrest. The church's collaboration with Salazar reached its climax with the appointment of a key clergyman, who was directing the Catholic Action Movement from Lisbon, as the auxiliary archbishop of Goa. Unfortunately for the Salazarist church, it failed to serve any purpose, since his appointment came in December 1961, the month in which India drove out the Portuguese.

With patrons gone, the church desperately turned to the patriots: a survival game had begun. The language of the clergy changed. The aims and objectives of the religious work were redefined. All Good Catholics were also to be Good Indians. In 1963, for the first time in the history of church in Goa, a son of Goa, Monsignor Francisco Rebello was appointed the archbishop-patriarch.

A Vigilant Church

With Liberation, the church also liberated itself from the Portuguese control. (In formal terms, however, the Portuguese control over the Goa church continued until the socialists took over power in Portugal in 1974 and declared the Pope's patronage granted to the Portuguese crown in the Age of Discoveries ended.) To exist in an Indian environment was the new challenge. Hindus were in an overwhelming majority in this country: the church had to find ways to make itself acceptable to them. A transformation was in the offing. What helped the transformation was the Vatican II held in the mid-sixties in which the Pope, announcing the end of Counter Reformation, called for a dialogue with the other faiths. "... The Church," elaborated the Vatican II statement, "has this exhortation for her sons: prudently and lovingly, through dialogue and collaboration with the followers of other religions, and in witness to the Christian faith and life, acknowledge, preserve and promote the spiritual and moral good as well as the socio-cultural values found among them."

The ecumenical revolution set off by Vatican II gave birth to the Theology of Liberation in Latin America, motivating Jesuits to join the armed struggles of Marxist organisations against the dictatorial regimes in the region. Alarmed at the unintended radicalism, the Vatican resorted to strict disciplinary measures to stamp it out. Although the postcolonial church in Goa participated in public protests over certain issues this had nothing to do with the Theology of Liberation. The postcolonial church has been a conservative church, in the sense that it does not go beyond the Vatican instructions. When it supported a cause it sought an ideological justification for it in one or the other of the Vatican documents or Pope's speeches. In the recent years the church has been taking up struggles and programmes for raising the awareness among the clergy and the laity of human rights, environmental protection, rights of the children, women and the marginalised, non-proliferation, peace, just society, religious freedom and inter-religious dialogue because these are causes which the Pope has championed in the post-Vatican II era.

Shortly after the Christian-Hindu alliance broke up with the formation of the state, the church, positioning itself behind the traditionally mutinous Christians of Salcete, plunged into agitation for the realignment of the Konkan Railway route. The Konkan region, comprising parts of four states, Maharashtra, Goa, Karnataka and Kerala, had no rail track running along its coastal route. The region was one of the world's most difficult terrains, full of interlocked hills, deep valleys, rivers and wet soil; laying of tracks was fraught with dangers; yet the Indian railway engineers had taken this up as a challenge, because this would not only make rail journey shorter and faster for the passengers from the four states but also spur economic development. In order to let things move faster, the Indian Railways had set up a separate corporation, called the Konkan Railway Corporation (KRC) which lived up to its mandate in the others states but got stuck up in Goa because of the opposition set up by Christians.

The Konkan Railway route, cried the Christians, would pass through thickly-populated villages, disrupting their life, economy, ecology, social harmony, internal travel and peace. Besides, they said, the route will disturb the *khazan* lands, blocking the natural tidal cycles, causing ecological imbalance. Then there were other reasons advanced why the Konkan Railway must do a realignment of its route through the hinterland: it will destroy the culture of coastal villages, it will attract squatter settlements along the tracks, it will encourage immigration of people from other states in Goa. The arguments had no logic whatsoever — a railway track had existed next to the Konkan Railway route for over a hundred years without disrupting life, economy, ecology or anybody's sleep; a highway next to the Konkan Railway route had not disturbed the tidal cycles; the railways or roadways had not been known anywhere in the world to have destroyed cultures; squatter settlements and immigration were possible even without the railways — yet the Christians received full-throated support from the church.

Overnight, an NGO, called the All Goa Citizens Committee for Social Action came up with the blessings of the church. Monsignor Alberto Luis, the director of Diocesan Centre for Social Action, who had a few years ago mobilised the Salcete Christians against the Carnival float parades in Margao, was named the key person in the committee, and he went about his job with a revolutionary passion. The protests he organised made the rail route realignment look like a matter of life and death for the Christians. Mutinous as the Salcete Christians had historically been, they demanded the resignation of the MLAs in support of their cause; and when they did not — they branded them as 'betrayers.'

They went to court with a plea to issue a directive to the railway ministry to change the alignment. Christian mobs attacked labourers and engineers at several track-laying work-sites, damaging the heavy equipment they were working with. Archbishop Raul Gonsalves dispatched strong letters to prime minister Narasimha Rao, asking him to intervene. In one of the letters, the archbishop accused the MLAs of the Congress (Rao's) party of betrayal, noting: "Many Congress MLAs have expressed themselves against the present alignment. Some of them have, however, regretted their helplessness in relieving the sufferings of the people on the excuse of party policy. Their insensitive attitude to the unfolding tragedy of the people exposes their interest in personal privileges rather than in serving the public for which they were elected … . In this grave situation of such magnitude rendered much graver by what we see as reasonless, feelingless and totally undemocratic attitude of our government I simply cannot remain a silent spectator … . (The church will) use every possible means within our democratic rights to obstruct and bring to a halt the works in progress."

However, the church failed to stop the track-laying through the coastal route because the majority of Goans backed it. The Hindus refused to see how the coming of the Konkan Railway could threaten Goa's identity or ecological balance. On the contrary, they hailed it as the cheapest, safest, most comfortable and environmentally least-polluting means of transport for the people of the coastal region. The majority of Goans believed the Konkan Railway would create jobs and economic opportunities for them. An unrelenting church, however, went on agitating, forcing the central government to set up a one-man commission to conduct public hearings on realignment. As the commission after its inquiry recommended the coastal route, the church and Salcete Christians reconciled to the coming of the Konkan Railway. Although even today the favourite NGOs of the church do not miss an opportunity to point out flaws in the coastal route, the Goans, Hindus, Christians and the NGO key persons alike, have found the Konkan Railway trains taking them to Mumbai and Mangalore quite useful.

The Clergy's Influence

Undaunted by the fiasco of its realignment agitation, the church went on taking up issues that primarily stirred up the Christians. By the mid-1990s the church had developed an ideology to guide its action. It was an ideology of resistance: its central thesis was that politicians were engaged in self-aggrandisement, ready to sell themselves to forces that were out to destroy Goa's ecology, culture, demographic profile and identity, and the church, as an institution concerned with the people, had to prevent this from happening in solidarity with others equally concerned. When archbishop Gonsalves drew the attention of prime minister Rao to the anti-people (undemocratic) attitude of the government, warning him that "I cannot simply remain a silent spectator," he was making a public announcement of church vigilantism.

Archbishop Gonsalves visualised a church which would not just minister to the spiritual needs of the people but also to their social and economic needs. "One must understand," explained Monsignor Albert Luis, "that the church does not mean only priests and nuns but also its flock, the people who form a community. And when the people fight any unjust or oppressive structures or forces, the church as a whole has always played an activist role .... It is totally irrelevant to talk of souls alone, for man is made up of body and soul and the two are inseparable .... The basis of Christ's teaching is found in the prayer that Jesus himself gave us, which refers to both body and soul, and (therefore) the question of leaving the social aspects to politicians and the ministering of souls to the church is meaningless. Any problem that affects a human being cannot be exclusively left to any particular agency or group and their failure to redress people's problems does not prohibit the other groups from acting to redress the wrongs. Since the politicians have miserably failed to attend to the needs, aspirations and cries of the people as citizens, every institution has a right to act in order to seek redressal of the injustices meted out to society."

During the elections to the state assembly in 1994, the church decided to launch a frontal attack on the class of unscruplous politicians. In his Justice Sunday message that year, archbishop Gonsalves virtually asked the Christians to vote out the politicians "(many of them Christians) who have been supporting projects detrimental to the good of Goa and Goans." The state was then being run by a Congress government headed by a Christian chief minister, and the archbishop's message hit him in the face. "The monster of corruption stalks the land," warned the archbishop. "Even to obtain a municipal birth certificate people are forced to grease palms." Let us "bring fresh character and conscience to the present corrupt society." The church followed it up with a circular, that shocked the wits out of politicians' heads, asking the people to cast their franchise in favour of candidates who were not corrupt and indifferent to their interests. The clergy worked very hard to persuade the lay Christians to follow the circular, turning it into some sort of a public impeachment of the MLAs who had opposed a realignment of the coastal rail route.

This campaign too ended in a fiasco, except for the fact that in some Christian-dominated constituencies the victory margin of the winning candidate was lower or higher depending on whether he was opposing or supporting the realignment. Most of the MLAs who opposed realignment got re-elected; and those popularly perceived as corrupt did not fare any worse. The 1994 election results had delivered a chastening message to archbishop Gonsalves and his fellow clergymen: The church did not have powers to influence public opinion in any significant manner. Restricted was their appeal, overly grandiose their thoughts. The Hindus did not heed their call, and, as the results clearly demonstrated, even most of the Christians voted according to their own preferences.

The results constituted a slap in the face of the advocates of the activist Church who had taken upon themselves the responsibility of ministering not only to the spiritual needs of the flock but also to their political needs. The majority of Christians had told them in unmistakable terms that they did not want the church to minister to their political needs as they considered themselves wise enough to make their political choices.

However, the church continued to issue statements and circulars to the clergy and laity in the subsequent elections too, asking them to support 'good' candidates. In the 2002 elections to the state assembly, which were held in the shadow of widescale Hindu violence against Muslims in Gujarat, the church called upon the people to vote against candidates who represented corruption and communalism; and in some Christian-dominated constituencies it worked. In at least one constituency (Cortalim) the church's call influenced the election of a third party's candidate in preference to the candidates of the Congress (who faced charges of corruption) and the BJP (who represented communalism).

Even in other times, the church criticised politicians at all available forums for self-aggrandisement and collusion with forces out to destroy Goa. Archbishop Gonsalves made it a practice to inject a few evocative words in every circular, asking the faithful to fight the politicians' misdeeds and other ills of society. In his Justice Sunday message in August 1997, just to take one sample, the archbishop warned: "We need not fall victim to that creeping sense of helplessness in the face of massive corruption. If the malady is within, so is the remedy. We must be on our guard against cynicism which cannot be the antidote to corruption and which in effect serves as the ally of corruption by bringing about a paralysis of thought and action. We are the church — we have well-established lines of communication through our vast network of institutions. We are in a unique position to motivate our brothers and sisters to launch the crusade against corruption from among ourselves and our immediate environs and link up like-minded people and groups across denominational barriers. To change the whole of society at one go is a tall order indeed, but to begin changing oneself is a feasible proposition."

The *Renovacao's* editorials and articles constantly portrayed a bleak future for Goa under the contemporary breed of politicians. They had no commitment to people or democracy, said the *Renovacao* in an editorial in August 1-15, 2000. Politicians frequently indulged in defections and counter-defections; and "this very lack of ideology has led the governance to be identified with corruption which has assumed monumental proportions."

The content of *Renovacao* was to become increasingly aggressive as the church got engaged in a confrontation with the state on some major industrial projects coming up in Goa. One of these projects, Meta Strips Ltd, was located in Sancoale, a part of a cluster of Christian villages, near Vasco da Gama. Seized by nightmares that effluents from the factory, which was to produce zinc and copper from imported scrap, would pollute the air, water and soil, the local Christians rallied behind an NGO called the Anti-Meta Strips Citizens Action Committee set up overnight. Daily press releases, village meetings, memorandums to the government, street processions: the committee within a few months seemed to have emerged as such a powerful public voice that the archbishop and his fellow clergymen began to see in it a consummation of their ideology of resistance. Just as the church had warned, the public anger was directed at the ravening politicians who had showered the factory with pollution clearances without the company putting effluent management machinery in place.

Inspired by the development, the priests plunged into the anti-Meta Strips agitation. They took part in processions, gave passionate speeches at village meetings, offered their presence in the front when the police cracked down upon a mob of stone-pelting agitators outside a Vasco da Gama court. It was a proud moment for the Activist Church when the photographs of two injured priests, clotheless down to the waist, showing the crisscross of red-brown wound marks of cane strikes on their backs, appeared in a local newspaper.

Not long thereafter, in March 2000, the priests were a part of the anti-Meta Strips public rally that turned violent. The agitators blockaded the traffic through the Zuari bridge, the sole link between North and South Goa, hurled rocks at public and private vehicles, damaging some of them. Failing to control the mob with a lathi charge, the police opened fire. The mob in retaliation lynched a policeman. Ignoring the savagery of those who killed the head constable and the vandalism of those who attacked public and private vehicles and the people inside them with rocks, the church assailed the police for "atrocities against innocent citizens," noting that the root of the problem lay in the government not showing concern over the serious threats to life and ecology that Meta Strips posed. The company was going to release pollutants that would kill fish and trees, the church said; not just that, there was also the danger of babies perishing in the mother's womb.

Following the mob violence, the members of the action committee put up a tent outside the state secretariat in Panaji and sat on a fast-unto-death, threatening to lay down their lives in a peaceful manner at the doorstep of the government. To add the weight of his office to their threat, to bless and encourage them, Archbishop Gonsalves paid a visit to them. By lending open and full-hearted support to the agitation, the church had won the sympathy of the Christians in the 'affected' villages. In many ways the archbishopric had begun to direct the activities of the action committee. The *Renovacao* had virtually turned into a journal of the 'people's movement' against Meta Strips; never before had the diocesan mouthpiece devoted so much space to non-religious writings fortnight after fortnight.

With the disquiet increasing in the villages around Meta Strips, the government decided in principle to set up a committee to inquire into the allegations of pollution hazards posed by the company. But a final decision, the then chief minister Luizinho Faleiro said, would be taken only after the archbishop approved of the idea. The archbishop rejected the idea outright. He wanted the Meta Strips factory to close down, and be dismantled and moved out of Goa. Faleiro was neither here nor there. The others attacked him for surrendering the government authority to the feet of the church. Who was the archbishop to take decisions in economic or administrative matters? Faleiro's critics said. The archbishop was a religious head and he must confine himself to religious affairs.

The Elusive Solidarity

Archbishop Gonsalves had made the church an institution to reckon with, and it requires to be noted here that his ancestors before conversion were not Brahmans but lower caste. Archbishop Gonsalves believed in a radical church, a church that attacked the roots of the problems society faced, and not the branches. The traditional church had been engaged in the service to the poor, the disadvantaged, the sick and the marginalised, without ever realising that poverty, discrimination, epidemics and callousness would not end unless the system based on exploitation was thrown out. The radical church would aim to eliminate the cause rather than the effects of social injustice.

The task before the archbishop was not easy. Most clergymen and lay Christians looked upon the church as a temple of faith, rather than an institution of social revolution. The church was a place where people came for mass, sermons, baptism and blessings. It was a prayer hall down which the Father led them into the shelter of God; it was where people came to confess and seek pardon for their sins, or to have courage instilled in them to deal with crises in personal life. The Christians who wanted to do more than pray for themselves and their families could join any of the associations or movements in the church, like the Legionaries of Mary or St. Vincent de Paul, each of which focussed on a particular area of Christian life, like charity or social care. For the Christians who wanted a still deeper involvement there were the Small Christian communities (SCCs) in the parishes devoted to working for the 'renewal' of the church, that is making people live in accordance with the Gospel values.

As none of these communities or associations would go beyond soul-ministering and altruism, the archbishop had to create a new mass organisation within the church to fight social injustice. It was called the Social Action Forum, and every parish was going to have one SAF. The aim of the social action forums would be to encourage the clergy and the laity alike to participate in 'social action' through a process of awareness, conscientisation and practical activity. In the forum, the parish priest had to play a central role.

The priests: they became the first target of the church radicals, especially the senior ones, who stuck to devotion and ritual and refused to speak out against social injustice; such priests were, the radicals said, not wanted. If they were not removed they would pollute the minds of the younger priests with their dogmatic effluents. Those among the senior priests who were willing to be radicalised could be called to counselling sessions and given a refresher course, so that they moved beyond ritual and devotion to social action. An even more radical prescription was the recasting of the formation process in the seminaries and novitiates in order to start producing priests who would devote themselves to social action.

The archbishop's radicalisation met with strong resistance not only inside the church but also outside it. The archbishop desperately wanted the Hindus to join the church's fight against social injustice, but they refused to accept the church's radicalism as universal. Not only for Christians, the church would say, they were fighting for all Goans, but the Hindus would not believe them. The church's desperation to involve Hindus had its root in the dramatically changing demographic profile of Goa. There was an alarming drop in the population of Christians in the postcolonial years. Once a Christian-majority state, Goa had become a Christian-minority state. Christians in large numbers had emigrated to other states of India and abroad; and the heavy inflow of migrants from the other states to Goa was predominantly Hindu.

According to the census figures, between 1961 and 1971, the Hindu population in Goa rose from 384,378 to 496,389, by over 100,000, while the Christian population rose from 227,202 to 270,126, or by only 43,000. As a result the percentage of Christian population fell from 38 to 34 per cent in the ten years after Liberation. (In 1900, the Hindus and Christians equally shared Goa's population.) Over the next census from 1971-81 the Christians were reduced from 34 to 31 per cent of the population; and in the subsequent census from 1981-91, from 31 per cent to 29.86 per cent.

Without the Hindus joining the Christians, the church could not take its campaign for social justice very far. But even when the church explained that the forces behind social oppression, economic exploitation, environmental degradation, and ill-effects of tourism did not discriminate people on the grounds of religion, the Hindus remained elusive. History stood in the way: having been tormented by a collaborationist church the Hindus could not accept the church in a leadership role.

And the radicals only made the matters worse by seeking a justification for their radicalism in the Christian traditions, rather than in secular and liberal traditions. God, insisted the radicals, originally created a beautiful world and made men managers of it. But men proved bad managers, and so God sent down his only son Jesus to earth to restore his original plan, to rebuild the Kingdom of God. Jesus gave every man the mission to rebuild this Kingdom. "And our job here on earth," said the radicals, "is to help Jesus in this work." Rebuilding of the Kingdom of God meant a struggle against the forces that had damaged the God's ecological plan, causing acid rain, browning of land, greenhouse emissions and ozone depletion. All men must work to restore 'eco-spirituality' on earth.

All these issues agitated the Hindus as well. They were organised in several smaller groups, like the Christians, to fight for the protection of Goa's environment. In Kerim, Ponda it was the Hindu villagers who had stopped the US multinational DuPont's Nylon 6,6 project coming up, because they thought the plant manufacturing thread for tyres would cause serious ecological damage. Agreeing on ecological vigilance, the Hindus disagreed on the church's role. And the radicals realized that history was not on their side.

Archbishop Gonsalves, in his Pastoral Theme for 1995, noted that communal harmony in Goa was more of mutual tolerance and peaceful co-existence than a 'positive attitude of true esteem' or a 'mutually enriching fellowship.' Hindus and Christians, he went on, lived in 'parallel' communities, communities which were 'friendly' but not 'fraternal.' Christians must bridge these differences, the archbishop said, asking them to 'respect' the beliefs and cultures 'which differ from our own.' Respecting was the first step, he warned; the second step was recognition of the 'positive contribution' the other beliefs and cultures had made to the 'common cultural, social and religious patrimony of mankind, especially in our Indian and Goan contexts.' The third step was to 'co-operate' with the people of other beliefs and cultures in 'causes of common interest.'

Undoubtedly, the archbishop's Three Steps to Goan Solidarity — Respect, Recognition and Co-operation — was inspired by the openness to the other faiths encouraged by the Pope in the light of Vatican II. They were to recur in the archbishop's messages with greater frequency. There was a 'vast domain of activities' in which Goans, forgetting the 'petty differences' that divide them and remembering the 'common basic elements' which unite them could engage together to tackle the 'wide range of social problems on whose solution depends the development of our beautiful land and the welfare of our peaceful population.' Goans, said the archbishop, formed one family with faith in one God, although He was 'invoked under different names' and in different forms. In his pastoral letters to the clergy, the religious and the lay faithful in the following years, the archbishop never forgot to lay emphasis on inter-religious dialogue, asking them to deeply cultivate an 'attitude of loving respect' toward their sisters and brothers in other faiths. "We should all work — in solidarity with them — for the establishment of a new society, the Kingdom of God."

In theory, they sounded magnificent, exalted, ideal, but in practice they were flawed. The post-Vatican II openness, from which flowed the archbishop's exhortations for multireligious solidarity, proved to be an illusion. It was not openness in the true sense; it was an openness of 'one window open, one window shut' kind. The Vatican did not give the non-Roman Catholic faiths more than a peripheral, superficial, academic respect. The Pope never recognised any ways of salvation outside Jesus Christ. According to this openness, the people of other faiths did deserve respect, but only because they were the children of the same God whose only son was Jesus Christ whose chief pastor was the Pope. Such recognition of the otherness made the men of other faiths look like misguided people, like objects of pity, who needed to be brought on to the right path. Such an attitude was inherently divisive and defective, as it presumed the philosophy, heritage and traditions of the Christian faith as the only manifestation of Truth, giving no importance to the philosophies of other religions.

And what the Pope was doing at the world level, Archbishop Gonsalves had to do in Goa. Never miss an opportunity for issuing exhortations on multireligious solidarity for enabling the mankind to meet common challenges but do not let the other faiths begin to think they can come, in thoughts and traditions, anywhere near the perfect divinity of the Roman Catholic religion. The archbishop never took initiative for an inter-religious dialogue with the *swamis* of the Partagali and Kavle *mutts*, the two most important religious institutions of the Saraswat Brahmans, or the heads of Hindu temples. And although he talked of fighting social injustice, he never even opened a dialogue with the Swami Brahmanand Ponda *mutt*, most of whose followers were poor and lower caste. In a few parishes a congregation with representatives of other faiths was organised, but the interaction remained confined to prayers and homilies.

While the archbishop promoted an illusion, some states of the country began to witness communal violence. Aggressive Hindu organisations, like the Rashtriya Swayamsewak Sangh, the Vishwa Hindu Parishad and the Bajrang Dal, set up a campaign against Christian missionaries who, they alleged, were converting Hindus by inducement, force and fraud. A series of attacks took place in an atmosphere of whipped-up hysteria on churches, church properties, individual priests, nuns and lay Christians in Gujarat, Uttar Pradesh, Bihar, Haryana and other states. In Orissa, rabid Hindus burnt an Australian missionary Graham Staines and his two young sons inside their car alive.

Christian organisations, led by the Catholic Bishops Conference of India (CBCI), held demonstrations and rallies in New Delhi and elsewhere, urging the central and state governments to stop the violent campaign. Offering an open dialogue with the Hindu organisations, they explained that the churches in India had a wholly native clergy who did not believe in conversions by force or fraud. Even though no violence against Christians took place in Goa — except for a minor bomb blast at the St Andrew's church in Vasco da Gama, oddly, by members of a small Muslim cult with its base outside the state — the archbishop and his fellow radicals were forced to give top priority to the concern over protection of the life and liberty of the Christians. The exhortations for multireligious solidarity for the time being took a back seat.

Ghosts of History

When the announcement that the Pope would visit India in November 1999 first came, it triggered off a new kind of protest, putting the Goa church further on the defensive. The aggressive Hindu groups demanded a public apology from the Pope for the atrocities the Catholic church had committed against the innocent Indians in the colonial past. This demand brought into focus the horrors of the Inquisition and threatened to reopen the wounds of the Goan Hindu community. Over the past some years the Vatican had been encouraging clerical discussions on a re-evaluation of its past role. On September 1, 1999 the Pope told that morning's general audience in the Vatican that "The church feels the need to recognise the sins of her own members, when they have been proved by serious historical research, and to request pardon for them from God and man." The Pope further noted, "Only in a continual purification of her members and institutions can (the church) offer the world a coherent witness of the Lord .... The recognition of the communal implications of sin impels the church to ask pardon for the historic sins of her children."

Terming the Pope's statement as too general, unsatisfactory and inadequate, the Hindu fanatics called upon him to offer a specific apology to the Indians before or during his visit. The clergy in Goa found the demand unjustified. First, they said, an apology is something that is offered voluntarily, not demanded of somebody. If the church in Jamaica had apologised for the role of missionaries in the genocide of the native Arawaks, the initiative had come from internal reflection and not as a concession to any demands raised by fanatical Arawak groups. There was no running away from the truth: the Catholic church saw itself as a Pilgrim Church which had its weaknesses, and hence was not averse to acknowledge and repent its sins or wrong-doings. Secondly, the atrocities referred to took place in a particular cultural context. If everyone started demanding apology of the other for historical mistakes, there would be no end to mutual recriminations. Thirdly, an apology would denigrate the glorious history of the church in India which began with the mission of St. Thomas. Fourthly, Pope John Paul II could in no way be held responsible for the 'historical mistakes' of the church. He was coming to India as a guest and he therefore deserved honour, respect and warm welcome, rather than the unpleasantness of a demand for a public apology.

Nevertheless, the aggressive Hindu groups went on filling the air with their chant: We want an apology, we want an apology. If you searched their hearts, they knew the Pope's apology would have no more than an academic value, but they insisted on it because they wanted to use it as an instrument to stop conversions in India. Once the Pope apologised for the past sins he would lose moral justification for any future sins. Most Hindu fanatics still had the crafty, colonial image of the missionary in their mind who rode on horseback through the country forcing helpless people to change their religion. "Conversions," said a Vishwa Hindu Parishad leader Giriraj Kishore, "not only change the religion of the converted but also their nationality."

The Pope offered no apology. Shortly after he returned to Rome, the Hindu fanatics revived their demand for a *swadeshi* or Indianised Church. They wanted the churches in India to declare independence from their central authorities who had seats in other countries. With that, assignments of foreign missionaries to India would also stop. In their view the best model of a *swadeshi* church was Kerala's Marathoma church, founded in the times of St. Thomas, whose entire authority was in the hands of local people, who had even continued with some of the old native customs. In the Roman Catholic structure, the Hindu fanatics said, the churches had to take the approval of the Vatican even for the smallest of things, like the manner in which a church property could be used or disposed of. Besides, the Roman Catholic faith did not allow revival of the native customs which had been banned by the Inquisition. The churches could continue taking spiritual guidance from their authorities abroad, but they could not become a truly Indian, a *swadeshi* church until they incorporated native customs into their faith and came to enjoy total autonomy in managing their non-religious affairs.

Absurd: that's how the Christian clergy described the demand for a *swadeshi* church. The churches had long been Indianised, they said. All the bishops were Indians, all the other clerics too. What hurt them, they noted, was the insinuation of extraterritorial loyalties of the Christians, of those who had fought shoulder to shoulder with members of other communities for the nation against all enemies before and after independence. Christians had more than anybody else proven their nationalism by promoting native languages, education, health care and arts. And contrary to the adverse propaganda, the Christian churches had incorporated native traditions in the liturgy. In many churches and chapels the mass was celebrated with symbols normally associated with Hindu spiritual and mystical traditions, like *pushpa aarti* (veneration with flowers), *dhup aarti* (veneration with incense) and *chandan tilak* (sandal mark on the forehead). "The Indian church," said an article in the *Renewal* of November 1-15, 1999, the month of Pope John Paul II's visit, "is making earnest efforts to flow along the Ganges and the Godavari."

A truly *swadeshi* church would not only stop at that but also stop conversions, said the Hindu fanatics. On this the Christian leaders differed. Evangelization, they said, was integral to the church, its raison d'etre: founded by Jesus to rebuild the Kingdom of God on the earth, it had a mission to fulfill; it must go on bringing the whole of mankind into its fold. Cardinal Jozef Tomko, the Prefect of the Congregation for the Evangelization of Peoples who represented the Pope at India's first national assembly of the Catholic church from September 20-24, 2000, told 10,000 Indian bishops and other representatives of the dioceses: " The incarnation and birth of Jesus Christ is the true sensational news for all time, the true Good News which must be proclaimed to every living being, to men and women of every age. Being members of the Catholic church you are also part of a church in mission. The church exists to evangelize just as a fire exists to burn: This is its nature."

During his visit to India, the Pope gave his apostolic exhortation to the synod of bishops' special assembly for Asia emphasizing that evangelization was the central mission of the church. The bishops, he noted, had read the signs of the times in Asia: the peoples of this continent were crying out for a saviour, for the 'door' that will lead them out of darkness. Jesus was the saviour and the door to life. Giving them a 'special responsibility,' the Pope asked the bishops to make "greater efforts to spread the Gospel of salvation throughout the length and breadth of the human geography of Asia."

A fire, the Pope went on, could only be lit by something that was itself on fire. The Gospel could be preached only by a clergy and laity who are "themselves on fire with the love of Christ and burning with a zeal to make him known, loved and followed." Observing that in parts of Asia freedom to proclaim the Gospel was denied or restricted, the Pope urged them not to be deterred by persecution, because the 'persecuted Christians' formed a continuity with the martyrs of the past and were the 'hidden pillars of the church.' He asked Christians to use the mass media, radio, news agencies and publications, as the new means of evangelization, as a means to integrate the Gospel into the new cultural of communication. A new dynamism was called for in the missionary activity, and the traditional missionary institutes must not 'waver in their missionary commitment.' The dioceses were to make mission an integral part of their pastoral plans. Every diocese should encourage opening of local missionary societies to promote the missionary cause.

In his homily the next day, still in India, the Pope gave a rousing call to Christians which the Hindu organisations found provocative and ominous. The Pope said: "Just as the first millenium saw the Cross firmly planted in the soil of Europe, and the second in that of America and Africa, so may the Third Christian Millenium witness a great harvest of faith on this vast and vital continent." Asia, the Pope had observed in his post-synodal apostolic exhortation, was suffering under political and religious oppression, economic misery and cultures of marginalisation which created an army of millions of poor people, exploited children, women treated as slaves, refugees, migrants, aboriginal people who were also deprived of health care. Under such conditions, the church had to teach its 'social doctrine,' take up the defence of human rights and promotion of social justice as an 'inescapable and unrenounceable' challenge and offer education and health care to them with a 'clear Christian identity.'

The Hindu fanatics severely criticised the Pope's 'Target Asia' call, warning that since China had banned Christian missionary activity and the Muslim nations did not allow it, the call for evangelization of the last remaining continent in the third millenium by the Roman Catholic Church was going to mean a concentration of proselytizing effort upon India, because the country guaranteed freedom for propagation of faith, making missionary targets achievable. It was in fact to fortify against the 'Target Asia' plan that the Hindu groups had started pressing for a *swadeshi* church. They wanted to convey to the Pope a message that if he ever tried implementing his 'Target Asia' plan in India he would face a retaliation.

This threat restrained the Catholic bishops in India, including the archbishop of Goa, from openly propagating 'Target Asia.' In fact, for a while, the church went on the defensive, denying it was engaged in conversions. An article in the *Renovacao* (October 16-31, 1999) argued that had the mass conversions been going on as alleged, the Christian population in the country would not have declined from 2.8 per cent of the total population in 1947 to 2.4 per cent in 1999. How could an 'insignificant religious minority like the Christians' threaten the religious majority with conversions? the article asked. And, had the educational institutions run by Christians been used to force or induce conversions, the article noted, why would parents from the Hindu community join the long queues to collect their admission forms and use all kinds of pressures to get their children enrolled into them?

The Goa church did not need to explain anything: conversions had not been an issue here. In spite of the fact that Christians made a large minority in the state they did not pose any religious threat to the Hindus. Here too the church had been running schools and charitable institutions but it was acknowledged by the Hindus that they had not been used for inducing or forcing conversions in the postcolonial years. Even though Archbishop Gonsalves and his fellow brothers affirmed and reaffirmed their commitment to the Pope's post-synodal exhortation at every forum they never really put his Evangelization-of-Asia plan into action in their archdiocese. They knew the church would be further isolated if they went by the letter and spirit of the exhortation.

However, the hardliners in the Vatican were to leave them with no choice. Following the Pope's 'Target Asia' exhortation came the sensational presentation by the Prefect of the Congregation for the Doctrine of the Faith Cardinal Joseph Ratzinger of *Dominus Jesus*. Endorsed by the Pope, *Dominus Jesus* proclaimed to the world that there was no salvation but in the membership of the Catholic Church, thus negating the proclamation of Vatican II that salvation was possible also outside the church.

Dominus Jesus held that Jesus was 'the way, the truth, and the life,' and the church founded by Him was 'the instrument of salvation for all humanity.' "Theories of salvific action of God beyond the unique mediation of Christ are contrary to the Catholic faith .... In fact the Kingdom of God which we know from revelation cannot be detached either from Christ or from the Church." While the Catholic church had 'sincere respect' for other religions, said *Dominus Jesus*, it could not accept that "one religion is as good as another." The other religions did not have a 'divine origin' or a destined 'salvation efficacy.' The uniqueness of the Catholic faith lay in the fact that the "canonical books of the Old and New Testaments ... are inspired by the Holy Spirit, have God as their author."

Ratzinger's *Dominus Jesus* had put a question mark over the 30 years of ecumenism and inter-religious dialogue encouraged by the openness of Vatican II. If the Catholic church was not to accept any other paths to salvation the leaders of other faiths would not consider it worthwhile any more to carry on the dialogue with it. Sensing this, the Vatican clarified that *Dominus Jesus* did not amount to closing of doors but only emphasized the fact of universality of salvation through Jesus Christ, without any prejudice to inter-faith dialogue.

In October 2000, on the occasion of Diwali, the Hindu festival of lights, Cardinal Francis Arinze, President of the Pontifical Council for Inter-religious Dialogue, sent a message to Indians, saying that "It is my sincere wish and prayer that we Hindus and Christians, through our mutual respect, esteem and friendship, may become concrete examples and a proof of harmony and peace for many others throughout India and beyond ... . We are convinced that together we can achieve much for the good of the world. We see, for example, that our two religious traditions ..., each according to its distinctive teachings, give the mystery of God the highest place in human life."

The Goa church echoed the Vatican messages such as the one from Cardinal Arinze but it was clear that with the revival of the ideology of absolute supremacy of the Catholic church with *Dominus Jesus*, the other religious and cultural communities, judged unequal and unfit, were alienated. There was only one way the Goa church could make a fresh endeavour to build bridges with the Hindu community; and that was by telling them frankly that although it did not consider their faith as equal, an alliance could still be built with them on the common threats faced by the Goans. If the Hindus accepted it, the solidarity might still become a reality. But the chances of Hindu acceptance were dim, because *Dominus Jesus* trivialised Hinduism, the Pope's 'Target Asia' threatened them, and the Goa church would not come out of its Christian constituency.

6

An Empty Pitcher

It is heartening to find that the dream of a uniform civil code in the country finds its realization in the Union Territory of Goa, Daman and Diu only. How many outside Goa are aware of this, I cannot guess .... A uniform civil code (in the country) remains today a distant goal. In my view it would be a retrogade step if Goa too were to give up uniformity in its personal laws which it now possesses.

— Y V Chandrachud, former chief justice of India, 1979

Goa's Uniform Civil Code

History bristles with ironies: if the Portuguese divided the Hindus and Christians in a thousand ways, so much so that the two communities are failing to bridge the chasm even in the postcolonial era, they united them in at least one way. They gave them a common civil code. While Christians enjoyed privileges in the domain of public affairs under the Portuguese regime, in the realm of personal affairs they were treated at par with the people of other religions. These personal affairs were covered under the family laws which dealt with marriage, divorce, succession, guardianship of children, gifts, adoption and such matters. People of all faiths found these family laws — loosely termed as the common civil code — so good and useful that even though they threw the Portuguese out they let this gift of theirs be permanently enshrined in their law-book.

Goa thus, was to be the only state of India where a uniform civil code would be in force. In the rest of India, the paradox with which the Constitution was born — the unceasingly painful wounds of discrimination on grounds of religion and gender being outlawed, yet allowed in personal laws — still governed the lives of the people. There were separate sets of family laws for members of every faith. It was only in accordance with these faith-specific laws that the courts were allowed to decide family cases. Politicians, fearing they might forfeit minority vote, would not even talk of bringing up a legislation to enforce a uniform civil code throughout the country.

In order to remind the politicians of their nightmares about losing minority vote from time to time, the high priests of some of the communities warned that God Himself had written their personal laws and no government or judge could change them. When in 1986 the Supreme Court granted maintenance to a divorced and helpless old Muslim woman named Shah Bano on the basis of provisions in the Quran, the Muslim clerics challenged its authority to interpret their holy scripture. Succumbing to their pressures, the then prime minister Rajiv Gandhi got a special legislation passed, shutting the doors which the Supreme Court had opened for the helpless Muslim women.

In the rest of India, the family laws were not only religion-specific but also subject-specific. Thus, Hindus were governed by at least twelve family laws: the Hindu Marriage Act, Hindu Adoption and Maintenance Act, Hindu Succession Act, Hindu Minority and Guardianship Act, Hindu Disposition of Property Act, Hindu Woman's Right to Property Act, Hindu Widows Remarriage Act, Child Marriage Restraint Act, Dowry Prohibition Act, Hindu Inheritance (Removal of Disability) Act, Hindu Gains For Learning Act and Arya Marriage Validity Act; the Muslims by two, the Shariat Act and Muslim Women (Protection of Rights on Divorce) Act; the Christians by two, the Indian Christian Marriage Act and Indian Divorce Act; and the Parsis by the omnibus Parsi Marriage and Divorce Act.

But in Goa family laws had been the same for all the religious communities since 1870 when the Portuguese crown for the first time introduced a comprehensive Civil Code making it uniformly applicable to citizens of Portugal as well as its overseas provinces — except for the fact that the Catholics were allowed a special privilege in marriage which was not allowed to people of other religions (after all, Roman Catholicism was the state religion in monarchical Portugal.) Under the new code only civil marriages were valid. But in the case of Catholics, marriages performed in the church were also granted validity. Marriages of Hindus conducted with Vedic rites or of Muslims with Islamic rites had no standing in law.

Behind the grant of privilege to the Catholics the work of the church could be seen. The church was afraid of losing its influence over the laity if marriages were performed in government offices rather than in churches. The church was also worried that if the civil code governed marriages of Catholics it would also govern divorces among them, weakening the community. If the marriages were solemnised in the church, a divorce would be out of question, since the Roman Catholic faith did not allow a break-up of a canonical marriage except by death.

In 1910, forty years after the civil code came into force, republicans seized power in Portugal and abolished the monarchy. Quickly getting down to business, they declared the state separated from the church and passed a set of family laws, ending the special privilege the Catholics had enjoyed. These laws — the Law of Marriage, the Law of Divorce and the Code of Civil Registration — laid down common procedures for all for the registration of marriage and divorce. Even the Catholics now had to conduct their marriage before the civil registrar which alone had a legal validity.

With this the divorce of the Catholics came under the jurisdiction of the civil courts, something the church profoundly dreaded. Accepting the irrevocability of a canonical marriage, the monarchical civil code had made no provision in law for the divorce of a Catholic couple. What it allowed in the extreme cases of marital discord was a judicial separation in which the marital ties remained intact but the man and wife were separated. It was called the 'divorce of the Catholics' and the process took years to complete.

Having been used for centuries to seeing marriages take place only in the church, the Catholics evolved a way of meeting the new challenge of the republican laws: they would first perform their marriage in the civil registrar's office and then go to the church to solemnise it with religious rites. It was not actually the Catholics alone who were doing it. Even the Hindus and Muslims had been getting married twice, once before the servants of the public and a second time before the ministers of god. The Hindus and Muslims had been doing it since the code was enforced in 1870. With the republic enactments, the Catholics also joined them in this dual propitiation of both the religious and political gods.

However, the church was not happy. It failed to reconcile to marriages of its faithfuls outside the church and kept on pressurizing the government to grant legal validity to canonical marriage. It ultimately succeeded in its effort in 1940 when Portugal and the Holy See signed an international treaty known as *Concordata*. This treaty ended the system of two marriages and allowed the Catholics to marry in the church after registering their marriage with the parishes or Catholic missions which were considered as offices of civil registration for the purpose of canonical marriage between natives. The missionaries were also empowered to issue no objection certificates before the solemnization of the marriage.

The non-native Catholics had to procure a no objection certificate from the civil registrar without which the minister of the church could not solemnize the marriage. The Concordata said: " The Portuguese state grants civil effects to the marriages celebrated in conformity with the canonical laws, provided that the record of marriage is transcribed in the competent registration of the civil status ... ." The Catholic minister who solemnized the marriage was bound by law to pass on a duplicate of the canonical registration of marriage to the department of civil registration. Failure on this count on his part could invite penalties.

As a natural corrollary to these provisions, divorce among Catholics passed out from the jurisdiction of the civil courts to ecclesiastical courts. The Concordata upheld the Vatican dictum that a canonical marriage was inviolable and indissoluble, except by death. Catholics seeking nullity of their marriage had to apply to the ecclesiastical courts and offices whose final judgement had to be sent for verification by the highest ecclesiastical court in Rome whose decree was to be forwarded to the competent High Court which had to "enforce them without revision and confirmation" and order that the decree be endorsed in the books of civil registration on the margin of the certificate of marriage. These provisions remained valid until 1974, when the judicial commissioner of Goa J Tito Menezes, hearing a petition on divorce, declared the Concordata article on divorce *ultra vires* Articles 14 and 15 of the Indian Constitution which guaranteed no discrimination on the basis of creed. The authority of the ecclesiastical courts in matters of divorce of Catholics was thus taken away and vested back in the civil courts.

Thus ended the special privilege the Catholics had enjoyed for nearly forty years since the enforcement of the civil code in 1870 and for about thirty years from 1946 to 1974. But certain privileges granted to the Hindus and other non-Catholics under the civil code continued.

Known as the Law of Usages and Customs, these privileges covered adoption, constitution and reconstitution of joint family, succession, religious oaths, a second marriage by the male spouse on grounds of an issueless first marriage, recognition of illegitimate children and other practices. The law gave the Hindus and other non-Catholics an option not to follow these usages and customs and opt by common agreement for the application of the provisions of the civil code. In an overwhelming number of cases the Hindus and other non-Catholics chose the option of general law, which was applicable to all the communities, thus making the codes of usages and customs virtually irrelevant. However, these codes continue on the statute book as they have not been repealed.

Aspects of the Civil Code

One of the most unique features of the monarchical civil code, which neither the republicans nor the Salazarists ever tampered with, was the relationship of marriage to property. The code required the spouses to make an ante-nuptial agreement before the marriage was solemnized on the regime by which they would like their properties to be governed. Treated as a contract, this agreement had to be recorded by public deed for legal validity. There were four regimes under which marital property could be governed.

One was called the *communion of properties*. Under this regime, all the properties brought by either of the spouses by gift, succession or a previous exclusive right from before the marriage as well as all the properties acquired or earned by either of them during the subsistence of the marriage were to be held as common property by the two spouses till the dissolution of their marriage by death, divorce or separation. No revocation of or changes in the contract was allowed during the subsistence of marriage.

The debts incurred prior to the marriage were to be paid from the respective share of the debtor spouse from the acquired properties, while the debts incurred during the subsistence of the marriage were to be paid by both the spouses where they had jointly incurred the liability. The ownership and possession of the common properties were vested in both the spouses during the subsistence of the marriage but the administration of the properties, without the exclusion of the exclusive properties of the wife, lay with the husband. The immoveable properties could not be alienated or charged in any manner without the consent and agreement of both the spouses. The husband was not allowed to renounce any inheritance without the consent of the wife. In the case of divorce, the properties of the *communion* were to be equally divided between the spouses or their heirs. The regime of *communion of properties* was also applicable to marriages in which no ante-nuptial contract was signed between the spouses.

The second regime was called *separation of properties* under which either of the spouses had exclusive ownership of whatever he or she brought, acquired or earned and was free to dispose them without the other's consent, except in the case of moveable properties. The third regime was a *mixed regime* of the first and second regimes in which the spouses agreed on *separation of properties* held from before the marriage and on *communion of properties* acquired during the subsistence of marriage. The fourth regime, called the *dotal regime*, applied to cases in which the wife or her family gave a sum in cash or kind to the husband, to be returned to her in the event of the dissolution of the marriage.

Although all these four regimes remained in force, in a majority of cases the spouses preferred not to sign any ante-nuptial contract with regard to the manner of allocation, administration and distribution of their properties. As a result, the regime of *communion of properties* applied to most marriages. Former additional solicitor general Manohar Usgaocar, who is an authority on Goa's family laws, notes: "… (The) fourth regime was very rarely used. The second and third regimes were in use, but they were not very common. (It is) to be noted that, even when the second regime was adopted, normally there was a condition that if there are issues from the marriage, the regime will not be of absolute separation but will be of *communion of properties*. The conclusion, therefore, would be that by and large the regime of *communion of properties* was followed. And it would not be an exaggeration to say that 98% of the population followed this regime."

The *communion of properties* did not mean common or joint property. In a joint property if one of the title holders dies his right ceases and passes on to the surviving title holder. In a common property if one of the title holders dies his right passes on to his heir or nominee; also, every co-owner has a right to ask for division of the common property for his individual share and to transfer his title to someone else. The *communion* is a unique common property in more than one sense. First, it is based on marriage. Thus two brothers or two friends or two partners desirous of holding a common property cannot opt for a regime of *communion of properties*.

Secondly, it gives right to one half of the property to either of the spouses. The Portuguese used to call this half share *meacao* or moity. Thirdly, it allows either of the spouses to hold individual properties that would not form a part of the *communion*. Such individual properties can include gifts or properties bequeathed to any spouse with a clear clause of non-communicability with the other spouse or jewellery, garments and other objects of personal use given to him or her before marriage. Fourthly, as far as the *communion* is concerned, the husband and wife jointly have one right to the common property and neither of them is permitted to transfer his or her share or to ask for separation during the subsistence of the marriage. Fifthly, the *communion* is reserved for the special purpose of providing for the expenditure for the maintenance of the couple and repaying the debts that they might incur. Since the right to hold this unique common property flows from the marriage only the dissolution of it could cause a partition of it.

When the marriage is dissolved by divorce each spouse gets one half of the property or moity. Irrespective of who has given the cause for divorce, an equal division takes place. When the marriage is dissolved by death, say of the husband, the wife gets half of the property and the remaining half is distributed among the children. The wife's moity is never divided among children, since succession is of the husband's side only. Property has to be divided equally between the two spouses even when there is a separation.

A spouse is entitled to equal share of the common property even if he or she has not brought any ancestral or previously-held assets from before marriage. If the husband brings assets worth ten rupees and the wife brings nothing, the wife becomes entitled to five rupees by the mere fact of marriage. Similarly if the wife brings assets worth ten rupees and the husband brings nothing, the husband gets the right to half the assets worth five rupees. Even if the marriage breaks on the morning following the wedding night the spouses will have to share the property equally. The moral philosophy behind the regime of *comm-*

union was to consolidate the marital bond by making the property common, indivisible and usable only for joint maintenance and by reducing the scope for marital discord with the threat of equal partition hanging over either spouse's head like a Damocles' Sword.

In principle, therefore, no discrimination was made on the basis of sex in the regimes of property acquired or held by the spouses. Neither was any discrimination on the basis of gender made in the civil code in succession. Sons and daughters stood on the same footing and were entitled to equal shares in the distribution of property. It was a common practice among parents to get a declaration signed by the daughter at the time of her marriage saying that she had received so much money by way of her share in their property. The idea was to deny her right to inheritance after the death of the parents and have the property distributed only among sons or their male successors. But the interesting thing was that the daughter did not lose her right to inheritance by any such declaration. Article 2042 of the civil code said: "No one shall, not even by ante-nuptial contract, renounce the right to succession of a living person, or alienate or charge the rights, which he eventually might have to be the inheritance of that person."

Usgaocar explains it with a very good example. Let us assume, he says, that a woman gets married in 1975. At the time of her marriage her parents give her Rs 50,000 in cash and take a declaration from her that this was the amount given to her by way of her future share in their property and hence she would have no claim to the inheritance. The parents die in 1991, leaving behind the married daughter and a son and an estate worth Rs 4 lakh without any will. The right to inheritance opens only after the death of parents. Consequently, the daughter becomes entitled to the half share of her parental estate only in 1991, the other half going to the son. But before the calculation of the two half-shares the cash of Rs 50,000 given to her at the time of her marriage will be added to the total value of the parents' estate after their death. The total value of the estate would thus be taken to be Rs 4.50 lakh and the same will be equally divided between the daughter and the son. The daughter's share comes to Rs 2.25 lakh. Since she has already received Rs 50,000, she will get only Rs 1.75 lakh.

The gender equality and religious neutrality that make Goa's family laws stand out from those in the rest of the country are not only guaranteed by the sharing of matrimonial and inherited property but also by the grounds allowed for divorce and maintenance. The Portuguese Law of Divorce, 1910 allows any of the spouses to apply for divorce or both of them to do so jointly. The latter is known as divorce by mutual consent and the former as contested divorce. The contested divorce may be obtained on the following grounds: Adultery committed by the wife; adultery committed by the husband; conviction and sentencing of one of the spouses to major penalties; illtreatment or serious injuries to any of the spouses; complete abandonment of the conjugal domicile for a period of not less than three years; absence, where nothing has been heard of the absentee, for a period of not less than four years; incurable unsoundness of mind when at least three years have elapsed after its pronouncement by judgement; de facto separation, freely consented to, for ten consecutive years, whatever the cause of separation; chronic vice of gambling and contagious and incurable disease.

Scene in Rest of India

In the rest of India divorce is largely governed by the personal laws of the communities — the Hindu Marriage Act, 1956, the Muslim Personal Law (Shariat) Application Act, 1937, the Dissolution of Muslim Marriages Act, 1939, Indian Divorce Act, 1869 and Parsi Marriage and Divorce Act, 1936 — but there is also a law providing for civil (marriages and) divorces called the Special Marriage Act, 1954. Only the Hindus, Parsis and the couples who get married in the presence of the civil registrar under the Special Marrriage Act are allowed, like the Goans, a divorce by mutual consent. The Muslims and Christians are not entitled to such divorce unless they have, apart from solemnizing a religious marriage, also registered with the civil registrar under the Special Marriage Act.

The Special Marriage Act is the only one law in force in the country which maintains religious and gender neutrality just as Goa's Law of Divorce does on matters of divorce. The grounds for divorce available to both the spouses under the two laws are quite similar. In fact, the Special Marriage Act goes a few steps further than the Goa law and provides for certain grounds for divorce available only to the wife. These grounds expand the meaning of 'cruelty' as the grounds for divorce to specifically include rape, sodomy or bestiality by the husband.

They also give her right to seek divorce on the grounds of non-cohabitation for a year following a court order for judicial separation.

Comparatively, the Hindu and Parsi personal laws give the wife more rights than the Muslim and Christian personal laws. Apart from the grounds of adultery, cruelty, desertion, mental disorder, disappearance, communicable disease and non-cohabitation, the Hindu Marriage Act makes two other grounds available to both the spouses for seeking divorce: one, conversion to another religion, and second, renunciation of the world for a religious order. It makes the following grounds available only to the wife: bigamy, rape, sodomy or bestiality by husband; a court order of maintenance to the wife, followed by a period of non-cohabitation of one year; and repudiation of the marriage.

The Parsi Marriage and Divorce Act, apart from the grounds of adultery, cruelty, desertion, mental disorder, communicable disease contracted from the spouse, non-cohabitation and imprisonment, makes three other grounds available to both the spouses for divorce: conversion to another religion, bigamy or unnatural offence and no intercourse for one year after an order for judicial separation, restitution of conjugal rights or maintenance has been passed by a court. This act makes two grounds available only to the wife: rape by husband of another woman; and the husband forcing her into prostitution. Unlike the Special Marriage Act and Hindu Marriage Act, the Parsi Marriage and Divorce Act gives the husband the right to divorce his wife if she is made pregnant by another man.

The Indian Divorce Act, which is applicable to Christians, is very unjust to the wife. While the husband is entitled to seek a divorce from his wife merely on the grounds of her adultery, the wife is not given this right. She can only file for a divorce if the husband has not only committed simple adultery but bigamy with adultery, incestous adultery, adultery with cruelty or adultery with desertion for two years or more. The grounds of imprisonment, communicable disease, insanity and desertion, which are available to the Hindu, Parsi and Goan women are not available to the Christian women in the other states of India.

Muslim women are trapped under the most unjust divorce laws. A Muslim husband can divorce his wife any moment in her life without giving any grounds. He gets this savage privilege from the Shariat Act, 1937 which lays down that all questions regarding marriage and dissolution of marriage will be decided according to the Muslim personal law. Muslim men usually resort to a divorce known in Muslim personal law as *talaq-ul-biddat* (and popularly as triple *talaq*). The man has to just make three pronouncements during a single 'tuhr' (period between two menstruation cycles) either in one sentence, e.g., "I divorce thee thrice" or in separate sentences, e.g., "I divorce thee, I divorce thee, I divorce thee" *(talaq, talaq, talaq)* to dissolve the marriage. The husband is not obliged to assign any reasons or to have witnesses for the pronouncement. He is not obliged to give any time for a change of mind or reconciliation.

According to Sanober Keshwaar, lawyer and Muslim women's rights campaigner, Prophet Mohammed did not approve of triple talaq. He permitted only two forms of divorce: *talaq hasan* or the good divorce and *talaq ahsan* or the best divorce. In *talaq hasan* the husband has to make three pronouncements of divorce over the period of a *'tuhr'* during which he will not have sexual intercourse with his wife or his pronouncement will become invalid. In *talaq ahsan* the man has to make just one pronouncement but it can become effective only after the *iddat* period is over. (*Iddat* is usually calculated as four months and ten days.) Women's rights campaigners have taken their plea to the All India Muslim Personal Law Board but the highest religious body has continued to be dogmatic in this matter.

Theoretically, the Muslim personal law treats marriage as a contract and provides for a *nikaahnama*, matrimonial settlement, in which the two spouses can stipulate the terms and conditions of the marriage. Theoretically again, the wife can ask the husband to agree not to take another wife, to pay the *mehr* (dower) partly at the time of marriage and partly later or to provide for her maintenance during the subsistence of the marriage. But in reality, neither the women nor their parents insist on such safeguards in the *nikaahnama*. Most women may actually be totally ignorant of the worth of the *nikaahnama*, and the Muslim theologians and qazis, who have been telling everybody the personal law is God's own law, have made no endeavour to educate them on the subject. In the end the women may end up getting nothing from their husband after divorce, not even their *mehr* which may be forfeited. With a one-sided *nikaahnama*, the Muslim woman must suffer injustices even during the subsistence of the marriage. Using the privilege given to him by the personal law the man can marry four wives, subjecting his first wife, and also the other ones, to various forms of discrimination and persecution.

A Muslim woman is entitled to sue for divorce under the Dissolution of the Muslim Marriages Act, 1939 on any of the following eight grounds:

    i. Disappearance of husband for four years or more
   ii. Denial of maintenance for two years or more to her by the husband
  iii. Imprisonment of seven years or more
  iv. Desertion for three years
   v. Impotence
  vi. Insanity or communicable disease
 vii. Cruelty
viii. Non-consummation of marriage until the age of 18.

The Act empowers the civil court to dissolve the marriage on any ground which the Muslim personal law holds as valid for dissolution of marriages. This shows that the list of eight grounds specified in the Act is merely illustrative. The main purpose of the Act is to confer on the civil courts of India the general power of the qazi in respect of judicial divorce as recognised in Muslim personal law.

As on marriage and divorce, so on maintenance, Goa's family laws are more reasonable and equitable than the personal laws. Goa's Law of Divorce gives the right to either of the spouses to claim interim and permanent maintenance from the other. The quantum of such maintenance depends on the 'needs' of the spouse who has to receive it and the 'circumstances' of the one who has to provide it. In no case the quantum of permanent alimony can exceed one-third of the net income of the provider. But the quantum fixed is not immutable.

If in the future the providing spouse proves that his circumstances do not permit him to continue paying the quantum earlier fixed or that her needs are lesser than this amount, the court may suitably reduce it. In the same manner, if in the future the receiving spouse proves that her needs are greater than the amount fixed as maintenance for her and that the other spouse can afford to pay her a bigger allowance in view of his improved financial position, the court can increase it. The right to maintenance ceases if the providing spouse is no more in a position to continue paying it or the receiving spouse does not need it. It also ceases if the receiving spouse remarries or "becomes unworthy of such benefit by his/her moral conduct."

The Muslim personal law is silent on maintenance. Some Muslim theologians have argued that the marriage of a woman in Muslim community does not change her belongingness from her natal home to her marital home; and therefore, her husband is not required to pay her any maintenance after divorce. This gives the husband an unquestionable privilege to throw the wife out of his home into penury, because the unquestioning responsibility to look after her is of her parents! The Muslim Women (Protection of Right on Divorce) Act, 1986, the mullah-pampering legislation forced through Parliament by Rajiv Gandhi, actually exonerates husbands from maintaining their wives after divorce and places the burden of maintenance on the woman's blood relations.

Behind the veneer of entitling divorced Muslim women to maintenance by their former husbands the Act handed them an extremely vague law, denying them a permanent alimony. Section 3 of the Act said: " A divorced woman shall be entitled to a reasonable and fair provision and maintenance to be made and paid to her within the *iddat* period by her former husband." But it is yet to be established by the Supreme Court whether this provision means payment of alimony only for the period of *iddat* or a 'reasonable and fair provision' for the whole of her life. High courts have given different verdicts, some interpreting it to mean maintenance only for the *iddat* period and others construing it as a lumpsum amount enabling the woman to have financial independence, in addition to the monthly payment of maintenance during the four months and ten days of the *iddat* period.

On maintenance, the Christian women too face several handicaps. The Indian Divorce Act sets a ceiling on the amount of interim maintenance at one-fifths of the husband's income, which means inadequate resources for her to litigate. The permanent alimony is decided after taking into account the wife's fortune and the earning ability of the husband. The court has powers to suspend payments if the spouse is unable to pay. Particularly unjust to Christian women are the sections 38 and 39 of the Act. Under Section 38 the court can appoint a trustee for the wife and direct that maintenance payments be paid to him. This takes away the independence of the woman about how to use her allowance. Under Section 39 the court can partition out the property of an adulterous woman between her husband and children.

A majority of court petitions for maintenance in the country are filed by indigent Hindu wives under the Hindu Marriage Act. Section 24 of the Act entitles the spouse to an interim maintenance depending on her needs and the other's income. Section 25 provides for a permanent alimony and it is left entirely for the courts to decide how much the indigent wife needs. Usually the courts have seen permanent maintenance as a subsistence or survival allowance and the amounts fixed have been small. Under another law called the Hindu Adoption and Maintenance Act, abandoned, deserted and indigent wives can claim maintenance from their husband without seeking a divorce. This law enables even the second wife, whose marriage was declared void, to get maintenance. But as under the Hindu Marriage Act, the maintenance awarded under this law has usually been meagre. The maintenance provisions in the Parsi Marriage and Divorce Act are similar to those in the Hindu Marriage Act, except for the provision, like the one in the Indian Divorce Act, for appointment by the court of a trustee to receive the maintenance payments on behalf of the spouse. The Special Marriage Act entitles only the wife to maintenance.

Clearly the principles governing the award of interim or permanent maintenance differ from personal law to personal law. They need to be changed, modified, standardised and strengthened with a view to providing justice to women of all communities. Even Goa's Law of Divorce is unjust to women on one count. Like some of the personal laws, this law makes the continuance of payment of permanent maintenance conditional upon the 'moral conduct' of the wife. Cessation of alimony on the remarriage of the wife may be a reasonable principle (although feminists consider this also wrong and unfair) but to stop paying maintenance to a divorcee who may have a sexual relationship with another man is plainly absurd. How can the law expect a woman to be faithful to her former husband? Why should a woman become a recluse after the dissolution of her marriage? The 'moral conduct' proviso requires to be knocked off the statute because this constitutes a curtailment of the human rights of women.

Muslims and the Goa Code

One of the Directive Principles of State Policy enshrined in the Indian Constitution (Article 44) lays down that, "The State shall endeavour to secure for the citizens a Uniform Civil Code throughout the territory of India." The State has refrained from making this endeavour for fear of minority reaction, so Article 44 remains on paper. Nevertheless, without an endeavour a uniform civil code has come into force in Goa, and the State has granted legal sanction to it. After Liberation the Indian State extended all the central laws to Goa but refrained from extending the personal laws. The Portuguese family laws were left untouched. Former chief justice of the Supreme Court Y V Chandrachud said Goa's family laws provided "an ideal for the rest of the country," hoping that they might one day "awaken the rest of bigoted India and inspire it to emulate Goa."

Chandrachud's commendation apart, Goa's family laws were never promoted as a model for a national uniform civil code by the State. None of the national political parties, whether in power or opposition, showed interest in raising popular awareness in the rest of the country about them. Even the political parties which made uniform civil code a part of their manifesto at every election would not propagate the Goa model. The judiciary alone showed concern, whenever the opportunity of a relevant case offered itself, over the non-existence of a uniform civil code in the country, never failing to urge the State to fulfill the commitment made in Article 44. But the elected representatives who lorded over the executive preferrred not to make any endeavour at all in this direction in spite of the court's urgings.

While Goa's family laws remained an unrealized ideal for the rest of the country the Muslim fundamentalists, for the fear of whom the State had not dared to enforce a uniform civil code, built up a campaign for the extension of the Muslim personal law to the state. The campaign was triggered by the appointment in December 1981 of a Personal Law Committee by the Goa government to examine the feasibility of repealing the Portuguese family laws and replacing them with the personal laws in force in the rest of India. The party in power then, both in Panaji and New Delhi, was the Congress led by Indira Gandhi who was known for placating the Muslim fundamentalists for her political survival. Incidentally, the law minister of the Goa government at the time also happened to be a Muslim who would not hide from anybody that the committee's mandate was to get rid of the "outmoded colonial laws and to replace them with our own laws."

Muslim fundamentalists of Goa thought their opportunity was here and now. They drummed up a raucous propaganda. How could a population of a few thousand Muslims in Goa be governed by a different set of family laws when the millions of Muslims in the rest of the country were governed by the Muslim personal law? Is Goa not a part of India? Are Muslims in Goa not part of the national mainstream? Do we not want uniformity of laws throughout the country? The All-India Muslim Personal Law Board passed a resolution deploring the fact that the Shariat Act had not been extended to Goa even though it had become a part of India, announcing that it would be asking the community and religious leaders to visit the state to educate Goans about the "importance, implications and efficacy" of the Shariat Act.

On display was dogmatism in the garb of nationalism, which did not fool the majority of Goan Muslims, who had enjoyed the fruits of the common civil code. Especially the women and youth came out with full force to torpedo the fundamentalist designs. A grassroots campaign was launched under the banners of newly formed Goa Muslim Women's Association, Muslim Youth Welfare Association and Margao Muslim Action Committee to make people aware of the dangers inherent in the Shariat Act. Members of these groups went from door to door, talking to people. There were supporters of Shariat among older men, but the women gave no room to the fundamentalists at all: regardless of whether they were educated or illiterate, whether they were young or old, or whether they were rich or poor, they backed the spontaneous movement for the retention of the Portuguese-gifted common civil code.

And quite befittingly, the movement threw up a young Muslim woman as the leader. Rashida Muzawar, who was a first year student of law, began to draw large crowds at public meetings with her fiery, unsparing speeches against the fundamentalists. Infuriated by her success a mullah at a mosque in Margao once tried to instigate the faithfuls gathered for a prayer to assault and chase away Rashida Muzawar who was scheduled to address a meeting in the city. Ignoring the threat, Rashida went on to address the meeting which drew a large crowd. A handful of fanatics from a corner tried to boo her but Rashida, and her audience, did not pay any attention to them.

The rest of India has not heard of Rashida Muzawar. Not even the feminists, liberal Muslims or the campaigners for enforcement of a national uniform civil code are aware of the remarkable and courageous role she had played in the preservation of the only model in the country we have of ideal family laws. Her name deserves to be written in letters of gold, for without her fearless, aggressive leadership the fundamentalists backed by their political patrons would have succeeded in putting the Muslim women of Goa in fetters. Rashida had a biting, abrasive, irreverent tongue, and it worked wonders; especially when she had to face the poisonous tongues of the mullahs. At a seminar on Muslim personal law she said: "Once a mullah told me: *Women are the 'chappals' of our feet.* I told him: If women are indeed *chappals* of men's feet, then men must seriously reconsider where they have come from!" She was called an infidel and blasphemer by the fundamentalists. She replied: "During my door-to-door campaign in Margao an elderly Muslim woman told me she wanted to beat the Shariat Act supporters with shoes."

For about three years Rashida and her fellow campaigners fought the fundamentalists at every forum: family, *jamaat* (Muslim community groups), mass media, and in the mosques, seminars and public debates. Every memorandum submitted by the diehards to the personal law committee was torn asunder, point by point, by them. Although the Christians and Hindus of Goa did not join the Rashida-led campaign they extended their moral support to it. When the personal law committee invited the archbishop and Hindu religious leaders to present their views on the replacement of the common civil code with personal laws they refused to oblige it. Gradually the Muslim fundamentalist camp began to weaken and disintegrate: quite a few of the older men and migrant Muslims who had formed the bulk of the camp withdrew, leaving the fight essentially to the mullahs. Buoyant, Rashida's campaigners started celebrating their triumph; at one of the public meetings organised by the fundamentalists, Rashida's yelling-booing campaigners rushed forward at the main speaker, forcing him to flee the scene.

One reason why the fundamentalists failed was that their arguments were fundamentally wrong. The large mass of Muslims found them irrational and unconvincing. They pleaded, for instance, that the Shariat was a divine law which had been handed to them by the Prophet (and hence it was the duty of all Muslims to accept it unquestioningly). The fact was the Prophet had not given any such law. On the contrary, the Shariat as practised by Muslims in other countries, and particularly the Muslim personal law that was in force in India had ignored, violated and distorted many of Muhammad's teachings. Muhammad never gave the followers of Islam the savage system of triple *talaq*. Up to four wives were sanctioned by him in the specific context of the wars of his times leaving behind too many widows and female orphans to be taken care of. But the Muslim patriarchs down the ages used it for amorous licence, and the mullahs justified it. India's Muslim personal law had not only this privilege but several other privileges of the patriarchs enshrined in it (immutably), reducing the women to playthings.

Down on earth, the fundamentalists found a legal sanction for the extension of the Muslim personal law. Article 25 of the Indian Constitution, they said, granted every citizen the "right to freely profess, practise and propagate his religion;" and the personal law being religion-based, this right must not be denied to the Muslims of Goa. Distortions these fundamentalists were indulging in again: the founders of India's Constitution did not include the right to choose civil laws relating to marriage, divorce, succession and other family matters in the right to profess, practise and propagate religion. The proof lay in the enactment of the Special Marriage Act. Without any prejudice to the faiths they professed, practised or propagated, citizens were free to solemnize their marriage under the act in the presence of the civil registrar. A civil marriage did in no way compromise the religious faith of the spouses. Instances in fact have not been rare where a man and woman of separate faiths have become husband and wife with a mutual understanding to continue practising their separate faiths. There was no contradiction, therefore, in being a good Muslim and being married under a common civil code.

Article 25 of the Constitution not only gave the citizen the right to freely profess, practise and propagate his religion but it also entitled him to 'freedom of conscience.' He was free to follow a religion or not to follow any religion at all. Even the men and women who were born

Muslims could follow their religion as well as their conscience; there was no cotradiction in it. If their conscience asked for a commitment to a common civil code in the interests of realisation of the principle of equality before law, of building a strong nation, of securing justice for women and of consolidating family as the basic institution of society, they could go ahead and follow it, because by doing so they would not cease to be Muslims. The separation of conscience from religion had been given the final seal by Article 44 of the Constitution, which directed the State to endeavour to secure for the citizens a uniform civil code throughout the country.

The fundamentalists also argued that Muslims treated marriage as a religious sacrament, and therefore, the common civil code trampled upon their religious sentiments by forcing them to solemnize their marriage before the civil registrar. There could be nothing farther from fact. Marriage under Islam was considered a civil contract and not a religious contract. "Marriage and divorce are social matters beyond the pale of religion," said Rashida's campaigners, asserting "they should be regulated by the State through a common civil code."

If the Muslim personal law was extended to Goa, warned Rashida's campaigners, the Muslim males of Goa would gain a licence to polygamy and triple *talaq*. When the feminists and liberals in other parts of the country were pressing the government and judiciary to end these horrendous privileges to Muslim husbands, it would be absurd to bestow them upon the Muslim men of Goa. It was due to the barbaric misuse of these privileges that a large number of Muslim women had been thrown into a life of indigence, and, not uncommonly, of prostitution. *Would you like to meet the same fate?* asked Rashida of the Muslim women. They replied in shrieks and squeals.

An awareness of harsh conditions of the life of abandoned Muslim women was in fact what had motivated Rashida Muzawar to fight the conspiracy of the politicians and mullahs to impose personal law. She had earlier undertaken social work in the brothels of Vasco da Gama where she was shocked to find that many of the sex workers were divorced Muslims from other states. With no institutions or individuals ready to help them and their children, not even their blood relations, and with no employers finding them fit for a job, they took to hiring out their flesh — away from their native states in Goa where nobody recognised them. Goa did not of course prove a paradise to them: at every step they had to suffer injustice at the hands of the customers, agents, policemen, government or the local communities.

Under the Portuguese civil code the Muslim women were safe, since it did not allow polygamy (except to the Hindus in exceptional circumstances, which we will discuss after a while) or divorce without reasons, witnesses or reconcilation time. A Muslim wife in Goa could sue her husband if he took another wife. If her husband wanted to divorce her he had to apply for it under the Law of Divorce. The wife was entitled to provisional as well as permament maintenance (that could be upto one-thirds of the income of the husband.) The Muslim personal law did not provide for any maintenance to the divorced wife, except for the brief period of *iddat*. No wonder, Rashida's campaigners won. The work of the personal law committee did not make much progress, and ultimately the politicians and mullahs stopped talking of repealing the common code and surrendered to the wishes of the women.

Goa : A Paradise for Women?

Although Goa has come undoubtedly the closest to the ideal of a uniform civil code it is worth examining how it has operated at the practical level. Have the Goan women benefitted from it? Can Goa be called a paradise for women? M S Usgaocar says that the philosophy behind the Portuguese civil code was to strengthen the family, the backbone of society, by inculcating a spirit of tolerance among its members. And accordingly the law had some inbuilt safeguards against intolerance and injustice. But have these safeguards been effective? Has the code fostered ideal marital relationships? Are wives in Goa protected from the cruelties the wives in other states are subjected to?

The answers to all the questions are in the negative. First, the law itself is unjust and unfair in certain respects to women. For instance, the Code of Usages and Customs of Gentile Hindus of Goa sanctions a second marriage for the Hindu husband if the first wife has not delivered an issue till the age of 25 or (even worse) if she has not delivered a male issue till the age of 30. This is an absurd and outdated provision, considering that neither the Constitution nor the liberal society sanctions gender inequality. Having a son for an heir was a feudal value; it has no meaning in contemporary life. Today a woman may not marry till the age of 25, and even if she does, she may elect not to become a mother till the age of 30, but the code of usages has already made her vulnerable to the licentiousness of her husband who may decide to marry again on the ground that she has crossed 25 and not delivered him an issue, or that she has crossed 30 but not produced a son.

Of course, the code of usages sets two preconditions before the husband can marry a second time: one, the circumstances of no issue or no male issue (or separation or dissolved previous marriage) must be proved in a court of law; and two, the previous wife must give consent to the simultaneous marriage in a public deed. However, both these conditions give a lot of scope for manipulation. If the husband does not like his first wife he might avoid sexual intercourse with her or force her to use contraceptives till she is 25 and then make her succumb to pressures from all around to give consent to his second marriage with someone else (who may be an old love predating marriage or a new fish.)

The Hindu women of Goa thus have to suffer injustice under legally sanctioned polygamy while those in the rest of the country are protected against it by Section 494 of the Indian Penal Code which punishes bigamy with a jail term of seven years with fine. The Code of Usages and Customs of Gentile Hindus stands totally contrary to the spirit of gender equality with which the family laws of Goa are imbued. Women's organisations have been pleading with the state government for years to amend the code of usages to end the scope for polygamy but the political parties in power have avoided considering the issue, fearing that they might lose Hindu support if they do it. But some political party has to take up courage and do it. Hindus of Goa are an educated lot and if the elite of the community is taken into confidence there is no reason why the government cannot do it. Former chief justice of India Y V Chandrachud noted: "... Polygamy in a very limited way and under strict conditions is countenanced by the family code of Goa. This is out of tune with modern thinking. But, with appropriate modifications, it would be worthwhile if Goa retained its uniqueness of a common civil code."

In actual practice, Goa's other family laws have not proved ideal for women of any community, either. In spite of these laws, women are often discriminated on the grounds of religion and subjected to injustice. Goa's family laws are like an empty pitcher lying by a well surrounded by hostile men: if the woman is dogged and spunky enough she can fill it with water and carry it home. But just the law being there does not guaranetee justice. It sounds surprising that in spite of high female literacy in the state, most Goan women do not know of the safeguards provided for them in the family code. They do not know even of the simple thing that there is compulsory registration of marriage in Goa, and that no marriage other than the one solemnized in the presence of the civil registrar is considered legally valid.

One of Goa's women's rights groups, the Bailancho Saad, recently found a young Christian woman who presumed that her marriage with an older man she had fallen in love with had been registered. In actual fact, the man had taken her to the registrar's office merely to sign the declaration of 'intent to marry' which was obligatory to invite objections to the marriage, if any. If no objections were filed the registrar gave them a no objection certificate, after which they had to register their marriage in his presence. In this particular case, the man never returned with the woman to the registrar to register their marriage. He lived with her for a while and then disappeared without a trace. It was later that she came to know that he had had himself transferred by his company to Chennai and was living with another woman.

When she came two years after his desertion to the Bailancho Saad activists to seek help for filing a divorce suit they asked her to bring the marriage certificate. Of course she did not have any marriage certificate; but, believing that they had signed marriage registration papers at the registrar's office, she said she would get one. It was when she went to the registrar's office that the truth hit her in her face. Now, the Law of Divorce provided her protection and maintenance, but she was not entitled to them because the marriage, not being registered, was legally not valid. (It was another matter that she felt happy she could marry again without going through the divorce proceedings.)

Sometimes a marriage can be solemnized with the religious rituals or in a token form, like exchange of garlands before a deity in a temple, and the woman may be led to believe that she has become the legal wife of the man. There is neither enough social awareness nor enough checks in the system to put pressure on the man to get his marriage with the woman registered. In the system of canonical marriages a Christian priest is permitted to solemnize a marriage in the church under certain special circumstances like 'imminence of delivery' or 'grave reasons of morality.' A man may get married with a woman under these special circumstances and never follow it up with a civil marriage.

The law is deficient on this point: the Law of Civil Marriage needs to be amended to make it obligatory for the priest of any religion to perform a religious marriage only after the couple has produced the certificate of their civil marriage before him. And this obligation has to have the force of penal provisions behind it in order to make the priests accountable. The priests today do not give any importance to the civil marriage, because they think only the religious marriage is sanctioned by God. The legitimacy and validity of marriage, according to them, is in the eye of God, not in the eyes of law. In the Muslim community this can make the situation worse for the woman.

Since the mullahs and orthodox Muslims of Goa favour the Shariat, they do not recognise civil marriages. If a Muslim decides to have four wives the clerics would be too willing to become his collaborators, since he is undermining the civil law and upholding the sanctity of the religious law. Cases are not rare in which a Muslim, who has a wife by registered civil marriage, has got married a second time with the blessings of a qazi without divorcing his wife. If the qazis were prohibited from conducting a marriage, first or second, without the couple producing the civil marriage certificate, there would be no scope for the husband to hoodwink the law. A man planning to take a second wife would never go to the civil registrar for a certificate for his second marriage, because it would not be legally permitted. (In one case in Valpoi, a small town in North Goa, a Muslim got both his first and second marriages registered in the same office! Call it foolhardiness or daredevilry; however, such instances are rare.)

It is not just Muslims. Hindus and Christians too are known to contract a second marriage without registering it. Some go to the other states to get married a second time, because unlike Goa there is no compulsory registration of marriage there. This makes it very difficult for the first wife to prove the second marriage, since there is no certificate, no document if she wants to sue him for bigamy or divorce and maintenance. Quite often, the first wife comes to know of the second marriage much later than it actually has been conducted. Husbands are morally and legally too wary to let the first wife to know of their liasion and cohabitation with another woman. Sometimes they, on one pretext or another, change their place of residence to live away from their first wife with their new woman. There are cases in which first wives have come to know of the second woman after she has delivered a child fathered by her husband. Instances are also not uncommon of the husbands resorting to violence against the first wife in order to force her to leave her matrimonial home or to make her reconcile to his licence.

The Virtual Widows

Notwithstanding the rights to women enshrined in the common civil code Goa remains a patriarchal society. The law may be egalitarian but the society is not egalitarian. The woman still remains the weaker partner in marriage and the weaker member of the family. She is looked upon as homemaker, which places unbearable burdens on her since she has to keep up the pretence of everything being all right even if nothing actually may be. She is not expected to cry aloud for neighbours to hear when her husband beats her; she is not supposed to complain to her blood relations if he mentally tortures her; she is not supposed to neglect her duties even if he neglects her. It is very common for the man who takes a second wife to justify his libertine adventure on the grounds that his first wife is negligent in her wifely duties, infertile, sexually inert, violent, vitriolic in her speech or adulterous. Even if she has nothing of these demerits she does not challenge the accusations, leaving the judgement to God since she has to adjust and make the marriage work.

For most of the women in Goa, as in the rest of the country, marriage provides social and economic security. Even if it is a bad marriage, they think it is far better than the life of a divorced, separated or deserted woman who is unwanted by everyone, including her blood relations. The blame for the failure of marriage is more likely to be foisted on her head, since she is supposed to be the homemaker. In many cases, therefore, women prefer to reconcile to the second woman in their husband's life, making an entreaty to him not to push her out of the home and to maintain a façade of a working marriage before the society while carrying on his relationship with the other woman in a discreet way. If there are children by the first marriage, the woman becomes even more compromising and submissive in the interest of their future.

Bigamy is not all the first wife has to live with. Marital violence is also quite common in Goan homes. A study by the Goa State Commission for Women found that the state police registered 2,754 cases of crimes against women in 1998 out of which 46 per cent were related to domestic violence. The types of violence listed in the complaints were: calling the woman names; indecent slandering of the woman's blood relations; assault which included slapping on the face, blows, hitting with iron rods or belts with metal buckles; pushing against the wall, throwing her down to the floor; confining her to a room or home; restriction on her visits to her natal home and other movements; beating in public.

"Domestic violence is prevalent in all the communities, irrespective of religion, and economic, educational or social status," said the commission study. " It is a myth that violence takes place only in poor families. 41% of women complainants were Hindus, 35% Catholics and 18% Muslims. There was an instance of a Catholic married to a Hindu. These women hailed from lower middle class as well as upper middle class families. They resided in slums, villages and towns. 28% of cases were of women who hailed from outside but are settled in Goa." It seems relevant to note here that a Bailancho Saad study on bigamy had arrived at a similar conclusion. The study said: "From the various cases we have been dealing with in Goa we noticed that bigamy is prevalent in all the communities, be they Hindu, Catholic or Muslim (and irrespective of) economic status, caste or place of origin."

The number of registered crimes against women does not give a full picture since several times more cases of violence go unreported. The woman has to withhold herself from approaching the police under pressure from her natal family and orthodox members of society even if her husband assaults her. The woman herself may not have enough courage in her to make her plight public. Fighting the husband would be like jumping into the world of unknown: she may shudder just at the thought of having to survive all on her own out in the big, bad world.

And the civil justice system has not made things easier for her. It starts with the police refusing to register her complaint and trying to force a reconciliation down her throat which she knows will not work, because her husband will not mend his ways. "In more than one instance," said the state women's commission study, "women complained that they did not get the required assistance from the police when they were thrown out of their matrimonial homes. Even though the law is very clear that the woman has an equal right to the matrimonial home, the police did not help to enforce the right. A case of wrongful restraint should have been registered if the women were prevented from entering. Instead of helping the women, in more than one case the police have gone out of their way and in connivance with the husband forced the women out of their houses when they re-entered."

If the woman has crossed the first hurdle, that is, got the police working on the case, she gets stuck up with the backlog in the courts. And the case is further dragged on by her husband's lawyer on one pretext or the other. It becomes a trial of her patience. If the woman wants to sue her husband for bigamy the burden of gathering proof of the second marriage is on her. The husband might get married in another city or another state and the priests who conduct the marriage or the new bride's relatives might refuse to give any information to her. Since bigamy is a non-cognisable offence the police are not obliged to make a prompt investigation into the second marriage. A woman who is traumatised by the mental and physical cruelties inflicted upon her by her husband just does not have the courage left in her if the police are hostile or indifferent to her.

As it is, she does not have the resources to pursue the complaint right through the prosecution in the court. The government's legal aid, if it is made available to her, is not of much help since the quality of legal talents she gets to represent her is poor. Her parents or brothers may extend full moral support but be reluctant to back her up with money to pay for her lawyer and her maintenance. If she happens to have children her position becomes weaker. Will she waste her money fighting for maintenance in the court or will she use it for the education and other needs of her children? The court case may go on for years and she might not gain anything at the end. Eventually, she gives up. And starts learning to live like a virtual widow.

7

Ethnic Fencing

The spectre of unemployment is looming large over the Goan youth due to the "packing" of non-locals in public and private sectors. The non-locals have shown a tendency to self-multiply .... With key positions in public and private sectors in the hands of non-locals, new employment opportunities have been systematically and deliberately denied to local youth who are equally qualified, skilled and talented .... The point is to protect the interests of a Goan. All our youth and their opportunities need to be protected from the mass immigration from the neighbouring states.
—A blueprint prepared by Konkani activists, 1999

The Great Konkani Wall

At the turn of the 21st century, a new group emerged on Goa's horizon: the Goa Hitrakhan Manch, or Forum for the Protection of Goa's Interests. This small but vocal group maintained vigilance against outsiders taking over jobs in the government or government-funded institutions in the state. If it came to their notice that a certain head of a department or institution was in the process of recruiting someone from outside the state the members of the Manch gheraoed him, crowding his office and preventing him from carrying on his work or leaving his room, until he gave them an assurance that he would terminate the process and recruit a Goan according to the government recruitment rules.

On July 9, 1991, "in order to ensure that the people of the state of Goa get a fair deal in this state in the matter of job opportunities," the government had issued a notification prohibiting the registration with the employment exchange of a person who had resided in Goa for less than 15 years. By another notification on March 7, 1996 the government had made knowledge of Konkani essential and knowledge of Marathi desirable for eligibility for government employment. The

Manch vigilantes wanted all the government departments, semi-government and autonomous bodies, like the university, the municipalities and planning and development authorities, to strictly follow the two clauses of the recruitment rules: domicile of 15 years and essential knowledge of Konkani. Rattled by the Manch's vigilantism, the chief secretary dashed off a circular on October 6, 2000, reminding all the concerned authorities of the two clauses, warning them that a failure not to follow them 'will be viewed seriously.'

Konkani had become the defining criterion of a Goan: even if someone had lived in Goa for 15 or 20 or 30 years but had not learnt to speak and understand Konkani, he would not be entitled to a government job. Konkani had become a form of border control — the high barbed wall of ethnic fencing. The Manch was an offshoot of the Konkani movement, an association of Goan youth, mostly Hindus, who felt the movement had only partially achieved its goal.

Although Konkani had won recognition as an independent literary language from the Sahitya Akademi, been enshrined as a prominent Indian language in the eighth schedule of the Constitution, and had become the official language of Goa, they felt their task was far from over. Konkani was steel-clad and in a safe sanctuary now but the Goan identity continued to be under threat. The battle for establishing the mother tongue in its homeland was over but the battle for making the homeland impregnable was on. When Luizinho Faleiro, a prominent figure of the Konkani movement, during his tenure as chief minister made the knowledge of Konkani essential for government employment in 1996 his objective was not to promote the language but to safeguard the Goan identity. "Konkani is not merely the language of Goan poetry, drama or fiction," said the Manch activists. "It is an instrument to establish Goans' control over Goan resources."

From the outset, the Konkani movement had a robustly ethnic subtext: a separate language, a separate state. "Mother Konkani is now safe in her homeland," the Konkani activists rejoiced when Goa attained statehood. However, the picture did not prove to be as rosy as they had thought. Statehood provided only inadequate protection to Konkani since the borders were open for people from other states, speakers of other tongues, to come in. And internally, the language scene remained extremely ambiguous. Devanagri Konkani had won recognition as the state's official language, but it had not won recognition as the common language of Goa. A large number of Goan Hindus preferred Marathi — they even recorded themselves in the successive censuses as Marathi speakers — while almost the entire population of Goan Christians would swear to know no other Konkani but Roman Konkani (although younger generations were studying Konkani and Hindi in Devanagri in schools and this could slowly replace Roman Konkani with Devnagari Konkani.)

How could Devanagri Konkani make itself the language of everyone? The Devanagri Konkani protagonists, who were mostly Hindus, adopted a dual strategy to meet the challenges from Marathi and Roman Konkani. They were very aggressive against Marathi; they would not mince words in condemning the existence of a large number of Marathi speakers in the censuses as a 'conspiracy' of a 'clique of fogey, diehard Marathiwadis;' no means would be spared by them to shrink the space for Marathi. However, their strategy against Roman Konkani was characterised more by friendliness than animosity; the wariness was the result of the painful awareness that if they pressed the Goan Christians to accept Devanagri Konkani at once, they would surely rebuff them and, maybe, walk out of the Konkani camp, ripping the façade of Konkani solidarity — or, in other words, inviting Marathi to take over. The wide chasm between Devanagri Konkani and Roman Konkani was never publicly discussed, because the Konkani activists did not want to present a divided house to the world.

For almost ten years since Goa attained statehood, the Devanagri Konkani activists used various channels to get Marathi out of the way but did not succeed. Thereafter the strategy of these activists began to show a distinct change. They would now focus on the external threats and work to awaken the Goans to the task of protecting the cultural, economic, demographic and political borders of Goa from the 'external enemies.' Thus was born the second phase of the Konkani movement: now, the Konkani activists declared, *let us not fight among ourselves over language or script or things like that*. They talked of a broader canvas and were full of eagerness to recognise the contributions Marathi had made to the cultural life of Goa as well as to grant Roman Konkani a distinct space. The need of the hour, the reborn Konkani activists concluded, was to unite against the 'common enemy.'

A Haunting Nightmare

A nightmare haunted them: *Goans will soon become foreigners in their own land;* and one thing was true: the outsiders were here, there, everywhere in the state. Before Goa became free, hardy, sinewy and low-paid labourers from Uttar Pradesh, known as *bhayyas,* handled the loading and unloading of cargo at the port of Mormugao, and that was about all that the Portuguese colony knew of immigration from India. Accommodated in small huts or rooms in *chawls* in the Vasco da Gama city, the *bhayyas* commuted to and from the port in trains that became famous as Coolie Trains, without arousing, among the natives, any fears of submergence. On the contrary, the local people showed an empathic attitude toward them, because a large number of Goans themselves, starving in a stagnant colonial economy, had emigrated to British India and abroad in search of livelihood. With the departure of the Portuguese this would change dramatically. The massive public funding for development projects — roads, bridges, public transport, construction, health care, schools, agricultural productivity — that followed Liberation necessitated import of a large number of skilled and unskilled labour — engineers, overseers, technicians, town planners, architects, headmasters, teachers, laboratory assistants, doctors, nurses, administrators, clerks, construction workers, coolies, town sweepers, domestic workers, drivers, and so on — from the other states.

These projects catalysed a spectacular transformation of Goa. At the time of Liberation Goa was producing 50,000 tonnes of food per annum; by 1985-86, the output trebled. As industry around Liberation there were just about 50 small units; by 1985-86, the number of small, medium and large factories had reached 3,500. There were only 17 government hospitals in 1960-61 and no private hospital; by 1985-86 there were 33 government hospitals and 69 private hospitals, excluding the 31 government medical dispensaries in the villages. By 1989, the doctor-population ratio in Goa had reached 1:750 against 1:5000 in India. By 1983-84, the birth rate had dropped to 21 per thousand against the all-India average of 33 per thousand. The enrolment in government primary schools rocketed from 18,900 in 1961-62 to 134,800 in 1984-85. The literacy rate increased from 35 per cent in 1960-61 to 75.5 per cent in 1990-91 and 82.32 per cent in 2000-2001, placing Goa next only to Kerala.

By 1985-86, every village in Goa had been connected by all-weather roads. The road density in the state was 155 km per sq km area, over three times the national average; and the road length 5,470 km per million population, almost double the national average. Electricity in villages was unthinkable in Portuguese Goa; but by 1986 every village had been connected by electricity. Less than 500 telephone connections existed in Portuguese Goa; by 1990 they totalled 50,000, and by 2001 to 155,000. Goa's net state domestic product at current prices increased from Rs 270 million in 1960-61 to Rs 3.15 billion in 1980-81, to Rs 10.24 billion in 1990-91, to Rs 18.49 billion in 1994-95 and Rs 25.74 billion in 1996-97. During the period from 1986-87 to 1994-95, Goa's growth rate was 8.2 per cent against the national growth rate of 5.3 per cent. Goa's per capita income, at constant (1993-94) prices, was Rs 15,602 against the national average of Rs 7,698 in 1993-94, and an estimated Rs 17,406 against the national average of Rs 10,151 in 1999-2000. Among states, Goa's per capita income was the highest after Delhi and Punjab.

A combination of three factors had brought about this amazing growth: the release of the suppressed energies of the native Goans, the enormous input of managerial and manual skills from other states and huge investments in public and private sectors.

High rates of economic growth came along with high rates of population and urban growth. Between 1900 and 1960, in six decades, Goa's population rose by less than 3 per cent, but in 1961-71 it swelled by 34.77 per cent against the national average of 24.78 per cent. In 1971-81, the growth was still high, 26.74 per cent against the national average of 25.75 per cent. Progress, said Luizinho Faleiro in his autobiography *My Goa*, came to Goans "at a price." It created problems of unplanned growth in the cities, congestion, slums and posed threats to 'our ecology, ethos and culture.' "Goa embarked, particularly in the first two trend-setting decades of our freedom, on a mindless building activity in the mistaken notion that the massive civil construction activity undertaken by the Public Works Department was by itself development," Faleiro noted, lamenting: "The result is there for all to see: ugly buildings and large scale influx of migrant labour which, one is told, could be in the region of 30 to 40 per cent of the total population."

Certainly Faleiro's immigrant figures were xenophobic. After the high growth rates during the first two decades following Liberation, the population in Goa had dropped below the national average. In 1981-91, it grew by 16.08 per cent against the national average of 23.86 per cent; and in 1991-2001, by 14.89 per cent against the national average of 21.34. A more reliable estimate of the size of immigrant population had been made by one of Goa's leading social scientists Dr. Nandkumar Kamat, who, using a comprehensive data including the records of numbers of births and deaths registered, put it at about 18 per cent of the total population. The official migration tables suggest that in 1961-71, 35,511 people emigrated from other states to Goa, in 1971-81, 74,682 and in 1981-91, 95,084. In the 1991 census, 169, 766 people recorded themselves as migrants. The figure is corroborated by a Goan economist Prabhakar Angle who notes: "Goa's population increased during the last three decades (1961-91) by almost 100 per cent against the all-India increase of 90 per cent. This circumstance leads one to believe that between 1.5 lakh and 2 lakh immigrants must have made Goa their abode."

Goa's urban population more than doubled by 1971. By 1991, in thirty years following Liberation, it had quadrupled, making up 41 per cent of the total population. This phenomenal and disturbing growth was attributable to migration — the migrants, both professionals and poor, preferred to pitch their tents in towns — as also to the village to city migration of the Goans attracted by new education and employment opportunities. Goa's first slum appeared in the mid-sixties, and now no major city is free from hutment colonies where migrants live. A significant share in the migrant population has been of Muslims who have taken up petty businesses.

Until mid-1970s the fruit and vegetable markets in Panaji, Margao and other cities used to have largely Goan vendors who would come with their goods in baskets and go back home with their emptied baskets in the afternoon. There were very few stalls. In the Panaji market there used to be a *bhayya* who was the only outsider among Goan stall-owners. But today 80 per cent of the stalls in the Panaji market belong to entrepreneurs from Karnataka. Similar is the case with the Margao market. And a majority of them are Muslims. Small wonder, the Muslim population in Goa has registered a phenomenal growth. In 1961, it made up 1.95 per cent of the total population; in 1991,

5.25 per cent. Most of the hawkers who today set up stalls at the Christian feasts and fairs are Muslims. In the recent years a number of Kashmiri Muslims have also migrated to do petty business on the beaches.

But it is not just Muslims. Ninety per cent of hawkers in the Anjuna Flea Market are from the states of Karnataka, Maharashtra and Rajasthan, and they include both Hindus and Muslims; selling their wares with them are also Buddhists from Tibet. In Vasco da Gama the dairy business is in the hands of the *bhayyas*; and so are all the *paan* shops. There are so many *bhayyas* in Vasco da Gama that people often tell a joke: if you see a knot of five people anywhere in the city, you can be sure three of them will be *bhayyas*. In the beach belt, increasingly, it is the outsiders who have taken over the curio, memento, garment and jewellery businesses directed at tourists. Luizinho Faleiro laments: "In Goa, the country's number one tourist centre, the handicrafts we offer the nearly two million tourists who visit us are: carpets from Kashmir, garments from Rajasthan, brassware from Uttar Pradesh and so on … . But once we were internationally famous for our walking sticks, the socks knitted in Goa were sought by discriminating London dandies, our Goan tailors could replicate the most intricate Parisian designs … ."

The Labour Paradox

Originally, the migrants filled the gap in the labour supply. Rapid economic growth required huge human capital, and Goa's small, and Portuguese-stunted, population was just not in a position to provide it. So, construction labourers were brought from Karnataka, primary school teachers from Maharashtra, high school teachers from Kerala and engineers and officers from everywhere. More than half of Goa's technical and general administrators during 1961-81 were 'deputationists,' officers loaned for specific but extendable tenures by the Centre or the governments in other states.

By the turn of 1980s, Goans, having benefitted from the spread of education, started raising a demand for replacement of outsiders with sons of the soil. The government jobs were the most sought-after because of the government's reputation as a blind and benevolent employer. Besides, it gave prestige and power. In Goa the madness gripped the men from labouring classes even more incurably, because they had seen the higher caste Hindus and Christians enjoy power as government officials during the Portuguese regime, and would like to enjoy the same now that the Constitution had declared everybody equal. They all wanted white collar jobs now.

Small wonder, Goa today has the highest government employee to population ratio among all states. From 3000 in 1961, the number of government employees in Goa rose to 60,000 in 2001. There has been no MLA in the past four decades who has not had a few hundreds to a few thousands of people recruited to government jobs for carving electoral support.

Goa's small supply of manual labour became scarcer with the growing snobbery of the Sudras. This was to have the effect of increasing the size of immigration. The vacuum the upstarts created was filled up by migrant labourers. So much so that the municipalities had to employ sweepers from other states. The coolies in the wholesale and retail markets were outsiders, and so were the masons, carpenters and blacksmiths.

Lambert Mascarenhas, a Goan novelist and journalist, observes: "Why are outsiders coming to Goa? Because the Goans are not ready to do the jobs they are doing. Ministers often shed tears for the educated unemployed. But should we shed tears for those who drop out of school after a few years and refuse to follow the profession of their fathers, such as cultivation, masonry, fishing and carpentry, because they think manual work is degrading?" Echoing his sentiment, Luizinho Faleiro observes: "The whole purpose of education will be defeated if the educated unemployed develop a contempt for manual work and a sense of arrogance and false pride that tells them not to soil their hands." Prabhakar Angle comments: "They all cry about the influx of migrants today. They are the same people who would not take up the jobs the migrants do. If the migrants were not there a building which is completed in one year will take three years to complete."

In the 1990s, on an average, there were more than 100,000 people on the live registers of the state employment exchange. And yet businesses had to depend on migrants for labour. The paradox of high unemployment and high labour import had been the result of four factors. First, the land reforms had ensured shelter and two meals a day to Goa's rural poor by guaranteeing against their eviction from their tenanted agricultural and homestead plots. Thus, they would not be desperate for daily wage employment. Secondly, freedom had been accompanied with a social revolution, unleashed by the political and government patronage extended by Dayananad Bandodkar to the *bahujan samaj*, the backward communities.

The proof of this was available in the spectacular growth in school enrolment during the first two decades of Liberation. Bandodkar, and later his daughter Shashikala who took over as chief minister, consciously encouraged recruitment of members of the *bahujan samaj* in government and private companies. The objective of the social revolution was to end the *Bamonn Raj*, the dominance of the Hindu and the Christian Brahmans in the administration and other fields, and replace it with the *Bahujan Raj*. The lower caste Goans who learnt to hate manual labour were products of this social revolution.

There was a third factor that made the lower caste Goans detest hard labour, and this was *sussegad*, an attitude prevalent in the land from the Portuguese times. This attitude had both positive and negative sides. The positive side of it was that it exhorted men not to join the rat race and be contented with a modest income. The negative side of it was that it motivated men to avoid work and indulge in leisure. "There is no work ethic in Goa," observes Lambert Mascarenhas, "only fun ethic, feast ethic and gossip ethic." Luizinho Faleiro calls the labour-shunning Goans "idle and parasitic." In the years after Liberation, the Mormugao port brought gangs of Christian Gauda workers from South Goa to do the job of loading and unloading of cargo the *bhayyas* from Uttar Pradesh had been doing since the inception of the port. The Gaudas could not endure the hard labour and went back to their villages. If you take the wrong route the *sussegad* leads you to alcoholism, incapacitating you for hard work, or any sustained work. Employers in public and private sectors alike bemoan the adverse effect on labour productivity of the negative features of the *sussegad*.

The fourth factor responsible for the high unemployment — high labour import paradox is the tradition of emigration among Goans. There are a large number of Goans who, after working abroad for some years, have returned with substantial savings, invested them in flats or fixed bank deposits to live off the rent or bank interest without having the need to take up a job. Between 1977 and 1991, the passport office in Panaji issued 166,000 passports, or an average of 11,000 plus a year, reflecting the outflow chiefly to the Persian Gulf. The majority of Goan emigrants are Christians. There would be a rare Christian family in Goa having no member or close relation working abroad. The jobs taken up by emigrants are of the lower categories: of domestic maids, nannies, plumbers, clerks, shop assistants, receptionists, telephone operators, cooks, roomboys, waiters, seamen. Quite often, the emigrants are pilloried for accepting the jobs abroad which they would refuse to do in their homeland. "Here they have let the sweepers' jobs in the municipalities be taken over by migrants, because they feel the work is below their dignity. But the same fellows would go to the Gulf and clean toilets and mop floors," you hear Goans saying commonly.

Money allures the emigrants. The wage differential explains the irony. A roomboy in a hotel in Goa gets Rs 1,100 a month, but in the Gulf he would get Rs 11,000. He tries to earn much more from his employer by working hard, his aim being to accumulate enough savings so that he does not have to work for his livelihood when he returns home. And indeed, it is not only he who finds himself comfortable when he returns home, but also the members of his family who have been receiving his remittances while he is working abroad. With the security of Papa's remittances, his sons and daughters do not feel the desperation to look for jobs for themselves. They would certainly have themselves listed in the live registers of the employment exchange but they would go on spurning opportunities for jobs which involve hard work or which they find below their dignity. (There are very few takers among Goans for jobs involving round-the-clock shift duty.) A large number of the 100,000 plus Goans on the live registers of the employment exchange are believed to be persons who are waiting for a comfortable and high-salary job. Errol D'Souza, a Goan professor of economics in Mumbai University, has termed the phenomenon as "luxury unemployment."

The irony was further heightened by the fact that most Goans did not have the qualifications for the comfortable and high-salary jobs they were waiting for. Thus they were caught up in a trap of their own: they did not want the jobs for which they had skills and they did not have the skills for the jobs they wanted. Of the 100,000 plus persons on the live registers of the employment exchange, nearly 85,000 were school dropouts or had not gone up to college. Behind the façade of high literacy, Goa's dropout rate was alarming: 7 out of 10 students discontinued their education before finishing school. These dropouts had no professional skills to qualify for a higher-level job. A Gujarati businessman from Vasco da Gama says: "Goans want jobs. But they do not have skills. If you wait for Goans with right skills to fill your vacancies you may have to wait endlessly."

The sorry plight of Goan labour was highlighted in a focus on the Kuskem village located in the Cotigao panchayat of South Goa. In 2000, 37 years after Liberation, not a single person from Kuskem had got a job either in the private or public sector. The village had 25 youths who had completed secondary or higher secondary education but were waiting for job offers after registering themselves with the employment exchange. At last when some of them got an interview call, the employer rejected them. They tried their luck with the enterprises located in the Sristhal industrial estate in Canacona which was not far from their village but they were turned down again for lack of qualification. The private sector employers did not want people who had studied in the Marathi medium. Disappointed, the 'educated unemployed' of the village returned to agricultural activities. Sometimes they took up odd jobs; once they hired themselves out as a labour gang to develop a football ground at Betul.

Indeed, the poorer communities — the Gaudas, Dhangars, Velips, Kunbis — who make up 20 per cent of Goa's population are in a pitiable situation. Most of them still live in isolated hamlets with no modern amenities in a depressing environment of poverty, illiteracy and sickness. By 1991 Goa boasted of a literacy rate of 77 per cent but only 10 per cent of the Gauda population had finished school education. The dropout rate among the poorer communities is very high. Most of them earn their livelihood working in the fields, though some of them also work in the mines, stone quarries or even as porters in small towns like Valpoi.

A few Dhangar families have taken up dairy in Valpoi, but such cases of self-employment are extremely rare. The youth from these communities have no professional skills. "Our boys don't go for technical courses because they can't find jobs," say some of the older men. Obviously there is no effort from the government's side to motivate the youth from the poorer communities to take up technical courses.

Government efforts to create a professionally and technically qualified Goan workforce have been eclectic and inconsistent. Ministers and MLAs — for building up electoral support, of course — have been taking individual initiatives to compel employers in their constituencies to train and absorb Goans in technical jobs. In the early 1990s Luzinho Faleiro as a minister prevailed upon the managements of a few five star hotels in South Goa to provide training in hotel management and housekeeping to 1500 youths from his Navelim constituency free of charge. After training, most youths found jobs in hotels in the state; and some went to work on the merchant navy ships. Owners of industrial and service enterprises in Goa have shown a general tendency to accept the recommendations for in-house training of candidates from the ministers and legislators on a give-and-take basis. The companies use the political clout thus acquired to advance their business interests.

On its own part, the state government has a Tool Room Centre, set up with UN funds, at Kundaim to provide technical skills to Goan youth. The training facilities here are good and those passing out of the centre are absorbed at a good salary by the industries. But the centre's trainee intake is small and its impact on the overall unemployment scene is only slight. The state directorate of employment also runs programmes to guide youths to vocations and self-employment, but its impact is negligible. The Economic Survey of Goa, 2000-01 laments: "The directorate (of employment) has provided guidance to 3966 applicants under vocational guidance programme and motivated 39 persons for self-employment. These efforts are not at all sufficient keeping in view the gravity of the problem." For several years the state government has been considering proposals for making education job-oriented; committees were also set up to recommend ways of linking university with industry; but no progress was made.

One of the most ambitious plans of the state government was to provide employment to over 100,000 unemployed youth during the Ninth Five Year Plan (1997-2002) through the "manpower development programme." This was to be achieved through skill development; the unemployed youth were to be trained under additional courses according to the requirements of the industry. The whole idea was to divert the manpower flow from non-technical branches to technical branches. In order to supplement the programme, the state governement also set up a Human Resource Development Foundation in 1997. However, according to the government's own admission, the programme has failed to achieve its grand objective. The number of youths helped to acquire technical skills under the programme was so miserable that the government never released the figures. It is in this light that people take with scepticism the state government's big promise of reaching zero unemployment by 2005.

Two Meals a Day

Call it Sudra snobbery or *sussegad*, when Goans refused to undertake hard labour, migrants streamed in. "During a recent visit to Goa," wrote senior journalist M V Kamath in 1987, "I was perplexed when the man at the Panaji ferry who offered to carry my two suitcases to the boat shook his head when I addressed him in Konkani. While I was trying to guess in which language, then, to speak to him, I heard him speak to a fellow coolie in Kannada. Since I happen to know Kannada I asked him where he came from in Karnataka and what he was doing in Goa. It transpired that he came from one of the drought-ridden districts of Karnataka and that he was doing reasonably well."

A majority of the migrant labourers came from Karnataka's Bijapur, Hubli and Dharwad districts and Maharashtra's Ratnagiri district. All these districts are known for their high unemployment rate, poor irrigation, uneconomical land holdings, insecure tenancies, landlessness and extreme poverty. There is not enough to eat at home and there is no round-the-year employment. Among the migrant labourers in Goa are the Lamanis, the gypsy tribals; and in March 2001 in their hamlets in Gulbarga district of Karnataka, they were found selling their infant daughters for a price. Although they told the police they had been doing it because they had no money to give as dowry when the girls became marriageable, the truth was that they had been selling the baby girls for Rs 1,500 or around to ward off starvation. A *Deccan Herald* reporter who visited the Lamani hamlets noted:

"The people in these hamlets cannot even afford two meals a day. Their only source of livelihood has been the forest (which they must enter) for collecting the Mouva flowers (which they sell to those who make out of them) an intoxicating drink and the leaves used (to make) *beedis*. The forest department has forced them to stop collection of the forest produce. More than 90 per cent of the people in these hamlets are landless labourers (and living in the forest region as they are) they fail to get work even for three days in a week, and even if they find work in the fields they are paid a paltry sum of Rs 10-20 per day. Also, the government apathy is obvious. Nearly 50 per cent of these hamlets do not have electricity, permanent drinking water and approach roads, leave aside transport facilities."

Not all the migrant labourers are as indigent as the Lamanis. A sizeable number of them are small and marginal farmers. However, poor rainfall and lack of irigation do not allow them to use new technologies to increase the productivity of their farms. When there is a marriage in the family, or somebody falls ill, they borrow from relatives or private moneylenders, and usually fail to pay back by the agreed schedule. Default in repayments to co-operative societies and rural banks is also common. Seeing no other way to end their misery, the families send their able-bodied men out as migrant labourers. Many of them prefer to seek employment in Goa, because the state is virtually a large city. Sometimes the family allows the migrant to take his wife along with him. If he works as a construction worker his wife gets helper's work at the site. At the rates prevalent in 2001, the man gets Rs 100 a day, and his wife Rs 50. That makes Rs 4,500 a month, which is a fantastic amount for them. Back home, for the same amount of work, they get less than half the wages.

And certainly, the wage differential is the main attraction. Goa may not have turned out to be a Land of Promise for the migrants, but it had definitely provided them opportunities to improve their life chances and to go up in social esteem. On their visits to their villages, they dress well, behave well and spend well. Quite a few of them have saved a few lakhs and built a house for themselves in their village, or bought cultivable land. They are the migrants whose wives, and often minor sons and daughters also work. The husband's income as a construction labourer, Rs 100 a day, takes care of the household expenses (and usually also of his alcoholic needs), while his wife and daughters, working as domestic maids in 10-12 homes, bring home Rs 3,000 to Rs 3,600 a month which goes into the bank as saving. Thus in a year the family saves Rs 36,000 to Rs 43,000. This is the kind of savings not even the richest landowner in their village could dream of.

Rukhsana came from a village in Dharwad with her husband in the late seventies when they had been married just six months. They stayed in a makeshift hut at Dona Paula and worked at the construction site at the Mahalaxmi temple in Panaji. She felt terribly miserable here, since there were very few people from Karnataka in Panaji, and she knew only Kannada. Once when she fell ill she could not explain her suffering to the doctor as she did not know Konkani and he did not know Kannada. Her husband took her to her village where her trusted traditional physician was. When she recovered she came back and they started working as construction labourers again. Soon, her husband turned alcoholic, and started spending all his and her earnings on liquor.

After a while she left the construction job and began to work as a domestic maid, but no matter how cleverly she would try to hide her earnings from him, he would find them for his drinks. After a few years, he contracted several diseases, did not heed doctors' advice, went on drinking and died. For the fourteen years that Rukhsana had lived with him in Goa she could not save a paisa. She could have saved at least Rs 2 lakh if he had not been that way, she feels.

As a widow and mistress of things, she started making savings. She made her first daughter, Zubeida, who was ten years old when her husband died, work as a domestic maid too. Together, in a few years, they saved Rs 50,000, which was kept aside for Zubeida's marriage. Soon Rukhsana also bought a plot of land for Rs 30,000 in the village, and leased it out for chilly cultivation to one of her late husband's first cousins. Away in Goa she often wonders whether the cousin is giving her, as promised, an exact half of the income he earns from the selling of chillies.

But she cannot help that. She has to continue living and working in Goa because of the enormous savings she is able to make here. Now her second daughter, Nazneen, who is ten years old, is sharing her work as a domestic maid. Her only son, Waseem, who is less than twelve, slogs virtually as a slave of a bar owner in the city's municipal market. The bar owner makes him drudge from dawn to midnight, does not allow him to visit his home, which is no more than a 15-minute slow bus ride, except on Wednesdays. Ignoring his slavery, Rukhsana expresses happiness that she and her two children bring home about Rs 5,000 a month, out of which Rs 3,000 goes for food, hut rent and medical expenses, the remaining Rs 2,000 going as savings into the bank. The medical expenses are quite high, complains Rukhsana, noting with resignation: "But this is normal for us who slog for long and odd hours without much rest, stay in dirty environs and eat food without thoughts of nutrition."

Rukhsana maintains strong links with her village. Festivals, marriage or death of a close one in the family, birth of daughter's first child: she has to go there two or three times a year. At 2001 rates, she pays Rs 180 for the bus journey from Panaji to Hubli, and Rs 20 for the bus journey from there to her village. On every trip, then, she spends Rs 400 only on ticket. Then she has to spend on her food and other things, like gifts to others, in the village. It adds up to Rs 3,000. However, Rukhsana does not mind spending Rs 6,000 to Rs 9,000 every year on her visits home. In spite of this, she beams, she saves quite a lot. She is a contented woman. She, like most of the migrants, has a dream to go back home and live off her own land when she is old. She giggles: "Who will give me work here when I am old!"

The Migrant Professionals

Like the labourers, several professionals also migrated to Goa for improving their life chances. But there was a difference. For the labourers, the main attraction was the wage differential; for the professionals it was the status differential. The salaries of professionals and technicians were lower in Goa compared to the other states. But the great advantage the middle class migrants enjoyed here was the absence of competition for higher posts. Goa was still considered too far from home by the professionally and technically qualified people in the other states. Owing to this there was a perennial shortage of such people in the state. The only way the Goan employers could get them was by offering them higher positions. The professional migrants were thus, more often than not, people who did not rate the chances of their promotion very high in the places they were working in in the other states. Even though it was a very hard decision to move to Goa, they were willing to make it, since it ensured them upward mobility.

At least 25 per cent of the general and technical administrators who came from other states after the Liberation opted for Goa government service because they were holding high positions and stayed on. Even in the private sector higher positions were held by migrants who preferred to stay on. In the years following Liberation, when the opportunities were available in plenty, the professional migrants also misused their offices to get one or more of their close relations employed in positions they could not hope to achieve in their own states.

Today there are quite a few doctors from Karnataka running their private clinics in Goa, as here they have found a good business among the Kannada-speaking migrant labourers.

No doubt, the professional migrants were gripped by a terrible sense of loss: a result of being cut off from their close relations and friends. This was not an ordinary loss: it was the loss of the environs in which their ethnic culture was nurtured. Having come to Goa to get a professional elevation, they were beginning to wonder whether it was worth letting their ethnic culture suffer a gradual erosion in the process, making the way for Goan culture to take over. The Goan culture threatened to imbue them, and even more dangerously, their children, with three cults: the cult of leisure, which frowned on literature and classical music; the cult of alcohol, which ate away evenings; and the cult of cosmopolitanism, which provided 'loose social norms' only a thin garb.

A Muslim professional migrant from Karnatka says he has been finding it difficult to get a boy from his native state to marry his daughter. "There, back home, they think girls brought up in Goa are too fast and free-willed for them to be able to control," he fumes. So as not to lose their touch with close relations and ethnic culture, the professional migrants keep visiting their native places on a regular or irregular basis. Even though almost all of them have bought a flat or built a house here, they keep their options open of selling it one day and going back to their native place if circumstances forced them.

Apart from professionals and labourers there are certain classes of people who have migrated to Goa for health reasons. A number of retired persons, both Indians and foreigners, prefer to spend the rest of their lives in Goa due to its excellent climate and natural beauty. This has earned Goa the name of 'pensioner's paradise.' There are some people, again Indians as well as foreigners, who have moved in for health-cum-business reasons. They run small enterprises catering mainly to tourists in the beach belt, like niche restaurants, curio shops and garment and jewellery outlets.

Hostility toward Outsiders

Goans are turning hostile to all classes of migrants (outsiders, *bhailos, ghantis*) because they feel they are taking over their land and space. "The beach villages have become totally unrecognizable," is a common Goan lament. "Greenery and open spaces have given way to hotels and apartment blocks." During the tourist season, in the beach belt, their alienation grows even more intense when they see more foreigners moving around than locals. It makes them feel they are in a part of Europe, not in Goa.

Every major Goan city has slums where migrant labourers and petty businessmen live, without any fear of eviction from the landowner who may be the government or a civic body. Even in the villages migrants have made encroachments on the *comunidade* or panchayat land. Industrialisation is changing the demographic profile of the cities. "Vasco da Gama was a port city and Goans were reconciled to its loss to migrants," says a Goan intellectual. " But today every city is becoming a Vasco da Gama. Ponda has in the recent years seen many industries come up within its vicinity. Today if you drive to Ponda and happen to need to ask someone for direction there are seven out of ten chances that you will run into an outsider rather than a local fellow."

A survey among expatriate Goans in mid-1990s recorded most of them lamenting that "Goa's social and physical environment was degraded by industrial growth, influx of migrants and mass tourism." Comments a Konkani playwright: "The conditions in Goa are deteriorating so fast we are beginning to feel like aliens in our homeland."

When a tourism promoter's proposal to construct a Japanese village in Pernem in North Goa — holiday cottages with a golf course, botanical gardens, sports facilities and a marina — came up in the early 1990s, the local panchayat rejected it, saying the 9.6 billion yen project would swallow land which was the villagers.' It would virtually be, said the panchayat, a Japanese enclave in a foreign country where their rich men would retreat and entertain themselves. And it would be an enclave of 750 acres, carved out of grazing land, cashew plantations and fields where medicinal herbs were grown. "The rich Japanese can go elsewhere for golf and relaxation. Why do they want to snatch our land from us? It is nothing but neo-colonialism," said the panchayat leaders.

One of the most famous Goan exponents of Hindustani classical singing, Kishori Amonkar, who lives in Mumbai, once told an interviewer: "Every year after our school examinations *mai* (Mother) used to take us to her native village Curdi (in Goa) for our summer vacations. We used to go up to Khatara by train and cover the remaining distance from Sanvordem by bullock cart. Curdi was one of the most beautiful places I have ever seen. There were miles and miles of paddy fields and the backdrop of the mountains was simply breathtaking. We used to go swimming in the lake and wandering in the fields. I still cherish those memories. But like my village which has gone, so too has Goa gone down in the dumps. When I come to Goa now I am pained to see the landscape altered beyond redemption. Goa has become over-modernised and too westernised. The roads are jammed with traffic .... I don't feel like coming here any more."

Goans in their collective mind carried the image of Goa as an idyllic paradise, and everything that changed looked like a threat to them. Much of this image was made up of the isolated, kingly verdant, undeveloped-hence-untouched colonial Goa, and it owed itself no less to the nostalgic imagination of the Goan emigrants, especially the Christians from feudal families who had made Mumbai their second home. Every year they would spend their summer vacations in the village, travelling from Mumbai to Goa by an overcrowded steamer that took twenty-four hours then, or by rail which took a few hours less but forced them to change trains twice. Then they had to get into a suffocating, shaking bus to reach the river crossing point from where a ferry or canoe took them across. There were no buses or cars thereafter: most of them walked home down the red dirt pathway carrying their tin trunks and holdalls on their heads or in their hands. But what still made the visit romantic was the thought of what was to follow. For two months now, an eminent Goan emigrant, George Menezes reminisces about the summer of 1948, "... everything flows. Rivers, gastric juices, sweat, tears of joy and sorrow. Wine flows into goblets, mango juice flows down the chin, cashew juice over shirt fronts, while on beaches and hills, girls are serenaded to the sounds of a million guitars."

Those were the times, George Menezes went on, when a fattened sow was let free, given a traditional chase and caught for slaughter; when the finest distillation from the cashew apple was transformed into an elixir called *feni* and stored in earthen jars; when old ink-bottles were filled with kerosene to be used as lamps; when water was drawn from the wells; when litanies at feasts were followed by boiled gram, coconut cubes and gossip. A Goan journalist living in Mumbai, Ervell Menezes often wrote of the times when the clop clop of the cattle setting out on their daily rounds past his village house was punctuated by the shrill cry of a kingfisher; when the baker with his basket on his head and the clang clang of his cane (stick with rings at the top for the sound) gave ample warning for the housewife to come to the door and get her daily bread (Today, he laments, the baker moves on a bicycle with his basket resting on its carrier and instead of the stick with rings he has a rubber horn hearing whose pom pom the housewife has now to come to the gate of her house); when the sons of the tenants went about in torn vests; when jackals used to come down the hills to the fields to fill their belly with the dried fish the landowners used as manure. "How to make Goa as green as it had been in the days when I as a child trudged my way through fields and trees to school, with the birds and butterflies as my guides and escorts?" laments Luizinho Faleiro.

Liberation had brought about a spectatular development, and there was no way Goa could have remained the same. Yet when the old sights disappeared, the Goans felt ill at ease. Instead of giving the fattened sows a traditional chase before slaughtering them Christians now bought pork from a shop; and instead of the elixir of *feni*, whisky and beer flowed at parties. Instead of serenading guitars what people heard was loud music from bars and cafes catering to tourists. Mothers complained to the government that loud music was affecting their children's studies during the exams. Goa was no more dependent on primitive agriculture and emigrants' remittances: mines, industries, tourism and other services were providing the bulk of income and employment. This shift had influenced changes in the caste hierarchy, social norms, family structure, housing patterns, demography and cultural values. The average Goan felt alienated by these changes, and, not taught how to understand them, focussed his anger on the migrants.

When Goan xenophobia takes over, sanity takes a back seat. Thus all crime gets associated with migrants. The Kashmiris, under the façade of carpet business, sell drugs on the beaches. The vagrants from Bihar and Kerala roam the beaches with hashish and charas in their pockets. (The involvement of Goans is ignored.) The pervert outsiders are promoting sex tourism in the state: the prostitutes at Baina in Vasco da Gama are from Karnataka, Kerala, Tamil Nadu and Nepal. (The fact that the number of AIDS cases has been rising among the local population in Goa is not discussed.) So in the case of child abuse:

the paedophiles who stalk Goa's beaches are all foreigners (no doubt, a Britisher and a New Zealander were sentenced to seven years rigorous imprisonment for paedophilia by a Goan court in July 2002); and the children they abuse are from other states. (The fact of paedophilia being common in Goan society is socially censored.)

Robberies, thefts and burglaries are committed by criminals from other states. It is a fact that mobile criminal gangs and thieves strike at targets in Goa, just as they do in other states, but this is used to portray the entire migrant population black. Crimes by outside gangs get prominently highlighted in the local media, which never fails to mention what language the robbers used among themselves or with the inmates of the house (and it is usually Hindi or Kannada or some South Indian language). A section of the local media unrestrainedly uses headlines, like 'Keralite held with charas,' 'Two Kannadigas in police net,' 'Man from Uttar Pradesh dupes woman,' 'Bihari booked for drug peddling,' 'Kashmiris caught with dope,' 'Two Gujaratis in fake passport scandal' which proves like a slap in the morning in the face of the migrant communities from these states. These headlines provoked the Goans in general, deepening their suspicion of outsiders. In early 2000, such headlines, which appeared in the wake of a series of armed robberies in the state, drove a mob to lynch a poor migrant to death in Taleigao on suspicion that he was a pickpocket.

However, the media only reported what the police told them, which showed that the enforcers of law had prejudices against the migrants themselves. It was a very usual practice for them to summon residents of slums to the police station for interrogation whenever dacoities or major thefts took place. The media never reported on the humiliation the poor migrant labourers suffered in silence. (If they set up a protest, the police might really put them inside, who knew?)

The politicians proved worse than the policemen: they thrived on people's prejudices. If the migrant was a permanent suspect in the Goan perception they would consciously reap harvests of this sentiment. In March 2001 the MLAs passed a legislation, called the Goa Employment (Conditions of Service) and Retirement Benefit Bill, making it compulsory for every job-seeker to register himself with the labour department. On registration he would get a Smart Card, with his photo, address and other details inscribed in it, with which he would open a savings account with the government. Into this account, his employer would deposit 5 per cent of his monthly wages without fail. If he changed his employer, the new paymaster had to deposit the 5 per cent of his monthly wages into the same account.

The declared objective of the legislation was to let the compulsory savings, on which the government will pay 6 per cent interest, be released as pension benefit to the unorganised labourer when he attained the age of 50 years. Behind this noble objective, however, there was also the plan of the government to build up a mechanism to monitor immigration through compulsory registration. The legislation had fulfilled a long-standing demand of the xenophobic Goans to force the migrants to carry identity cards. The aim behind issuing smart cards, the government said, was to make identification of migrant labourers easier and help police check crime.

In some of the villages in the coastal belt, the panchayats passed resolutions asking the residents to demand photo and personal details of the migrants they wish to employ as servants or hire out accommodation to. The panchayats also wanted them to submit their personal details to their offices, so that they can ask the police to verify their antecedents. "The verification," says Anthony Pinto, the sarpanch of Varca, "serves a dual purpose: one, police comes to know of the bad elements, and two, it instills fear in the minds of the migrants." The whole exercise, naturally, has made every migrant an object of suspicion. If a few of them hang around in the main village bazaar past nine or ten o'clock, just for gossip, or for a drink, they might be taken to be thieves. Obviously the verification campaign was aimed at striking terror in the hearts of the migrants.

It was grossly unjust to blame crime entirely on the outsiders. Records showed that Goa had one of the highest crime rates, that is, the ratio of total crimes to total population, and the role of outsiders in this was marginal. Most of the crimes were committed by Goans: murders, attempts to murder, extortions, criminal assaults, rapes, paedophilia, domestic violence, robberies, cheating. During the nine years ending 1999, 62 cases of paedophilia were registered by the state police of which only 4 or less than 7 per cent involved foreigners. The largest number of cases, 37 or about 55 per cent involved neighbours, family friends and close relations. A police study of the 35 murders that took place between January-October 2000 found that most of them were committed by close relations. The daily *Gomantak Times*, commenting on the police study, said: "We face threats to life not from the non-Goan burglars — traditionally associated with crime and murder — but from our very dear own family members who include husbands, brothers, sisters-in-law, girlfriends and boyfriends (that is all those) whom we were taught to love (and adore)."

Corroborating it, a senior Goan journalist, Mario Cabral e Sa wrote in *Sunday Navhind Times*: "As for the so-called outsiders who are blamed for all the crimes taking place in Goa, a visit to the Aguada and Sada jails should be educative — unless the suggestion is that the outsiders are smart and don't get caught. Being a jail visitor I know for a fact that if one breaks the figures ethnicity-wise one will find that there are more locals cooling their heels behind bars than outsiders. The statistics: of 49 lifers in Aguada jail 33 are Goans; of those jailed for serious crime from 10 to 15 years, 36 out of 52 are Goans. There are less Goans convicted for drug-related cases, i.e., ten in a total of 46. But so far as undertrials are concerned there are 37 Goans in a total of 47."

School dropouts in Goa, who remained idle because they did not want the jobs they deserved and were not qualified for the jobs they wanted, had been the ones most commonly involved in organised crime. They needed a motorcycle, and they needed money to buy fuel to run it, money to spend on buddies and dames, money to drink, money to show off: and, quite naturally, they could get money for all these things only from burglaries, robberies and extortions. Houses, whose owners lived abroad or had gone on a holiday, often were found broken into and emptied of encashable properties. Businessmen's families were robbed in daylight.

And extortions are becoming common. Gangs, small to big, exist all over the state that thrive on extortions from hotel owners, real estate developers, builders, scrap dealers and shopkeepers. Until recently these gangs were traditionally armed, but in January 2001 the police seized 62 illegal firearms with 700 rounds of ammunition from 34 persons, and that showed that guns had become the common weapon of the extortionists. There was in fact, police found, a well-established network of gun-running through states of which the Goa link was provided by some motorcycle-borne, princely-life-seeking school dropouts.

The police have not found it easy to prosecute the extortionists because their victims are not ready to give evidence against them. In the first place, the victims rarely lodge a complaint with the police; but even if they do in the initial flush of their anger, they retract their statement at a later stage fearing a retaliation by the extortionists. A most notorious extortionist of Panaji had at least 12 criminal cases registered against him but chargesheets could not be framed in any of them, because the complainants or witnesses were too scared to depose against him. The whole of Panaji knew how he had accumulated his wealth, but nobody could do anything. When once the police put him in preventive detention under the National Security Act, he hired one of the topmost Supreme Court lawyers to argue his case in the Bombay High Court and got himself released. He never stopped extorting.

As gun-running showed, the criminals in Goa had set up active links with criminals in other states. Not long ago, a Goan and a Kannadiga were caught stealing cash and other properties from shops on the ground floor of a building; having spent some time together in the Aguada jail they had become partners in crime. In July 2002 a group of Goans and outsiders were caught in a major case of pilferage of petrol from the oil industry pipeline at the Mormugao port. There are at least 5,000 Goans involved in the illegal *matka* business in which people gamble on numbers. The criminals who run this business in Goa have strong links with criminals in Mumbai and other cities. Other examples of profitable criminal relationship between Goans and outsiders are: smuggling of consumer goods, drug peddling, money laundering and female trafficking.

The Second Class Goans

The migrants being objects of suspicion they have not received any sympathy from the people, the government or the media, in spite of the fact that they live in less-than-human conditions. More than 100,000 people or about 8 per cent of the state's population lives in slums, and they are nearly all migrants. In Panaji alone, there are 37 hutment colonies where the city's domestic maids, sweepers and contract labourers reside. The most wretched is the plight of the construction workers who are forced to live, often with their wives and children, in a camp of tiny, low-roofed plastic tents without ventilation, electricity, water, drainage or toilets close to the work sites. They have to live in such conditions as long as the work on the building is not complete, and in times of downswing in the real estate market this may mean an indefinite number of years.

Although the laws provide for punishment to builders who do not provide proper accommodation to workers, the builders have never cared. Neither does the labour contractor, who has brought them to work on the site, take any responsibility for their housing. He leaves it to the labourers to find their accommodation. What the labourers do is set up a colony of makeshift huts not far from the work site, to which the builder or labour contractor turns a blind eye, especially if it is on public land. The laws require the builder to provide drinking water, bathing and washing facilities, crèche, toilets and other amenities to the workers, but they do not. The labourers, including the women, have to use public spaces to answer calls of nature. In the beach belt, where the construction activity has been most intense, the labourers often use the shrubs around the sand dunes to ease themselves and then go and wash their bodies on the beach.

For no fault of theirs, the migrants get smeared black in their face again: "There is no fresh morning breeze from the beach any more. It is laden with the stench of the migrant's nightsoil." Of course it is true that most of the migrant labourers come from villages and they feel more comfortable answering the nature's call out in the open. At the same time, it is also true that the builder has left them with no other alternative. The government has not enforced the law against the builders. Even the municipalities, which require the builders to fulfill conditions like proper amenities to labourers before a construction licence can be issued to them, seldom take the trouble of making an actual check at the site. The most law-abiding builders in Goa would be those who put up a few gunny cloth or wooden mat enclosures around a hole in the ground near the site. Not only the number of the enclosures would be inadequate for the large number of workers, but their maintenance would also leave much to be desired.

Considering the conditions in which they live, it is hardly surprising that the construction workers become a common victim of malaria, and hence also a common carrier of it. A report, titled, the *State of Goa's Health*, released in April 2000, pointed at strong links between the high growth of construction industry and high growth of malaria. Till 1986, malaria had not been a serious problem in Goa. Then the first outbreak occurred in Panaji's Miramar and Campal localities, both scenes of frenetic building activity. It later spread to the other parts of Panaji and the villages around, Taleigao, Santa Cruz, Chimbel and Betim. In

1985 only 80 cases of malaria were reported in the whole state; in 1988 this figure rose to 6,732, and in 1998 to 25,390. What was more alarming, during these 13 years, was the proportion of *Plasmodium falciparum*, the most dangerous form of malaria, to the total number of cases increased from 3.75 per cent to 34 per cent. In 1996, 10 persons died of malaria, in 1997, 57 and in 1998, 19.

Researches into the epidemic found that the common malaria vector, *Anopheles stephensi*, bred in the curing waters, rainwater pools, unfinished WCs, roof gutters, open drains and masonry tanks at the construction sites. The vectors feasted on the bodies of the labourers who slept close to their birthplaces, in shanties or out in the open, usually with a minimum of clothing. Moved very often by the builders or contractors from one work site to another in the state, the labourers carried the disease to other parts, making the local residents and tourists also vulnerable to it. Even when the epidemic thus spread, the state government did not take action against the builders. Under the law, the builders and contractors were obliged to carry out regular anti-larval measures at their construction sites to stop *Anopheles stephensi* from breeding in the curing waters, tanks, roof gutters and other places. There were going to be regular checks, and every time breeding was found at his site, the builder was to pay a fine of Rs 5,000.

Then the government made the screening of construction labourers for malaria compulsory. The health officer of the area would issue every labourer a health card, noting the dates and results of every screening in it. Every time a labourer failed to produce the card, he would be fined Rs 1,000. If he failed to produce a card continuously he was to pay a penalty of Rs 50 per day until he got one. All these penalties remain on paper. The report on the state of Goa's health blamed political interference for it. Builders were among the principal benefactors of the politicians. Whenever the health officer tightened the screws on them they lobbied with the local MLA or ministers to get him off their neck.

However, there were infrastructural problems as well. The government propaganda about the legal provisions was poor. Confronted by the wily builders, the health officers sometimes did not know how to proceed next. And there was no legal cell in the health department to guide them. Neither did exist any system of vector surveillance at the breeding sites. Unless these weaknesses were attended to, the health officers could not make regular checks and issue on-the-spot notices to the defaulters.

However, the construction workers were not the only hosts to the malaria mosquitoes. A majority of workers in the restaurants and bars were migrants, and given no accommodation by their employers, they slept on the footpaths or spaces outside their work places, exposing themselves to insect bites. And *Anopheles stephensi* not only bred in stagnant waters at the construction sites but also in the wells, choked drains and water accumulated in scrap pieces, abandoned tyres or barrels at the slums where the migrant labourers live, but also in the overhead tanks, ornamental fountains, disused swimming pools, waterlogged cellars, basements and lift depressions in the middle class flats or houses where their women and children work.

Good housing was the first bulwark against malaria, and most migrant labourers do not have it. Even those who came over two decades ago continue to live in huts on government or private land. They have no houses to call their own. Middle class people living in bungalows or flats are told to shut their doors and windows at 6.30 p.m., so that the malaria mosquitoes do not enter their homes. The migrant labourers have too many openings in their tenements to stop the insects that come preying in. They cannot bring about improvements in their dwellings, since neither the huts nor the plots on which they stand belong to them. Even the poorest of villagers have a sense of hygiene and aesthetics, but they must have a sense of belonging to the place first. Although, after lobbying with the elected representatives, most of the migrant labourers have managed to get electricity and water connections to their tenements, and even a ration card on the address where they live, the ownership or secured tenancy of the land on which their huts stand eludes them.

And it has not been easy getting those connections or ration cards. They have to visit the offices several times before things start moving, and often they have to pay a higher bribe to the officials than a Goan will have to. Wage earners as they are, running to the offices means that many days of wages lost. Besides, the bribe demanded, Rs 2,000 to Rs 3,000 at current rates, might not be affordable for them.

There is no redress available to the migrants higher up in the government, because invariably the question — who's the victim? — comes up, and if it happens to be a *bhailo* or *ghanti*, an immigrant, the

Goan partisanship takes over. Some years ago a co-operative bank, called the Citizen Co-operative Bank, was set up in Vasco da Gama with the objective of providing credit to the poorer sections. A large number of the original shareholders of the bank, about 500, were *bhayyas*. But when elections to the board of directors were held, the *bhayyas* were left unrepresented. All the directors were Goans. Despite the persistent demand of the *bhayyas*, the composition of the board has not changed. In credit disbursement too, the *bhayyas* have not benefitted. The government has refused to intervene to safeguard their interests.

The migrants are victims of double alienation: removed from their native home and not accepted in their adopted home. They are forever in search of an identity, because they are neither here nor there. They do not belong anywhere. A terrible feeling of insecurity grips them. It affects their physical and mental health.

It is not the labourers alone, however, who face double alienation. Migrants holding government offices have serious complaints too. Quite a few of them, despite having the required rank, merit and experience, have been bypassed for promotion to make way for a (junior and undeserving) son of the soil. Some of them had been waiting for the elevation for years; they felt so frustrated they quit the service and joined private companies. A painter from Madhya Pradesh who joined the Goa College of Art as a lecturer was never given a promotion: he retired as a lecturer. A man from Uttar Pradesh, who was selected by an expert panel for lectureship in a Vasco da Gama college, was shocked to find no students in the classroom when he arrived for his first lecture. When he inquired, he was told that the students were boycotting his classes in protest against an 'outsider's' appointment in preference to a Goan. He was amazed, since the panel had selected him out of ten candidates. The students had the backing of some Goan teachers.

Unable to break through Goan prejudices, the migrants have come to nurse their own prejudices against Goans. Behind the outward camaraderie at workplaces, there is a subterranean hostility between locals and outsiders. Often the employers have to do a tight rope-walking to keep the hostility under control. The migrants' interaction with Goans generally does not move beyond the boundaries of the workplace. The socialising of migrants is confined to their linguistic, religious and cultural communities, which have their own temples, *mutts* or mosques.

Children of Migrants

Discrimination does not spare the migrant children, especially those of the labourers. There is no crèche at the work site. So, while the parents work, the children play around the site. Older children have to carry around the tiny tots. The children are not sent to school, because their parents do not have time to take them there or bring them back. Out in Goa they do not have any other relation of the family to escort their children to and from school. One or two NGOs have been running non-formal schools for migrant children but they have proven like a drop in the ocean. Attempts by the migrant communities to set up schools in their own tongue, so that their children did not have difficulty grasping the lessons, have been thwarted by government indifference. The three prerequisites for their sustenance, land for the building and playground, recognition of its courses and financial assistance, have been denied to them.

The children of the middle class migrants are fortunate because they go to the English medium schools which are in plenty. The labourers' children find English too difficult a language to understand. Neither can they go to the Konkani or Marathi medium schools where poorer Hindu Goan children are sent to. Asking them to study in any medium other than their mother tongue is asking them to learn two things at the same time: a new language and a new syllabus. And this when their parents are not of much help at home, since they have never been to school themselves.

No recreational facilities are available to the migrant children, either. They do not have money to go to movies or to buy toys. Local sports groups do not allow them entry. A majority of them are forced to do odd jobs to bring supplementary income to the family, like selling of plastic bags to customers in the market, ragpicking, assisting motor mechanics, or working as domestic help and waiters in bars and restaurants where the employers subject them to physical violence and verbal abuse.

Some of them wander about the beaches hawking sundry things or looking for odd jobs. It is among these children that the paedophiles look for their prey. These children are all boys, since even the poorest of migrant parents do not generally let their daughters lounge about except under their vigil. They do not want anything to happen to her which will bring her a bad name, making it difficult for them to find a boy for her. Taking advantage of poor parental vigil over the wandering boys, the paedophiles entice them with chocolates and little gifts. Pampering them day after day they begin to get closer to them: like they would stroke or hug them, squeeze their arms or cheeks, exhibit their organs to them, all the time making the relationship look fatherly and innocuous. Once they think they have won their confidence, they take them to their rooms where they sexually molest them.

A social worker who ran a non-formal school for migrant children in Mapusa observed that the children would not be able to concentrate on studies as they had been corrupted by the gifts showered by the paedophiles. A child once went missing for days: when he returned to school he had a watch on his wrist. Such examples 'inspired' other children to take the same route to good life.

Knowing no other way to get those good things their sexual exploiters give them (a 54-year-old German paedophile gave his 14-year-old victim a cellular phone) the boys never let their parents know what was happening. Even though they know what they are doing is not right, they find it impossible to deny themselves the temptation. They grow up as traumatised, morbid human beings. Studies of these children have found that they do not talk about the abuse unless they get caught and are confronted with circumstantial evidence. There are cases in which the paedophiles worm their way into the childrens' parents' hearts by offering them gifts, inducing them to lower their guards. In some other cases the father may be a drunkard, and oblivious of the childrens' indulgences. Studies have noted a rise in the number of liquor addicts among migrant labourers. Even those who never touched liquor started drinking under the influence of the local culture which glorified drinking.

There are 8,500 licensed bars or liquor shops in Goa. If you counted the beach shacks and homes with a few tables set up on the sides that sell liquor illegally, the number would come to 10,000, or one bar or shop for every 130 persons. In such an atmosphere the male migrants cannot remain unaffected. They quickly learn to rationalise that they must drink to kill fatigue. Alcoholism has taken such strong hold on several of them that they cannot stay very long in the native village on their visit; they have to rush back to Goa because they have been missing their drink. Addiction takes away most of their earnings.

And it makes them sick and feeble and unwanted at work. Then they start demanding money of their wives and daughters to buy their drink. And thus the very purpose of emigration — saving enough for the future — gets defeated.

Migrant women have to bear insults, verbal abuse, violence and emotional torture from their alcoholic husbands. And on the top of it, they are expected to work harder than men. They have to wake up early to cook some breakfast, march off to work, buy the day's rations on their way back home, start cooking as soon as they step in, and all the time never letting the children go off care. There is no piped water supply in the shanties, so water every morning and evening has to be brought from a well or public tap where invariably there is a long queue. Living in squalid environs and surviving on low-nutrition or contaminated food, the women fall prey to diseases, like anaemia, respiratory infections and malaria. What makes their life worse is the denial of privacy of bathrooms and toilets to them. The Goa State Commission for Women and the women NGOs have been pressing for measures to give migrant women better housing, education and sanitation but nobody has paid any attention to their call.

The Goan Sovereignty

No organisations exist in Goa to protect the migrant women's — or, for that matter, men's — human rights. There are enlightened Goans of course, Goans with exposure to other parts of the country, who bear an empathic attitude toward the migrants, but their number is small, and, what is still sadder, they are not the kind who join organisations to fight for causes, popular or unpopular. Therefore, those who dominate the horizon are people who consciously or unconsciously, see the *bhailes* and *ghantis* as eaters of their grains and drinkers of their waters, in short, as merry-makers on their land. They want barriers to be put to stop any more migrants coming.

For the Goan, the alienation starts from the street, where today several languages can be heard. When the average Goan hears Hindi, Kannada or Malayalam on the streets, he fears his mother tongue Konkani might become a minority language in its own homeland. A threat to Konkani is considered as a threat to Goan culture. That is why the Konkani movement today has become a movement for monoculturalism. Konkani activist groups do not want the government to give any encouragement to the other languages or cultures. They have been opposing the telecast of Maharashtra's cultural or literary programmes on the Panaji Doordarshan in preference to Konkani programmes, saying that this prevents the local talents from blossoming. They want the government to send replies to citizens who write to them and to print invitation cards for official functions in Konkani.

By mid-1990s the monocultural safeguards were provided in the system of recruitments in the government, which required knowledge of Konkani and a 15-year domicile for a candidate's eligibility over and above his other qualifications. This was a hundred per cent job reservation to Goans by another name. In theory, employment in the government was also open to outsiders who had made Goa their home and could speak Konkani, but in practice it remained in the hands of the selection panels whether to choose them in preference to native Goans even if they fulfilled the two essential criteria. English continued to be the state language in reality (even the Assembly proceedings were conducted in English) with no sign of Konkani ever replacing it; yet, the Goans had used their official language status to Konkani as a tool to keep non-Goans out of the government services. Konkani was serving the ethnic interests of Goans. It ensures their control over their resources. Outsiders had to be excluded from jobs and business opportunities (the 15-year domicile was made compulsory for self-employment schemes too); and they would be denied access to land and housing.

For the existing private companies in the state in the mid-1990s the government, much to the delight of the Konkani activists, made a new recruitment rule, which became known as 80:20 ratio. This required every company to have 80 per cent of Goans in their workforce. A penalty clause was incorporated into this rule: if the company did not comply with it the government would withhold the disbursement of investment subsidy to it. And an inspection of every company was to be made by the director of employment on whose report would depend the release of the subsidy. Unless he was convinced that a company had "valid and adequate reasons" to recruit less than 80 per cent Goans it could not escape the penalty. The new rule put the companies in a great dilemma. They had recruited people from other states, not because they loved them more than the Goans, but because talents were not available locally. Even the leading Goan industrial houses had a large number of outsiders on their payrolls precisely for the same reason.

Soon, the two qualifying criteria for government employment — knowledge of Konkani and a 15-year domicile — were also made applicable to the private companies. The government has kept up the pressure by sending reminders from time to time to the private companies on the subject. It has asked the employment exchange not to register anyone who has resided in the state for less than 15 years, and the private employers have been asked not to recruit anyone who is not registered with the employment exchange. Members often raised questions in the Assembly on the 80:20 ratio, accusing the government of showing a lenient attitude toward the defaulting private employers. On January 22, 2001, in reply to the members' queries, the labour minister said that 2,038 of the 2,750 employees in the five star hotels in the state, or about 74 per cent, were Goans, who knew Konkani and had resided in Goa for 15 years. But the members disputed the labour minister's figures, saying even the waiters and other seasonal staff recruited by the five star hotels were outsiders. They doubted if the recruits had produced their employment exchange registration cards at the time of employment.

Around the same time, the MLAs also raised questions about the Prime Minister's Rojgar Yojana (PMRY) scheme in which educated unemployed were provided credit by banks for self-employment through the state government's Economic Development Corporation. They alleged that most of the beneficiaries had been youths from other states and demanded details on how many Goans had availed of the scheme. In its defence, the government said that the PMRY was a central scheme and it required only a 3-year domicile for the educated unemployed in the state where he availed the credit. The MLAs pressed the government to apply the 15-year domicile criterion to the scheme, but the government said it was an all-India scheme and it was not within its powers to apply its own rules to it.

Under constant pressure from the Konkani groups, the men in the government and opposition competed with each other to put stricter border control; and the panchayats have not lagged behind. Private companies require a variety of licences from the panchayats, and they would not give them without a commitment from them that they would have 80 per cent Goans in their workforce. The Goa Hitrakhan

Manch is now pressing for an industrial policy under which the government will sanction an industry not because it provides revenue to the state exchequer, but because it provides employment to locals. In other words, only such enterprises could exist in Goa for which manpower is locally available.

The Manch's ideology — Goan sovereignty over Goan resources — has much in common with that of the Christian groups which have sustained themselves on the submergence fears of the community. Behind the Christian groups' opposition to the coastal alignment of the Konkan Railway was the nightmare that it would open floodgates to immigration, as also the anger that the railway ministry was pushing through the proposal in total disregard of 'Goan sentiments.' They wanted the Meta Strips Limited to go out of the state not only because it would spawn hutment colonies around the factory causing problems of sanitation, health and overcrowding for the local communities, but also because this polluting metal scrap recycling plant had been set up 'without the consent of the people.'

The proposal for a Free Port in Goa was opposed not only because that the entrepreneurs would bring cheap labour from other states, but also because Goan sovereignty would cease to exist in that part of Goa. The groups attacked the state government for agreeing to the Free Port proposal, demanding that a referendum be held to know the views of the citizens of Goa. Goans, said the groups, must have a right to decide the course of their development, cultural and physical environment and destiny. The church backed the groups openly. Archbishop Gonsalves in his pastoral theme for 1995 said: "Our (Goans') proverbial hospitality is being challenged today by the ever growing influx of non-Goans into our state threatening our security and comfort."

The Rotten Apples

In the eyes of Konkani activists and Christian groups, the Goan sovereignty, despite the grant of statehood, has remained partial. As a union territory for more than 25 years since Liberation Goa remained in the hands of the Centre, and thereafter too, the Centre's administrators have exercised control. Due to the smallness of its size the state does not have its own cadre for officers selected by the Union Public Service Commission, but is clubbed with two other small states, Arunachal Pradesh and Mizoram, and the union territories. The officers of this combined cadre — popularly known as the AGMU cadre, or cadre for Arunachal, Goa, Mizoram and union territories — keep moving on transfer from one state/union territory to another state/union territory within this group. And for this reason primarily they are not liked in Goa. They have been nicknamed 'tourists,' because they come to Goa not for work but enjoyment during their tenure, or 'suitcase officers,' because they keep themselves ready for a transfer. Politicians freely use these nicknames, feeding the deep-rooted prejudice in the Goan psyche against 'officers from Delhi.' The officers of the AGMU cadre come from various states and work in various states, yet they are lumped together in the politicians' rhetoric as 'officers from Delhi' who have very little interest in the development of Goa. Shortly after Manohar Parrikar took over as chief minister in mid-2000 he made a public statement that most of the civil servants of the AGMU cadre left behind their family in Delhi and found one excuse or the other to catch a flight to spend weekends with them.

Parrikar forced his chief secretary to quit Goa, because he was 'indifferent and incompetent.' Luizinho Faleiro had thrown out his chief secretary for not attending his *janata durbars*, where he wanted him to come to answer people's questions, a responsibility, the chief secretary said, which did not form a part of his duties as a civil servant. Other chief ministers had removed their inspector-generals of police (IGPs). Each of these officers had been driven out of Goa in a humiliating manner, and with derogatory tags slapped on their back: 'mad,' 'communal,' 'corrupt,' 'unfit,' 'derelict.' Bound by service conduct rules as they were, the officers left Goa without telling their stories to the Goans through the media. So, the dirty stickers stuck, reinforcing the prejudice against 'officers from Delhi.'

Politicians had succeeded in finding a scapegoat for their failures and mismanagement — since in the system, the ministers remained supreme, the civil servants being servants — yet the Konkani and Christian groups would throw their weight behind them rather than the officers. They shrieked in agreement when politicians attacked the Centre for treating Goa as a 'dumping ground' of 'rejected officers,' officers whom no other state or union territory of the AGMU group would accept. Such affront to Goan sovereignty frequently found its reflection in the media. The editorial in July 1993 issue of *Goa Today* said : "Indeed, Goa has been singularly unlucky in its IGPs, saddled as it has been with a string of incompetent and politically pliable marionettes. It would seem from the attitude of the central government that Goa is an inconsequential dumping ground to banish inconvenient officials to, in police and in other departments .... Goa can no longer afford to be the repository of New Delhi's rotten apples."

Prejudices against officers from Delhi date back to the union territory days when they were all-powerful. All the funds flowed from the Centre, whose officers, naturally, also managed them. Even after the democratically elected government led by Dayanand Bandodkar took over, the real powers lay in the hands of the Lieutenant Governor, the chief executive officer of the central government. All the financial authority was vested in him and he even had the powers to overrule cabinet decisions. His secretary attended cabinet meetings and could often influence decisions by his suggestions.

Stories abound in Goa about lieutenant governors taking away antiques, paintings, curios and precious furniture from the Cabo Raj Niwas. There are stories about them and their subordinates having bought huge areas of land for speculation. A reader recently wrote a letter to a local newspaper, saying, of course without any proof: "In order to satisfy IAS officers from New Delhi, the industries department set up a centre at Panaji to produce carved furniture, and every IAS officer who served the Goa government went with a booty of carved furniture." The image of the 'officers from Delhi' being arrogant, overbearing, dominant and greedy has persisted even though Goa has become a state and the elected representatives call the shots.

In the recent years, politicians have frequently advocated the formation of a separate Goa cadre for all-India officers. This cadre will be composed of candidates passing the Union Public Service Commission exams who opt for service in Goa. They can be transferred only within the state and, in senior positions, posted at the Centre.

The idea has found strong support among the Konkani and Christian groups, because in this they see the consummation of self-rule. There is a consensus among Goa's political camps on the issue. In early 2001 when Manohar Parrikar's Bharatiya Janata Party government was threatening to pull Goa out of the AGMU cadre and establish a separate state cadre, the Goa Pradesh Congress Committee set up a panel headed by its former president Shantaram Naik to examine the issue. Within a few weeks, the panel concluded its examination and came out with a strong recommendation for a separate state cadre on five grounds: One, the Goa statehood legislation passed by the Parliament in 1987 envisaged an independent state cadre. Two, the Constitution gave every state the right to form a separate cadre: even the three newly formed states, Jharkhand, Uttaranchal and Chhatisgarh, had their separate cadres. Three, the officers of the AGMU cadre could never contribute much to the development of Goa, as they were transferred before they could even understand the topography of the state: in contrast, the separate cadre officers would be residing in the state and committed to the land. Four, the controlling authority of the AGMU cadre was the central government, which fact encouraged its officers to defy a state minister in particular or the state government in general. Of the state cadre the controlling authority would be the state government authorities; they would be writing their confidential reports; and this will prevent the officers from neglecting the development works.

In September, 2002, the state cabinet began a process of deliberation on the formation of a State Cadre. Behind the idea of a separate state cadre was the dream to have an all-Goan bureaucracy. Although Goan youths showed no inclination to compete for all-India civil services, the politicians hoped that the formation of a separate state cadre would make them change their attitude. Thus would the high offices in the state bureaucracy get occupied by sons of the soil. The state civil services had already stopped recruiting non-Goans. The general and technical administrators from other states who had been absorbed would retire in a few years, leaving the state civil services entirely in the hands of Goans. Goa was on its way to achieve full sovereignty.

The war against outsiders in the bureacracy had started in the 1970s, when the United Goans Party (UGP) led by Jack Sequeira set up an agitation asking Bandodkar's Maharashtrawadi Gomantak Party (MGP) government to send the officers on deputation back to their parent states. The agitation had been fuelled by resentment among Christians (literacy among whom was higher than among Hindus) that Bandodkar was discriminating against them in government recruitments and filling the posts with officers from other states. The MGP led a counter-protest, arguing that these officers were here because qualified Goans were not available for those posts: accepting the UGP demand would mean allowing mediocres and unfit people to run the government. Insisting that it was a conspiracy to deny the Christians the right to employment, the UGP started mobilising small gatherings of Christians outside the government offices to chant the slogan: *Deputa-tionists, go back. Deputationists, go back.*

In the later years, the battle against outsiders in the government was to take other forms: denial of promotions despite the qualifications, less important postings, insidious smear campaigns, taunts, barbs and contemptuous nicknames. This battle represented a part of the broad campaign against immigration. And this broad campaign has not always remained insidious or peaceful. Unable to get at the middle class immigrants, xenophobic gangs have attacked the migrant labourers. In 1972 the city of Vasco da Gama was rocked by violence of Goans against the *bhayyas*. Mobs attacked the *bhayyas* in their homes, set their kiosks ablaze, demanded they get out of Goa. The *bhayyas* were so frightened they all headed toward the city's railway station to catch the first train out of Goa. Shrieking mobs arrived there too to assault them when they sat in the compartments and hurled their luggage here and there.

Certainly, it was not only xenophobia. A complex web of factors was working. In the ten years preceding a powerful trade union leader called Mohan Nair had emerged in the city. He was god to the dock labour and barge workers. At his instance all movements of iron ore and loading of cargo could come to a halt and this bothered the exporters, stevedores and other businessmen no end, because he frequently made them hike the workers' wages.

In order to fight his terror, the Goan bourgeoisie began a 'Goa for Goans' campaign, demanding that Goa must be cleansed of outsiders. Their front was led by a stevedore who also had other businesses; and this front in no insignificant way built up a hostile atmosphere against Mohan Nair and the migrant labourers — the *bhayyas* as well as those whom he had brought from Karnataka and Kerala — who had rallied behind him. Then there was another factor. Mohan Nair belonged to the Indian National Trade Union Congress which was the labour front of the Congress party. During elections he campaigned for the Congress candidates in Vasco da Gama.

The party which competed with the Congress in the port city was the MGP, whose leaders, during the elections in 1972, were pressing the *bhayyas*, who constituted a large segment of the electorate, to vote for them. Anger rose in the MGP ranks when they saw that the *bhayyas* would stick to Mohan Nair. This offered a good opportunity for the 'Goa for Goans' campaigners and, with their and the MGP leaders' blessings, mobs launched the offensive to drive the 'traitors' away.

In the following years Mohan Nair became physically and organisationally weaker and moved to his home state Kerala where he soon died. For the Goan bourgeoisie the battle was over. The 'Goa for Goans' campaign was wound up. After all, the local bourgeoisie needed outside labour. They wanted their work done and did not mind whether the workers were locals or outsiders.

However, the interests of the poorer classes of Goans who constituted the MGP ranks in Vasco da Gama were different. A large number of them had migrated to the port city in search of livelihood from predominantly rural talukas, like Pernem. They nursed grievances in their hearts that the labourers from the other states were eating up their space and growing prosperous. The migrants were buying properties and entering businesses.

In 1982, riots broke out in the city again. This time mobs targetted the migrants from Karnataka. The immediate provocation was a dispute over a piece of land between local people and Kannadiga labourers. Violent mobs beseiged the Kannadiga colonies and attacked those that fell into their hands, ransacked the huts. Thousands of Kannadiga labourers took shelter on the platforms of the city's railway station. Having carried whatever of their wretched possessions they could along with them, they cooked, ate and slept on the platforms for about 15 days without any help coming to them. It was only after the government of Karnataka intervened that the Goa government was forced to provide police security to the Kannadiga labourers and restore order and calm in the city.

8
Writings on the Wall

We, the workers and builders, traders and industrialists, the executives and engineers, the doctors and social workers (from other states) who have been living in the state of Goa for decades and made it our homeland, giving it our heart and soul, our sweat and intelligence, and exchanging love and affection with it ... are forced to speak with profound sorrow and feeling of insecurity against (moves by the state government to make an) employment policy that guarantees employment only to Goans as sons of the soil, leaving us as strangers in our own Mother India.
— An ad. published by the Goa National Integration Forum in 1992

Fading Colonial Influences

Goa has changed a lot in the over forty years since Liberation. The Portuguese influences on Goa's culture are fading and may only survive as a minor exotic inscription on the history's gargantuan tombstone. The obscuration is attributable not only to the declining size of the Christian population in Goa, which absorbed most of these influences, but also to the fact that the generations of Christian elite who considered themselves as true inheritors of the glorious Iberian culture are dying out. The aggression, the solidarity, the zealotry with which these native *fidalgos* combated a revengeful Hindu India to preserve the unique identity, the Indo-Portuguese identity, of Goa are flagging.

Today when a Goan Christian speaks of identity he does not speak of the Indo-Portuguese identity but of Goan identity. Nobody knows what Goan identity is, since Goa has a dichotomous culture with unbreakable Hindu-Christian walls, yet the Christians would go on speaking of one, because they realise that it is only by establishing solidarity with the Goan Hindus that they can survive the onslaughts of the bigger forces represented by 'India.' If they went on harping on a unique identity bequeathed by the colonial experience, the Goan Hindus, bitter about the Portuguese era, would never unite with them.

And the government of India had made their task easier by incorporating the monuments of the Indo-Portuguese era, like the churches of Old Goa, into Indian heritage. The government of Goa had granted Corridinho and Mando an equal place with Hindu performing arts, opened a department of Portuguese in the Goa University and had given a commitment to promote the 200-odd mansions built in Indo-Portuguese style as places of tourist interest and to patronise Carnival as a tourist event.

Nostalgic memories of Goa Portuguesa might still enliven a few evenings at the formal or informal gatherings at the Portuguese consulate in Panaji, what with its invitees' list never missing out on the 'true inheritors' of the glorious Iberian culture, but the reality is that even their children might have studied in the English medium rather than in Portuguese and were settled in America or Canada rather than in Portugal. Although there are more centres teaching Portuguese in Goa now than there were in the '60s or '70s, English has become the most favourite language even of Christians, pushing Portuguese to the margins.

In 1991 barely 3 per cent of the Goans knew Portuguese. Sunday mass is no more held in Portuguese anywhere in Goa except in the Panaji church. Until recently there used to be a mass in Portuguese also in the chapel at Fontainhas, a residential district of some of the ardent Lusophiles in Panaji, but it was discontinued due to the non-availability of priests conversant with Portuguese. The dearth of Portuguese-knowing clergymen was only a part of the problem; the bigger problem was the growing preference for English among the church hierarchy and the laity.

Even the Indo-Portuguese architecture, a blend of the exotic and the vernacular, is out of popular favour today since nobody has the taste, time or money for this style. Churches are no more built in the Baroque, Manueline or Neo-Gothic style. The 200-odd feudal mansions stand as private monuments to fusion, no doubt, but as only that: they do not inspire grand architecture any more. Many of them in fact may go out of existence themselves, because the *bhatcars* who built them are gone and their progeny are scattered on all parts of the globe, spinning in their grooves, while the mansions are locked up and decaying in disrepair. These mansions used to have a giant reception hall where the *bhatcar* hosted parties for Portuguese civilians and soldiers and Goans of social standing. Even the most affluent Goans today do not make a giant reception hall in their homes but host parties in hotels or public halls.

An integral, indispensable part of not only these mansions but every Goan house built in the Indo-Portuguese style was the high sitting porch up a short flight of steps at the entrance called *balcao*. The *balcao*, comprising a pair of stone benches facing each other, was not only a status symbol but also a favourite haunt for the inmates. It was airy, and it served as a good observation post for the comings and goings on the street, providing opportunities for a chitchat with acquaintances passing by.

In the Goan satire, the *balcao* is as hallowed as the pulpit, taverna and soapbox: a place for high talk and no action. However, in the Goan Christian nostalgia, the *balcao* finds a respectable mention, because it hosted a get-together of the family every afternoon at which young boys and girls sang or played music. In those days life was rural, rustic and exposed; today the mantra of family life is privacy. People do not sit out at their entrance exchanging pleasantries or gossip with the passers-by. In the new bungalows, the *balcao* has given way to the welcome porch, a small flight of steps at the entrance leading up directly into the house. These bungalows may sometimes try to incorporate some of the elements of the fusion style, like the balustraded balcony, tiled roof or multiple windows but these are embellishments, not integral to the architecture. Even the tiles are artificial these days.

In music too, the Portuguese component is whittling down. The Goan Christians are evolving a new, native grammar. Among all the Goan song-and-dance forms, it was in Mando, in which men and women dance in parallel lines, the men brandishing a colourful handkerchief and the women a hand-fan, both moving rhythmically toward and away from each other in a wavy form, that the Portuguese influence was most pronounced. Sung usually in a public performance, the Mando songs, which reflected the sentiments of the romantic lover, were all written in Portuguese. Today Mando is performed on all social occasions: weddings, birthdays, parties, village gatherings. The songs are no more written in Portuguese but in Konkani and they do not only reveal the lovers' hearts but also satirize the contemporary political and social life. In the colonial times musicians and dancers from Portugal would frequently come to Goa to entertain soldiers and civilians. Today visits by Portuguese performers are rare. Most Goans would not know what *fado* is.

Goans have made the Portuguese influences on their way of life also their own. It was from the Portuguese of course that the natives learnt to drink liquor, but if today drinking has become a part of food for many Goans the Iberian habitues could not be blamed. (The per capita annual consumption of soda in Goa is 120 bottles as against 6 bottles all-India, according to a market study, and why should so much soda be needed, except for mixing with whisky?) The Portuguese way of life influenced Christians, but today a large number of Hindus also drink and serve liquor on social occasions, except at wedding receptions. People from other states who have settled down in Goa also serve drinks on all social occasions, including childbirth celebrations, something that is unthinkable for their communities back home.

It was from the Portuguese again that the Goan Christians learnt to lend their spirits to music, feast and fun. Churches and clubs during the colonial times used to frequently organise fiestas and feasts, inviting the people to fine food, good fun and lots of games and prizes. However, it was the fast growth of tourism that made not only the Christians but also Hindus to build upon this tradition. Today in the coastal villages there may sometimes be difficulty in finding an electrician or a barber but there is no dearth of event managers, singers, drummers, guitarists, sound equipment suppliers, comperes, masters of ceremonies, rostrum-makers, decorators and game masters. It is tourism again which has helped promote and preserve the traditional songs and dances — not only Mando and Corridinho, but also the Hindu folk forms — by creating a demand for performances on the river cruises and in the hotels. Small wonder hundreds of groups of traditional performers have emerged in the villages.

The Invading Cultures

As the Goan culture was breaking free from the Portuguese dominance, it got caught up in two strong currents, one of the Indian mass culture and the other of American mass culture. Goan popular music no longer remains only Goan or indigezined Portuguese; it is, for the most part now, influenced by Bollywood and American pop. In the Christian families during the colonial period, it was a custom for young girls to sing Portuguese songs to entertain their guests. The young men's indulgence was serenading — playing clarinet, violin and drums with sweet, romantic humour outside the window of damsels. No more do Christian girls sing songs for guests and no more do Christian boys go serenading. Their favourite music comes from Eng-lish and Hindi pop. And in this there is no communal divide. Round the year, in one or the other place in Goa, one or the other group is holding a Hindi Film Singing Contest in which the best copycat renditions of the Bollywood songs are awarded prizes: in senior, junior, male, female categories. Some Goan bands have lead singers who can sing Bollywood as well as American pop songs. Cinemas in Goa usually exhibit Bollywood movies. The sales of Bollywood albums are high in the state.

Although the Portuguese television channel RTP is available through cable operators in Goa, it is the Hindi channels that top the viewership charts. Goans, much to the Konkani activists' dismay, are hooked on to the serials, Bollywood-based programmes, game shows and news bulletins on the Hindi channels; they can turn to the English channels for a change, but they never go to the Konkani programmes on the Goa Doordarshan. Together, the Bollywood movies and the Hindi TV serials have introduced the Goans to the Indian mass culture, motivating them to learn Hindi and try North Indian cuisines. In dress too, the styles of North India have invaded Goa. Today all young and not-so-young women, Hindu, Christian or Muslim, have started wearing *salwar kameez*, the traditional dress of Punjabi women of all ages. In Goa married women used to wear *saris*, but no more. Even the women who have become grandmothers can be seen moving about in *salwar kameez*. The change in dress style has been accompanied by the liberal social and family environment with a rising number of women going to schools and colleges and taking up employment.

Similarly, the American mass culture daily invades the Goan environment with movies, music, television and consumer goods. The event managers hire bands for hotels and public concerts that can play American pop in fabulous imitation, making the crowd dance to the African or Latin beats. Live shows by American pop singers draw huge crowds in the coastal cities. A large number of Goans annually emigrate to the US for employment or education and this makes them, and through their examples their contemporaries back home, very susceptible to the influences of the American mass culture. Pepsi and Coca Cola have a pervasive presence in the Goan way of life, which is characterised by the frequency of parties. The two cold drink giants have painted Goa red and blue: it is impossible to miss these colours on the walls of bars, liquor shops and roadside kiosks as you travel through the villages of Goa.

The Konkani groups have been organising 'yuva mahotsava,' youth festivals, to encourage Goan talents to perform and develop the traditional forms of music and drama. The Kala Academy regularly hosts festivals of Goan performing arts. But the younger generations are drawn to the American mass culture (or Indian mass culture, depending on the upbringing) like iron filings to a magnet. The festivals promoting local cultural forms do not attract audiences. Four major colleges in Goa organise annual festivals which draw huge crowds of students from all over the state; their programmes are strongly influenced by American pop and Bollywood; folk forms do not find favour with them. Neither do the Indian or western classical music. Gone are the days when the Old Goa church's eight-voice choir was considered as good as the Vatican choir in Rome and when the Goans were called the 'Italians of the East.' Although the Kala Academy runs a western music department, it has had neither good teachers nor good students. Goa, which has been known for its musicians, does not have a single orchestra.

The English Annexation

And the American mass culture has not stopped at influencing music or dress. It is threatening the heart of Goan culture, the Konkani language. Goan parents are sending their children to English medium schools. The enrolment in Konkani medium schools is miserable and falling. The circulation of the only Konkani daily has not gone beyond a few thousands in spite of the fact that Konkani is the mother tongue of 95 per cent of Goans and is dropping, whereas the English newspapers have registered high rates of growth in readership. The readership of Konkani fiction is declining while that of English fiction is rising.

Konkani lived in exile in the Portuguese times. And before it could find its place in its homeland again, English is threatening to exile it again. The first signs were available in 1989, just two years after Konkani became Goa's official language. The coalition then in power issued an order asking all the primary schools to adopt Konkani or Marathi as their medium of instruction, warning that if any school continued to impart education in English the government would stop payment of their annual grant. This brought the church's Diocesan Society of Education, which ran 130 primary schools in English medium, under tremendous pressure. Their request for a year's time to make the switchover was refused by the government.

On the other side were the parents who, organised into a group called the Action Committee on the Medium of Instruction (ACMI), asserted their right to choose the medium of instruction for their child. "Who is the government or the diocesan society to decide the course of our children's development?" the ACMI asked. Attempts by the diocesan society to resolve the problem through a series of parent-teachers meetings failed. The parents wanted the church schools to continue teaching in English even if the government stopped aid to them.

Provoked, the Konkani activists demanded that the English medium schools refusing to switch over to Konkani be derecognised. However, even the Goans who had fought for the literary, constitutional and official recognition of the Konkani language remained indifferent to the demand. Ultimately, the government surrendered: the state decided to follow a policy which would allow schools in different media to exist, leaving it to the parents to decide where to enrol their children. Konkani had lost the battle. Not only did the church's 130 schools continue to teach in English but several new private English medium schools also sprung up to fulfil the growing demand. Even in the villages people now wanted English medium schools for their children. Official figures had it that about 95 per cent of students appearing at the state's secondary and higher secondary examinations answered the questions in English. Parents said English prepared their children for global exposure.

At the gatherings of Konkani writers, lamentations would be heard over the displacement of Konkani by English in the schools, mass media, music and culture; whiplashes would crackle on the backs of Goans who chose to use English even where they could do without it — like the Christians who conducted their weddings in English, printed their invitation cards in English and said their mass in English — and bugles would be blown for waging a war against English. But deep within their hearts they knew it was impossible to stem the tide of English. There was betrayal in their own ranks: many of them had got their children admitted to English medium schools. English, they said, was the language of science, technology and world culture, and hence the language of progress. Agriculture was on the decline in Goa; the families were changing from being land-based to job-based; and in this transition the younger generations had to be looking outward rather than inward, because no property was to be taken care of in the village. The conservative patriarch of yesterday, who took pride in domesticating his son, had to give way to the liberal father of today who believes in exposing his son to the big, wild world, because he thinks this alone will train him in the art of survival.

Small wonder, the number of families speaking English at home is growing at a fast pace. The thinking is, if you do not speak it at home you won't be able to speak it in the street. "It's like a sport: unless you play it every day on your home ground you won't be able to play it on other grounds," they say. "If you eat with your hands at home can you eat skillfully with knife and fork at parties?" In Kerala, they say, the government promotes English medium schools. What can learning through Konkani or Marathi bring — not more than jobs of clerks in the state government or municipalities. How do Goans who want to take up jobs in other parts of the country or abroad compete or communicate with other Indians and foreigners — in Konkani or Marathi?

Goans of a New Kind

If English is banished from Goa, the wheels of emigration will screech to a halt. And emigration is crucial for improvement in the life chances of Goans; so English will grow in importance. A labour-supplying state cannot set its own terms; it has to conform to the demands of the labour-receiving states or countries. Most Goans would prefer to give their children a solid English-based education with Konkani as the second language. English will make the medium for their professional flight and Konkani the medium for their cultural rootedness.

Goan expatriates have their special problem too. If Konkani were to make the metrology of Goan identity, most of them would not qualify as a Goan. Edward D'Lima, who teaches English in a Mapusa college, recently published a 53-page guide to the Konkani language for the Goan expatriates and foreigners (hardly indistinguishable, if Konkani is the measuring rod) giving them readymade sentences in Konkani to deal with local language problems at the post office, hotel, pharmacy, railway station or snack bar during their visit. Professor D'Lima presented 19 episodes imagining various situations in Roman Konkani, which indicated for sure that the guide had been aimed at the Christian expatriates. "I was inspired to write this self-learning guide," said D'Lima, "when several of my cousins who are second generation Goans in England, Canada and Australia expressed a desire to be able to speak Konkani while on holiday in Goa."

A survey of the Goan expatriates spread over different countries published in the *Goan Overseas Digest* (London, issue 5.4, 1997) found that 14 per cent of them had "no attachment to Goa." Most noted that the traditional Goan values were breaking down due to the weakening of the parental authority, leading to interracial marriages and making mixing acceptable. Goans no more socialised only with Goans; they mingled with other Indians, Pakistanis, Sri Lankans, whites, Afro-Caribbeans and Chinese. In the past Goan social life meant the community association, sometimes based on common village origins, which organised songs, dances, feasts and festivals following the customs of the native culture.

But the new generations of Goans found no excitement at the association gatherings. Cosmopolitan rather than Goan as they thought they were, they preferred cross-ethnic companies. "I fear," Tony DeSouza, a Goan settled in Australia told the *Digest* "that once the older generation passes away there will be no cultural legacy left to pass on to our children. A visit to Goa may be just a holiday — with little to gain culturally except for reminiscences. The Goan ethos is likely to fade. An Indian identity may be more appropriate to assume rather than the tag 'Goan' in the next millenium. It may also command more respect."

"There is no single way of being Goan," says Joao da Viega Coutinho in his book *A Kind of Absence*. "We must learn to live without roots ... we have been severed, disconnected from the soil and its presences, a history in which we have been no more than guests, victims, auxiliaries, that make us turn to an India before that history began. But the India we can relate to is in the process of creating itself .... *Roots have been replaced by horizons*. (emphasis ours)"

A report from Toronto (*Goa Today,* March 1994) said a large number of Goans settled in the Canadian city felt that their youth identified with the values predominant in North America. Although "we may occasionally wear Indian dress and acknowledge our brown skins, most of the time we are trying to be western .... Social events are so western in flavour that they could be taken for Italian or Irish. We consider a suit more 'civilised' than a *sari*; we would rather say we are Goan, not Indian. Our Indianness is only acknowledged in our food. In almost every other area — language, culture and traditions, we are western. We speak English, gyrate to western music and our social activities can hardly be distinguished from those organised by westerners."

It is not only the Goan expatriates that have gone over to the camp of English and the world of western culture, but also the repatriates from Africa and the Gulf. And together they constitute a force the state government cannot ignore. Not only have they done Goa proud but they have also fuelled the economy with their remittances. For the first time in March 2001, they got the chief minister to set up a special cell in the home department for the NRIs in order to address their needs in a more efficient manner. This cell would also "maintain a comprehensive data base which would serve as a potential talent pool to assist the development of the state." With the increasing influence of Goan migrants on the government decision-making, there is no chance of English losing state patronage.

The Language Ghettoes

In the years to come, more and more Goans will prefer to read, write and speak English and thus their exposure to Konkani media and literature would be reduced — although owing to its strong roots the *tiatr*, the theatre in Konkani popular among Christians will not lose ground, which cannot be said of the Konkani *natokk*, theatre in Konkani sought to be popularised by Goan Hindus. The Goans will become like the domestic *avataars* of the Goan expatriates, speaking English and following the modes and moods of the American and Indian mass cultures. Konkani will fail to stand up to the challenge owing to its inherent weaknesses, like the dichotomy of script. The Hindus and Christians of Goa cannot communicate with each other in Konkani, except, though not without difficulty, orally. Christian Konkani and Hindu Konkani do not only differ in script but also in style, structure, grammar and lexicography. Christian Konkani carries a lot of words of Portuguese origin and Hindu Konkani a number of words from Marathi.

It is owing to this dichotomy that Konkani will never become the official language of Goa in practice. The official language legislation accepted Devanagri as the script, but it would be too unrealistic to hope that the Christian government employees will make their submissions in the files in Devanagri Konkani. If they are forced to write, they will write Roman Konkani. The Hindu employees will write in Devanagri Konkani. Neither will understand what the other one has written. In order for Konkani to become the official language, every employee will have to have the ability to write and understand both Devanagri and Roman Konkanis, which is rather asking for an impractical qualification.

Leaders of the Konkani movement assert that the Christians are slowly switching over to Devanagri. However, a familiarity with Konkani as a subject at lower school level does not assure a wider readership of books, periodicals and newspapers published in Devanagri Konkani. The readership of books and magazines published in Roman Konkani has been rising at a steady rate, but not so that of the literature and journals in Devanagri Konkani. What is actually happening, and which the Hindu Konkani leaders do not want to publicly admit, is that the Goan Hindus are switching over from Konkani to Marathi. The readership of Marathi books and newspapers is also growing.

There is a ghettoisation of languages in Goa. The prospects for Devanagri Konkani to be accepted universally by all Goans are bleak. The languages that look destined to become stronger in the future are English, Marathi and Roman Konkani. Devanagri Konkani in all likelihood will survive as the cultural language of the Hindus. English will of course be on the top, followed by Marathi and Roman Konkani. English will be backed by globalisation, Marathi by the power and glory of Marathi in Maharashtra and revival of the traditional relationship of Goan Hindus with its cultural heritage, and Roman Konkani by the ideology of survival of the Christians reflected in a resolute minorityism.

A Multicultural State

English has an extra advantage: it is also the favoured language of the middle class migrants in Goa, who, through this preference over

Konkani, have been resisting acculuturation into Goan society. Poorer migrants, however, might prefer to place their children in the schools teaching in their mother tongues. The state government does run a few mixed language schools where education is provided also in migrant tongues but their number is not enough. In the coming years migrant pressures will mount on the state government to provide land and grant for more and more minority language schools.

The numbers of speakers of minority languages are rising in Goa. There were 16,504 Kannada speakers in the state in 1971; in 1981, their number rose to 33,473 and in 1991 to 54,323. The number of Urdu speakers, which was 18,910 in 1971, rose to 27,580 in 1981 and 39,944 in 1991. In 1971, 11,375 registered Hindi as their mother tongue, in 1981, 20,498 and in 1991, 37,073. Malyalam, Telugu, Tamil, Gujarati, Bengali and Punjabi had also shown a similar rise.

There is no running away from the fact that Goa has now become a multilingual and multicultural state. The Konkani groups that have set themselves the aim of creating a monolingual and monocultural Goa may soon realise the futility of their battle. Even without the migrants, they would have failed to set up a monolingual, monocultural Goa due to the segregation of the Hindu and Christian cultural spaces. Whenever, at government or private initiative, Goa's culture is showcased in exhibitions, music festivals or float parades, the separate streams of Hindu and Christian cultures have to be prominently represented. In the recent years, government showcasing has started including Goan Muslim festivals and art forms too. Not for very long can the government ignore the festivals and art forms of the migrant communities who have made Goa their home.

On their own, the migrant communities have maintained their cultural distinction by observing their festivals and patronising their arts. Raising donations among themselves, every community has built its own temple where its revered deity is installed and whose priests come from their native states. The community life revolves around the temple. Members come to pay their obeisance to the deity mornings and afternoons and families gather for special *pujas*. Some of the communities even take out their traditional religious processions every year, like the devotees of Ayappa. The communities also have their cultural associations which regularly organise religious discourses and musical or poetry festivals at the temples or in public halls to which devotees, singers, instrumentalists or poets are invited from the states of their origin. With the increasing population of Muslims from other states the number of mosques has increased, and now Muslim religious preachers come from outside, which is a new phenomenon since Goan Muslims had been self-dependent in their religious affairs.

Of course, how long it will take for the migrant communities to force the government to accept Goa as a multicultural state will depend on circumstances. In the first place, the migrant communities must work toward this common goal; but these communities are anything but a homogenous lot. They do not share the same experiences, and they are divided by language, religion, economic status, caste and year of arrival. Broadly they are grouped according to the states of their origin: there is a lack of cohesion among them, and they hardly meet on the same platform.

An organisation called the Uttaranchal Society has been trying for years to bring together migrants from different states north of Goa — Bihar, Uttar Pradesh, Madhya Pradesh, Himachal Pradesh, Gujarat, Punjab, Haryana and West Bengal — under one platform but not with much success. Huge crowds of migrants from these states gather at the Ram Mandir at Vasco da Gama on the days of Dussehra or Ram Navami but they are lacking in courage or motivation to establish a solidarity for lobbying with the government for cultural spaces for immigrant communities. The largest segment of migrant population in Vasco da Gama comes from Karnataka, the second largest from all the states north of Goa put together; the Uttaranchal Society's efforts to set up a coalition of the two segments have borne no fruit.

Despite the lack of unity, by the very fact of their rising numbers and of the growing acceptance among Goans of their contributions to the development of Goa in the postcolonial years, the migrants are beginning to make their presence felt. In the years to come Goa would have to give them a cultural space — and, in order to protect that, more political space. Although they constitute 18 per cent of the population, the migrants do not have any political representation. None of the political parties have thought of nominating migrants as their candidates in the past four decades of electoral politics in the state. (Some political observers cite the example of Simon de Souza, who came from Mangalore in Karnataka and was elected as an MLA and even held office as the deputy speaker of the state assembly, as an exception.)

To the municipal councils of Panaji and Vasco da Gama migrants have been elected as members. But these are very rare examples. The spectre presented to Goans by the Konkani groups is: "Non-locals are taking up political leadership at the panchayat, municipal and state levels and finally they will be the decision-makers in our democratic institutions." But this is far from the true picture, as nothing of this sort is happening or can happen. This is a way of stopping the political parties thinking in terms of political representation of the migrants.

In the two Assembly constituencies of Vasco da Gama and Mormugao the migrants make 55 per cent of the electorate, that is, a clear majority of the electorate, but the two seats have always gone to Goans. None of the political parties, the Congress, MGP or BJP, have ever nominated an migrant as their candidate in these constitutencies (except again, Simon de Souza). For many years most of migrants voted for the Congress candidates. "They took their votes and then forgot them for five years, until the next election came, when they repeated their deception with a few thousand rupees for a community temple or meeting hall," notes an embittered D P Tiwari, a businessman from Uttar Pradesh who has been president of the Uttaranchal Society for a long time. Disillusioned with the Congress party, the migrants in the recent elections shifted their patronage to the BJP. "But here too, behind the façade of nationalism, no sympathy could be found for the children of Mother India from other states," says Tiwari. In order to keep the migrants in good humour the BJP made Tiwari a member of the party's state executive "but when the state council meets I am not allowed to speak because they know that I am going to plead for the political representation of the migrants."

When the announcement for the Assembly elections of 1998 was made, something happened which Tiwari carries a very bitter memory of. There was a meeting of the top state leaders of the BJP at his residence in Vasco da Gama; the agenda was to start making preparations for the elections and to decide the election strategy for the two migrant-majority constituencies of Vasco da Gama and Mormugao. Among those present were Manohar Parrikar who was to become chief minister and Digambar Kamat who was to become his power minister two years later. In the course of the discussions Tiwari brought up the subject of political representation of the migrants, pleading that they had voted for the party but not been given a chance to elect one from among themselves. Hearing this, one of the BJP leaders lost his temper and told Tiwari: "You came to Goa to do business. Now you want to rule us!"

Migrants in the Courtyard

The game — use the migrants for vote but refuse them political representation — has been going on not only in the two Assembly constituencies in the port city but also in the Panaji, Santa Cruz, Margao, Fatorda and Cortalim constituencies. Some politicians, in order to win, have in fact been encouraging migrants to settle in their constituencies and getting their names entered in the electoral rolls, so that they have one assured big segment of electorate with them. They help them get water and electricity connections for their hutments, ration cards, and licence and space from the municipal council for setting up a roadside kiosk or doing any other petty business. When the demolition squads of the municipal councils come armed with orders to raze their illegal hutments down, it is these politicians who intervened with the authorities to stop them.

But when it comes to nominating candidates from the migrant communities all doors close. However, if the refusal of the political parties persists, a day may soon come when the migrant communities will decide to set up their own candidates for the Assembly, municipalities or panchayats. Goa being a small state, its constituencies are also small; with low-percentage and fragmented voting, a person needs to mobilise only a few thousand of votes to win the election with a margin of a few hundred votes. Despite their linguistic and cultural divisions the migrants can get a candidate elected to the Assembly from Vasco da Gama or Mormugao. There are newer areas threatening to fall in the migrant hold. The Margao Assembly constituency, for instance, today has 9,000 Muslims among its 25,000 voters.

And there are all the signs that the migrant population in Goa will increase in the coming years. First, globalisation will bring in outside labour. If Goa will allow technology, capital and goods from anywhere to enter freely how can it stop labour from coming? Global capital and technology will not come without the freedom to decide the quality of human resource it needs. Goans have the reputation for poor work culture and low productivity: under such conditions, entrepreneurs would not be inclined to give 80 per cent of total employment to local people as the government and Konkani groups want. It is certain therefore that the economic growth of Goa will be accompanied by migrant population growth.

Not only the outside entrepreneurs, even the Goan entrepreneurs prefer a mix of local and migrant labour: builders, fishing trawler owners, shrimp exporters, mineowners, industrialists. Harsh economic logic overrides the emotionally ethnic concerns. A Goan sells his land or house to an outsider, rather than to a Goan, because he gets a better price. Goan patriots have been urging Goans to sell their properties only to Goans, so that the "outsider does not enter our homeland," but nobody listens. For the simple reason that if Goans alone are going to be buyers the demand will be low, bringing the property prices crashing down: the seller may get 20 per cent or less of the price a similar property might fetch in Karnataka or Maharashtra. In Jammu and Kashmir, which does not allow outsiders to buy land in the state, property prices are ridiculous.

Goans who own properties prefer migrants even as tenants, because they fear if they lease out their houses or rooms to local people they may never leave and go to court. "In our Goa of today," Reginald Diniz, a school teacher from Velha Goa, advises the Goans, "if you have a room or a house to let on hire who would you give it to? Would you hire it to someone who knocks at your door and asks you in Hindi: *Hai ek room rehene ke liye deneko aapke pas?* Do you have a room to rent out? You will find a lot of people of this category approaching you; their tribe is increasing. These are non-Goans on business trips and they leave Goa as soon as their assignment is over. They are harmless creatures with good intentions. You can hire your place out to them. The second category consists of non-Goans who are job seekers. They stay on in Goa and later build their own house. It is safe to rent your accommodation to them too. The third category is of our fellow Goans. They ask you: *Fatlean room assa to biradak dina?* Do you have a room to rent to a member of your own community? Beware of these tricksters. They are the dangerous ones. They are not homeless. They have houses in Goa. They pay a paltry rent. They refuse to move out and drag owners to court."

All along the coastal belt Goans have made legal or illegal extensions to their old houses to construct rooms to hire out to the tourists and migrants. The coastal belt has in fact been very hospitable to the migrants, seasonal or long-term. When the hippies first invaded the beaches the local population agitated against them. But when they offered them opportunities to earn an extra income and change their lives hostility turned into hospitality. A similar change of attitude took place with respect to the people from the other states. Today there are a large number of migrants surviving on tourism in the beach belt, either as businessmen or as labourers.

A case in point is the flea market at Anjuna. When the hippies started selling their personal goods every Wednesday to get cash to survive a little longer in Goa or to leave with some money in their wallets, people from all parts of Goa turned up to buy them original and cheap: cameras, transistor radios, wrist watches and original Levis. Soon it became also a haven for drugs. Drugs are still peddled on the fringes, but the market is no more a flea market: it has been transformed into a crafts mela, with most stalls or spaces taken by vendors from Gujarat, Rajasthan, Kashmir and Karnataka who sell crystals, figurines in wood, metal, ivory, ethnic garments, beachwear, jewellery, hammocks, footwear to the tourists.

Despite the fact that there are only a few Goan vendors in the market, the residents of the Anjuna village want it to go on. Whenever the government tries to close the market on the ground that it is a haven for drugs, the Anjuna panchayat sets up resistance and foils the government bid, arguing that it not only provides livelihood to the majority of villagers but also provides Rs 4 lakh every year to the panchayat by way of auction of the lease of the plot on which the market is held, which fund is used for the development of the village.

Every panchayat in the coastal belt has been earning considerable revenue from tourism-related businesses: hotels, construction, plot leases. Despite pervasive corruption, these panchayats have been able to provide a number of amenities to the villagers, like street lights, drainage, community hall, roads with the money they receive from the industries. Coastal villages are far more developed than the villages in the hinterland. For the reasons that they provide scope for corruption as well as for mobilisation of funds for the development of the village and hence mustering of the vote for winning elections, the officials of these panchayats are among the most ardent advocates of free flow of capital.

Local non-government organisations have been agitating against the negative effects of tourism — the water table is falling in the coastal belt, there is constant shortage of water, the concrete jungle is expanding, the green cover is dwindling, there is congestion and squalor all around, Goans are becoming a minority in their own homeland, crime has increased, the local culture is polluted — but the coastal population has refused to give them support. They have seen their villages and their families prosper with the income from tourism. The benefits far outweigh the losses.

And, indeed, Goa is not in the imminent danger of facing an Apocalypse, as some of its most pugnacious patriots would shriek out to the world it is. During the eight months beginning every October the state's population almost doubles with the arrival of tourists. But it has not produced any real crisis. There may have been strains on the local resources, but the doubling of population has not led to shortages that the coastal population cannot cope with.

As for the rise in crime and cultural pollution resulting from the fillip to migration that tourism gives, the coastal people have their own perspective. Migrants are required, they say, because local youths are not available. The local youths are working or waiting to work abroad, in countries or on ships; or they do not like to do manual jobs; or they just do not like to do anything. A panchayat declared a construction in the village as illegal and set a date for the demolition of it, which could not take place because there was no labour available locally. The panchayat announced another date for the demolition; again no labourers were available. A third date also saw the illegal construction remain unscathed. Ultimately, the panchayat had to bring in migrant labourers to execute their order.

The Future of Goa

The mismatch in demand and supply of labour necessitates its import from other states. Goans are forever seeking jobs abroad, at sea or in the other states of India, thus creating a vacuum which is filled in by the people from the other states. Emigration is so institutionalised in Goa that there is now a well-established migration industry, with a number of overseas recruitment companies or agents engaged in manpower export. They have offices in Goa, Mumbai and also in the countries with substantial Goan population, like the US, Australia, Canada and the Persian Gulf. In his autobiography Luizinho Faleiro laments: "A large number of our youth are ready to mortgage their house and estate, pawn the family's jewellery, beg and borrow, steal if inevitable, to secure a job in the Gulf, risking, often enough, being cheated by unscruplous and crooked job agents and finally landing in jail as illegal immigrants in the host country and being repatriated in veritable cattle boats." And what kind of jobs they go for? Faleiro asks and answers himself: often of menials, construction workers — the very jobs they consider beneath their dignity in their homeland.

If only 4 per cent of Goa's population is below the poverty line against the national average of 26 per cent the emigration to other countries is one of the key factors. There is another important economic indicator of the importance of emigration. The rate of savings in Goa is very high. As on March 31, 2001 the total deposit in banks in the state stood at Rs 84,160 million, an increase by 22 times over the previous two decades. About 80 per cent of the deposits came from the three talukas of Salcete (headquarters, Margao), Tiswadi (hq, Panaji) and Bardez (hq, Mapusa). Almost 30 per cent of the total bank deposits came from the Goans working abroad.

The desire to find "good jobs" and earn "much higher pay" drives Goans to emigrate. And in the era of globalisation emigration is going to increase: especially with the air fares and telephone tariffs declining and customs barriers and foreign exchange restrictions relaxing. Then there is global connectivity through the internet, which eases the emotional stress in the migrant.

Then, Goa's fertility rate among the states is higher only than Kerala. In the next 25 years, a typical Goan couple would be living in an apartment in the city with a single child. This will mean reduced supply of local labour. The literacy rate being high and the opportunities and standards of professional and technical education being unsatisfactory in the state, more and more Goan youths would be forced to go out of Goa to study and be inclined to seek jobs outside the state. That would make the labour shortage really acute in Goa, necessitating increased migration.

There is no way the migration of unskilled labourers can be stopped in Goa, because the Goans continue to consider it *infra dig* to do manual jobs. But the state could perhaps find a way of keeping the migration of skilled people within limits by moving toward technology-driven, capital-intensive and labour-saving investments. In the ten years since the beginning of the New Economic Policy in 1991, about 15,000 industrial workers were retrenched, laid off or retired with a golden handshake in the state. The shift was obviously toward technology giving most of the output with a small number of technically skilled people monitoring it.

Goans preferred jobs where machines gave the output with the minimum of human manipulation. The best example of it was the Mormugao port at which all cargo loading and unloading work was handled by the *bhayyas*, nearly 4,000 of them, until the grabs were introduced, reducing the labour requirement to 700. With grabs for the first time Goans entered cargo handling and today they make up 50 per cent of the cargo handlers. At the mechanised ore handling plant at the port, where most things are done by technology, 90 per cent of the 1,500 workers are Goans. In the big foreign and Indian industries in the states, like Syngenta, German Remedies and Zuari Agro, almost the entire regular workforce is composed of Goans. All of these industries are driven by high technology.

Agricultural productivity is fast declining in Goa due to several factors: predominance of small, uneconomical holdings, poor irrigation, low use of modern inputs like fertilisers, competing demands for land due to industrialisation and urbanisation, migration of labour to other sectors due to high literacy rate. The share of agriculture in the net state domestic product (NSDP) was only 8.4 per cent in 1997-98, whereas the share of manufacturing sector was 32 per cent and that of the tertiary sector 51.8 per cent. The share of tertiary sector has been steadily rising over the years due to growth in tourism and other services.

Tourism by 2002 employed about 20 per cent of Goa's workforce, which is hardly surprising, considering the fact that a number almost equal to the state's population visits it as tourists every year, bringing billions of rupees as income.

Goa does not have much scope for growth in the manufacturing sector due to various factors. Conventional factories require large areas of land, which Goa does not have. Then, as a location it is uncompetitive, because it is very far from the sources of raw materials as well as from the markets for finished products. Conventional manufacture survives on low-cost labour which is not available in the state. Besides, factories that come to Goa must be non-polluting, since environmental activism is very strong in the state.

In view of these factors, the state is going to be very choosy about the type of industry to be allowed. The ideal major investments in this field should come for pharmaceuticals (which already has a significant share of the investments in organised industry in the state), software, biotechnology and agro-based products. As far as agriculture is concerned, cereals have no future in Goa. Farming in the coming decades is going to mean horticulture, floriculture and animal husbandry. Close to 60 per cent of the total cultivated area in the state is already under horticulture, the primary crops being nuts — coconuts, cashewnuts and arecanuts. The horticultural coverage is going to expand with government-subsidized inputs, like drip and sprinkler irrigation, crop improvement techniques and export-promotion services. There is a huge market in the state for vegetables and animal husbandry products, like milk, eggs, chicken and meat. Hotels and homes alike have to import these daily necessities from other states. Slowly Goan entrepreneurship is likely to grow to take a share of the huge market.

The service sector is expected to grow faster in the state. Goans, who hate manual labour, queue up for jobs in the service industries. The state government in its policy announcements has been laying emphasis on the development of services, because "Goans are suited for light jobs." The IT-enabled services are being encouraged in a big way; and so are enterprises in the health and education sectors. The state government has given its approval to the proposal for a special economic zone in which offshore banking and other services would be provided.

However, the development of the service sector will depend on the availability of trained manpower in the state. The state government will have to bring about a qualitative change in education and training. The students will have to be trained in information technology from the earliest stage; the government has promised to provide computer and internet facilities in schools; the established educational institutions would have to be encouraged to set up facilities in the state to provide courses in IT, management, engineering and medicine. It is with these human resource development initiatives alone that Goans could be enabled to get satisfactory employment in their homeland. However, the infrastructure, like roads and transport, and power and communications are still very poor and unreliable in Goa. So far for the state to take a quantum leap in the service sector, particularly, the IT sector, will need quite a lot of doing, apart from creating manpower.

A Glossary of Goan Terms

Bahujan Samaj, a nomenclatural aggregate for lower caste Goans, used both in normal and pejorative senses

Balcao, a raised porch above a flight of steps outside the entrance door of the house built with Portuguese influence. It had concrete benches on either side where the members of family and guests sat for a chat as they watched the movements on the road that passed their house

Bamonn, a colloquial term for a member or members of Saraswat Brahman community, sometimes used in a derogatory sense

Bamonn Raj, a term used to describe the heydays of Hindu and Christian Saraswat Brahmans during the Portuguese rule.

Bhailo, non-Goan, outsider, migrant

Bhandara, community-built reservoir of water for irrigation

Bhatcar, landlord

Canarin, term used by the Portuguese to refer to Goan native. Derived probably from the word Konkani, which was the mother tongue of the natives

Chardo, man from the Kshatriya caste among Christians

Cocote, balloon filled with white powder hurled by people celebrating Carnival at each other

Comunidade, association of the male members of the families of first settlers in the village, later also including non-resident and shareholding members. Known before the Portuguese came as gaocari (see Gaocari)

Concelho, Portuguese name for sub-district

Cuntocar, new settlers in village with no rights in gaocari

Devadasi, literally servant to god; young woman ritually married to the deity in a temple and in several cases compelled by circumstances into illicit sexual relationship with the wealthy men in the village

Devakudd, God's home, family shrine, prayer room in household

Descendente, Eurasian, person of mixed parentage

Feni, hard drink brewed out of green cashew or coconut

Fidalgo, Portuguese term for nobleman

Firangi, derogatory term used by Goans (and Indians) for foreigner

Gaocar, member of gaocari

Gaocari, association of male founders of a village that managed the lands, cultivation, irrigation and other affairs

Ghanti, derogatory term used by Goans for manual labourers from other states

Goa Portuguesa, Portuguese Goa

Goawadi, Goans who supported a separate political status for Goa in opposition to the agitation for its merger with Maharashtra in the mid-'60s

Jono, share of profit among members of gaocari, comunidade

Khandy, a measure of 160 litres

Khazan, salty, muddy lands located by riverside, prone to inundation by high tides of the sea

Kher, alluvial tracts located inland

Konkaniwadi, supporter of supreme status for Konkani among languages in Goa

Konkanno, term used by Goan Christians to refer to Marathi used by Goan Hindus

Kutcha, made of clay, earth

Mand, a sacred place earmarked in the village from ancient times for community celebration of festivals and staging of theatrical and musical performances

Maharashtrawadi, Goan supporting Goa's merger with Maharashtra in the mid-'60s

Marathiwadi, a partisan of Marathi, used to distinguish the person from Konkaniwadi, a partisan of Konkani

Mund, a small loan

Mundkar, a landless, homeless man who was given a small plot and a loan (mund) to construct a dwelling in lieu of his services as caretaker of his plantations and other properties

A Glossary of Goan Terms

Mundkari, relationship of mundkar with landowner; the tenurial system bonding the mundkar to the landowner
Naikin, landowner's concubine
Nala, channels for traditional irrigation
Nova Conquistas, New Conquests
Patrao, master
Pedaco de Portugal, piece of Portugal; term used by the Portuguese under Salazar to describe Goa
Ramponkar, traditional Goan fishermen who used to catch fish by sweeping the catch with a net
Sorpotel, minced pork curry
Sudir, lower castes among Christians
Sudra, lower castes among Hindus
Sussegad, an easygoing attitude to life Goans are believed to have acquired from the Portuguese; a philosophy of contentment with small earnings or gains; complacent, laid-back, leisure-loving
Taluka, sub-district
Velha Conquistas, Old Conquests
Zamindar, one holding zamindari
Zamindari, a system of landownership in Bengal in which the revenue to be paid by the landowners to the state was fixed permanently at a low level by the British East India Company in order to encourage cultivation

Bibliography

The West Invades

Azavedo, Carmo, *The Goa Question: Salazar's Bluff Called,* Delhi, 1956

Borges, Charles, *The Economy of Goa Jesuits,* 1542-1759, New Delhi, 1994

Boxer, C R, *The Portuguese Seaborne Empire,* 1415-1825, London, 1973

Danvers, F C, *The Portuguese in India,* volume I and II, London, 1894

D'Costa, Anthony, *The Christianisation of the Goa Islands,* Mumbai, 1965

De Souza, Teotonio R, Christianisation and Cultural Conflicts in Goa, 16th-19th centuries, *Boletim do Instituto Menezes Braganza,* Panaji, No. 170, 1974

Dhume, Anant Ramkrishna Sinai, *The Cultural History of Goa from 10,000 BC –1352 AD,* undated

Gaitonde, Pundalik and A D Mani, *The Goa Problem,* New Delhi, 1956

Gune, V T, *Ancient Shrines of Goa: A Pictorial Survey,* Panaji, 1965

Kosambi, D D, *Myth and Reality,* Mumbai, 1962

Mitragotri, V R, *Socio-cultural History of Goa from Bhojas to Vijaynagar,* Panaji, 1999

Pereira, Rui Gomes, *Goa : Hindu Temples and Deities,* volume I, Panaji, 1978

Priolkar, A K, *The Goa Inquisition,* Mumbai, 1961

Richards, J M, *Goa,* New Delhi, 1982

Shirodkar, P P (ed), *Goa's External Relations,* Panaji, 1992

Subrahmanyam, Sanjay, *The Portuguese Empire in Asia, 1500-1700 : A Political and Economic History,* London, 1993

Xavier, P D, *Goa : A Social History, 1510-1640,* Panaji, 1993

A Unique Identity

Braganza, Alfred, The Counting as I Saw It : An Account of the Historic Opinion Poll, *Goa Today,* August 1996

Borges, Charles and Helmut Feldman (ed), *Goa and Portugal : Their Cultural Links,* New Delhi, 1997

Boxer, C R, *Race Relations in the Portuguese Colonial Empire,* Oxord, 1963

Carvalho, L Cotta, Goa: *The Anatomy of Merger Politics,* Delhi, 1966

De Cunha, Tristao B, *Denationalisation of Goans,* Mumbai, 1940

Esteves, Sarto, *Goa and its Future,* Mumbai, 1966

Esteves, Sarto and Vatsala de Sousa, *This is Goa,* Mumbai, 1983

Gaitonde, Pundalik, *The Liberation of Goa: A Participant's View of History,* London, 1987

Government of Goa, *Operation Vijay in Goa,* released in Panaji in 1999

Jorge, Evagrio, *Goa's Awakening : Reminiscences of the 1946 Civil Disobedience Movement,* Panaji, 1971

Khedekar, Vinayak, Maand, in *Govapuri,* Bulletin of Institute Menezes Braganza, July-September 1999

NCAER, *Techno-economic Survey of Goa, Daman and Diu,* New Delhi, 1964

Priolkar, A K, *Goa Rediscovered,* Mumbai, 1967

Rubinoff, Arthur, *The Construction of a Political Community : Integration and Identity in Goa,* New Delhi, 1998

The Navhind Times, Panaji, January-December 1963, and January-December 1967

Fruits of Freedom

Almeida, J C, Government of Goa, *Aspects of the Agricultural Activity in Goa, Daman and Diu,* Panaji, 1967

Department of Agriculture, Government of Goa, *Advances in Agriculture,* Panaji, 1996

Dias, A L, Government of Goa, *Report of the Goa Land Reforms Commission,* Panaji, 1964

Directorate of Planning, Statistics and Evaluation, Government of Goa, *Statistical Handbooks of Goa,* 1986, 1993, 1998 and 2000

Fernandes, Tony, Government of Goa, *Report of the Study Committee on Agrarian Conditions,* Panaji, 1966

Karapurkar, H Y, Agricultural Scenario in Goa, *Boletim do Instituto Menezes Braganza,* no. 176, 1996

Naik, Vaman R, *A Study of Agrarian Relations in Goa,* unpublished PhD thesis, Goa University, 1991; also Thinking Afresh on Land Reforms, in *Govapuri,* Bulletin of Institute Menezes Braganza, Panaji, April-June 1999

Tombat, Ashwin, Margao's Leaking Lifeline : What Ails the Selaulim Pipeline, *Goa Today,* Panaji, April 1997

Paranjpe, Vijay, *Selaulim Dam: An Ecological and Economic Analysis of Selaulim Irrigation Project in Goa,* Goa Research Institute for Development, Panaji, 1991

Perils of Progress

Albuquerque, T, *Anjuna : Profile of a Village in Goa,* New Delhi, 1988

Anderson, C, *Our Man in Goa,* London, 1995

Angle, Prabhakar S, *Goa: An Economic Review,* Mumbai, 1983; also *Goa : An Economic Update,* Mumbai, 2001

Dempo, Vasudeva V, Mining Industry in Goa : Historical Background, *Boletim do Instituto Menezes Braganza,* Panaji, no. 176, 1996

D'Souza, B G, *Goan Society in Transition : A Study in Social Change,* Mumbai, 1975

Ecoforum, *Fish, Curry and Rice : A Citizens' Report on the State of Goan Environment,* Mapusa, 1993

Economic Development Institute, World Bank, Tourism and *the Environmental Case Studies on Goa, India and the Maldives,* Washington, 1998

E Sa, Mario Cabral (ed), *Winds of Change,* Panaji, 1987

Goa Chamber of Commerce and Industry, *Bridges Constructed before and after Liberation,* 90 years commemorative volume, Panaji, 1999

Goa Government, *Regional Plan 2001 A.D.,* Panaji, 1988

Kamat, Pradeep V, When Hippies Roamed the Beaches, *Govapuri,* Bulletin of Institute Menezes Braganza, Panaji, April-June 1999

Kirloskar Consultants, *Report on Study of Tourism Industry in Goa,* Panaji, 1994

Malgonkar, Manohar, *Inside Goa,* Panaji, 1982

Mascarenhas, Lambert, Goa's Changing Face : The Good, the Bad and the Ugly, *Goa Today,* August 1995

Panandikar, V A Pai, A World to Win, *Goa Today,* August 1995

Pendse, D R, Goa after Liberation : Looking Back, Looking Forward, in Mario Cabral e Sa (ed) *Winds of Change,* Panaji, 1986

Phaldessai, Pandurang, An Escape Route, *Govapuri,* April-June 1999

Sequeira, Devika, Charter Tourism : Flying High, *Goa Today,* January 1993

Wilson, David, Paradoxes of Tourism in Goa, in Norman Dantas (ed) *Transforming of Goa,* Mapusa, 1999

Road to Salvation

Barbosa, Alexandre M, Konkan Railway on a Trying Track, *Goa Today,* Panaji, November 2000; Are the Japs Coming, *Goa Today,* March 1995; Off the Track? *Best of Goa Today,* August 1996; Free Port : Dropping Anchor in Goa? *Goa Today,* December 1992

Borges, Charles J and Helmut Feldman (ed), *Goa and Portugal : Their Cultural Links,* New Delhi, 1997

Chowgule, Ashok V, *Christianity in India : The Hindu Perspective,* Mumbai, 1999

D'Costa, Anthony, *The Christianisation of the Goa Islands,* Mumbai, 1965

De Souza, Teotonia R, *Goa to Me,* New Delhi, 1994; also the essay, The Church in Goa : Giving to Caesar What is Caesar's? in Norman Dantas (ed) *The Transforming of Goa,* Mapusa, 1999

Hindu Vivek Kendra, *Religious Conversions : Frequently Asked Questions,* Mumbai, 1999

Mendonca, Delio de, The Inquisition of Goa, *Govapuri,* Bulletin of Institute Menezes Braganza, Panaji, October-December, 1999

Mesquita, Menezes Wilfred, *Why Maharashtrawadi Gomantak Party Supports the Present Konkan Railway Alignment,* a memorandum, Vasco da Gama, 1992

Priolkar, A K, *The Goa Inquisition,* Mumbai, 1961

Robinson, Rowena, *Conversion, Continuity and Change : Lived Christianity in Southern Goa,* New Delhi, 1998

Shirodkar, P P, Hopes from New Century Generations, *The Navhind Times Millenium 2000 issue,* Panaji, 2000

Vempeny, Ishanand, *Conversion : National Debate or Dialogue?* Ahmedabad, 1999

Xavier, P D, *Goa : A Social History, 1510-1640,* Panaji, 1993

An Empty Pitcher

Almeida, Albertina, Women : Beyond Hearth and Home, *Goa Today,* August 1995

Bailancho Saad, Bigamy : The Hushed Issue, *Saad,* volume II (6), Panaji, undated

Dantas, Norman, Shariat Act Instead of Common Civil Code : For Better or Worse? *Goa Today,* July 1986

D'Souza, Carmo, *Legal System in Goa,* volume I and II, Panaji, 1994 and 1995 respectively

Fernandes, Joaquim, Cruelties against Wives : Myth of Happy Homes, *Zest, The Navhind Times Saturday Magazine,* May 5, 2001

Fernandes, Linken, Muslim Personal Law : For Better or Worse? *Goa Today,* September 1984

Goa Foundation, *The Goa Law Reference,* Mapusa, 1997

Gracias, Fatima de Silva, *Kaleidoscope of Women in Goa,* New Delhi, 1996

Jaising Indira (ed), *Justice for Women : Personal Laws, Women's Rights and Law Reform,* Mapusa, 1996

Martins, Sabina, *Cognisance of Non-cognisance : Report of the Goa State Commission for Women on Registered Crimes against Women in Goa,* Panaji, 2000

Mitragotri, V R, Life and Women in the Pre-Portuguese Period, *Govapuri,* Oct-Dec 1999

Natekar, Ujwala, Women: Long Way to Go, *Goa Today,* August 1995

Salgaoncar, Pramod, Empowerment of Goa's Women, *Gomantak Times,* September 23, 2000; also Men Don't Like Empowered Women, *Sunday Navhind Times,* March 25, 2001

Sardessai, Libia Lobo, *Glimpses of Family Laws of Goa, Daman and Diu,* Panaji, 1982; also Women: From Abala to Sabala, *Goa Today,* August 1995

Usgaocar, M S, *Family Laws of Goa, Daman and Diu,* volume I, Panaji, 1979; *Family Laws of Goa, Daman and Diu,* volume II, Panaji, 1989; Family Laws of Goa: collection of articles published in the *Sunday Navhind Times,* volume I, Panaji, 1996; Property Law in Goa (With special reference to Law of Inheritance and Matrimonial Property in Goa), presented at workshop on property rights of Hindu women : proposed reforms, Pune, August 28-29, 1999; and *Merits and Demerits of the Portuguese Laws in Force in Goa,* part I-VII, Institute Menezes Braganza Lecture Series, Panaji, February-September 2000

Ethnic Fencing

Azavedo, Carmo, Home and the World, *Goa Today,* September 1994

Bhembre, Udai, Language : Such a Long Journey, *Goa Today,* August 1995; also Government Promoting Pig, Peg, Pros Culture, Insight, *Herald Saturday Magazine,* Panaji, February 10, 2001

Census of India 2001: *Goa, Provisional Population Totals,* Panaji, 2001

Diocesan Service Centre for Social Action, A Free Port for Goa, *Renewal,* Panaji, August 15-31, 1996; also A statement on Meta Strips Ltd, *Renewal,* August 1-15, 1999

D'Sa, Eddie, Community Survey, part 2, *Goan Digest,* London, no.5.4, 1997; also Spewing Hatred, *Goa Today,* January 1994

D'Souza, Errol, Economic Policy and Development in Goa, in Peter Ronald deSouza (ed) *Contemporary India : Transitions,* New Delhi, 2000

D'Souza, Joel and Alexandre M Barbosa, The Green Grass at Home, *Goa Today,* September 1994; Tribal Tribulations, *Goa Today,* October 1995

Faleiro, Luzinho, My Goa: An *Autobiography,* Margao, 1999

Fernandes, Remo, *O, Panjim, a poem and song,* in *Panaji : A Search for Identity,* published by the North Goa Planning and Development Authority at a seminar on October 4, 1997

Gonsalves, Raul Nicolau, Archbishop of Goa, Pastoral Theme for 1995, *Renewal,* Panaji, April 1-15, 1995

Horsfall, Pierre, Economic Growth : The Reasons Behind Jersey's Enduring Success, *The Parliamentarian,* London, July 2000

Kamat, Nandkumar, The Demographic Transition in Goa, *The Navhind Times,* February 26, 2001; also Making Sense out of Census, *The Navhind Times,* April 16, 2001

Mascarenhas, Lambert, The Goan Today, *Goa Today,* March 1995

Menezes, Ervell, Paradise Lost, *Indian Express,* Mumbai, February 11, 1989; The Old Order Changeth, *Goa Today,* March 1995; Those Were the Days, *Indian Express Magazine,* July 5, 1981

Morse, Jane, Slaves of Paradise, *Sunday Navhind Times,* Panaji, November 5, 2000

Official Language Implementation Adhoc Action Committee, A Blueprint, undated

Patel, Vikram, et al, *State of Goa's Health : A Report,* Panaji, 2000

Phaldessai, Pandurang R, Goa's Music : Multi-cultural Traditions, *The Navhind Times Millenium Supplement,* 2000

Pereira, Nicolau, Higher Education in Post-Liberation Goa, *Boletim do Instituto Menezes Braganza,* no. 176, 1996

Rodrigues, M F, Kishori Amonkar : Deep in the World of Notes, *Goa Today,* January 1994

Sequeira, Devika, Goa : Migrants Harassed after Dacoities, *Deccan Herald,* April 3, 2001

Third World Network, Globalisation and Migration, *Herald,* Panaji, November 22, 2000

Tombat, Ashwin, Interview with Luizinho Faleiro, *Goa Today,* May 1995

Yamnur, Anand Y, Area of Darkness, *Deccan Herald,* Bangalore, April 6, 2001

Writings on the Wall

Angle, Prabhakar S, *Goa : An Economic Update,* Mumbai, 2001

Bounsulo, Damodar, Health and Medical Care in Goa, *Boletim do Instituto Menezes Braganza,* no. 176, 1996

Cabral, Richard, The Fading Bustle, *Goa Today,* June 1998

Crawford, James, A Nation Divided by One Language, *Deccan Herald,* Bangalore, March 11, 2001

Coutinho, Joao da Viega, *A Kind of Absence : Life in the Shadow of History,* Stamford, USA, 1997

De Sousa, J R Ralino, Goan Architecture and Environment, *Boletim do Instituto Menezes Braganza,* no. 176, 1996

Goa Today, A Question of Identity, March 1994

Gomes, Olivinho, Konkani at the University of Goa, *Boletim do Instituto Menezes Braganza,* no. 176, 1996

Government of Goa, *Economic Survey,* 2001-02

Herald, Konkani Writers Lament Drop in Readership, a report, April 22, 2001; Fight for Mai Bhas, an editorial, March 13, 2001; Erosion of Identity, an editorial, April 25, 2001; Sun, Sand and Shopping ... Goa Emerging as a Market for Designer Wear, a report, April 23, 2001

Kamat, Prakash, Tackling Unemployment with Self-Employment, Town Talk, *The Times of India,* May 9, 2001

Kelekar Ravindra, Concern over Survival of Konkani, *Boletim do Instituto Menezes Braganza,* no. 176, 1996

Keni, Chandrakant, Turning over a New Leaf, *Goa Today,* March 1995

John, Sarah, Portugal's Goa, *Hindu Sunday Magazine,* April 22, 2001

Mascarenhas, Mira, Impact of the West on Goan Music, in P P Shirodkar (ed) *Goa : Cultural Trends,* Panaji, 1988

Naik, Vaman R, Impact of Globalisation on Goa's Economy, *Gomantak Times,* Panaji, December 27, 2000

Newman, Robert S, The Struggle for a Goan Identity in Norman Dantas (ed) *The Transforming of Goa,* Mapusa, 1999

Noronha, Jorge de Abreu, Lisbon Calling, *Goa Today,* August 1995

Priolkar, A K, *Goa Rediscovered,* Mumbai, 1967

PriceWater House Coopers, *Recommended Industrial Policy Statement for Goa,* submitted to Government of Goa, September 4, 2000

Sanvordeker, Dilip Ramrau, Goenkars : Fall from Virtue, *Sunday Navhind Times,* March 11, 2001

Stephen, Shannon, *Globalisation and Forced Migration, Commonwealth Currents,* London, no. 4, 2000

The Navhind Times, *Conduct Functions in Konkani, Christians Urged,* a report, April 23, 2001

The Parliamentarian, Small Countries Conference — September 19, 2000, *Jersey,* issue no. one, 2001

Weekender, *Govt Must Not Waste Money on Other Languages : Naik,* a report, April 22, 2001

Index

A

Academy, Kala 214
Agriculture 15, 16, 30, 33, 34, 51, 67, 68, 74, 75, 80, 81, 83, 84, 86, 88, 89, 90, 91, 97, 104, 113, 189, 216, 228, 229
Agricultural land 71
Albuquerque, Afonso 19, 20, 21, 31, 45
American mass culture 212, 213, 214
Amonkar, Kishori 187
Angle, Prabhakar 87, 175, 177
Anjuna 98, 107, 176, 225
Anti-Narcotics Bureau 102
Antruz 27
Arambol 98, 110
Archbishop 25, 116, 122, 123, 124, 125, 127, 128, 129, 130, 131, 132, 133, 134, 135, 136, 137, 141, 142, 160, 203
Archbishopric 132
Archdiocese, Goa 114, 122, 124
Architecture 33, 34, 42, 104, 210, 211
Arinze, Cardinal Francis 143
Arpora 98
Augustinians 122, 124
Ayappa 220

B

Baga 94, 95, 96, 97, 98, 107
Bahujan raj 178
Balcao 211
Bamonn 32, 33, 65, 74
Bamonn raj 178
Bandodkar, Dayanand 43, 44, 50, 53, 58, 59, 60, 64, 65, 66, 67, 75, 76, 77, 78, 79, 81, 82, 83, 86, 91, 97, 178, 205, 206
Beach 94, 95, 102, 103, 104, 106, 109, 110, 112, 113, 114, 186, 194, 199
Beach areas 108
Beach belt 100, 102, 106, 111, 112, 113, 176, 186, 187, 194, 225
Beaches 93, 94, 95, 96, 97, 98, 99, 103, 105, 107, 108, 109, 110, 112, 176, 198
Beach front 108
Beachside villages 102, 107, 110, 112
Bengali 220
Bhatcar 50, 68, 72, 73, 74, 78, 210
Brahmanand, Swami 137
Brahmans 21, 26, 29, 32, 33, 50, 65, 73, 121, 133, 178
Brazil 29
British 19, 20, 22, 38, 74
British system 38, 40
Buddhists 176

C

Calangute 94, 95, 96, 97, 98, 103, 107, 110
Candolim 98, 107, 143
Carnival 27, 41, 100, 116, 117, 127, 210

244 Index

Caste 16, 23, 32, 33, 47, 50, 66, 69, 73, 97, 98, 133, 137, 177, 178
Catholics 33, 114, 136, 137, 139, 140, 142, 143, 145, 146, 147, 168
Chardo 32, 33, 74
Chavan, Y B 48, 56, 57, 58, 59, 61, 63
Chitpavans 50
Christian 22, 23, 24, 25, 27, 28, 29, 33, 34, 37, 40, 41, 42, 43, 46, 47, 48, 53, 55, 63, 71, 73, 74, 92, 114, 115, 116, 117, 118, 119, 120, 121, 122, 125, 126, 127, 129, 130, 131, 133, 134, 135, 136, 137, 139, 140, 141, 143, 145, 153, 156, 165, 166, 178, 179, 203, 204, 205, 206, 209, 212, 213, 217, 219, 220,
Christianity 15, 23, 24, 32, 34, 39, 40, 56, 73, 117, 124
Christians 15, 17, 27, 28, 29, 32, 33, 34, 35, 37, 40, 41, 42, 43, 44, 45, 46, 47, 48, 49, 50, 53, 54, 55, 56, 57, 58, 60, 63, 64, 65, 73, 74, 85, 92, 100, 114, 115, 116, 117, 118, 119, 120, 121, 125, 126, 127, 128, 129, 130, 131, 132, 133, 134, 135, 137, 139, 140, 141, 142, 143, 144, 145, 152, 153, 156, 160, 165, 166, 172, 177, 179, 188, 189, 206, 207, 209, 210, 211, 212, 215, 218, 219
Church 15, 16, 17, 21, 22, 25, 26, 28, 29, 32, 41, 73, 74, 114, 115, 116, 117, 118, 119, 120, 121, 122, 123, 124, 125, 126, 127, 128, 129, 130, 131, 132, 133, 134, 135, 137, 138, 139, 140, 141, 142, 143, 145, 146, 147, 166, 203, 210, 212, 215, 218,
Church, Marathoma 139
Coastal zone 108
Code, Goa's Uniform Civil 144
Code, Monarchical Civil 146, 148
Code, Portuguese Civil 163
Code, Uniform Civil 17, 144, 145, 158, 160, 162, 163, 168
Colaco, Abel 37
College of St. Paul 22
Comunidade 24, 68, 69, 70, 71, 72, 75, 76, 77, 79, 82, 83, 187
Cultivators 83, 84
Cuntocars 69, 70

D

Dal, Bajrang 137
Descendentes 31
Dominicans 20, 122, 124
Drugs 95, 96, 99, 101, 102, 193, 225
D'Souza, Errol 179
DuPont 135

E

Ecclesiastics 25, 122, 123, 124
Education 69, 93, 119, 141, 169, 175, 176, 177, 180, 181, 200, 213, 227, 229
Emigrants 110, 179, 188
Emigration 16, 31, 74, 110, 172, 178, 200, 216, 226, 227
English 38, 39, 61, 119, 198, 201, 210, 214, 215, 216, 218, 219
Esteves, Sarto 61
Eurasian 31, 33
Expatriates 216, 217, 218

F

Faleiro, Luizinho 132, 133, 171, 174, 176, 177, 178, 181, 204, 227
Farmers 78
Fishermen 96, 97, 118
Franciscans 20, 122, 124

G

Gandhi, Indira 108, 158
Gandhi, Rajiv 110, 145, 156
Ganesh 22
Gaocari 30, 68, 69, 70, 80

Gaocars 70
Goan diaspora 70
Goa Techno 100
Goa Trance 99, 100
Goembab, Shenoi 119
Gomantak 50
Gonsalves, Raul 127, 129, 130, 132, 133, 135, 136, 203
Governor General 36, 85
Growth rate 90, 105, 174
Gujarati 180

H

Hindi 172, 200, 213, 220
Hindu 15, 17, 20, 21, 22, 23, 24, 25, 26, 27, 28, 29, 30, 35, 40, 50, 53, 58, 63, 64, 73, 74, 92, 113, 114, 115, 118, 119, 120, 121, 126, 128, 130, 134, 135, 137, 140, 141, 142, 143, 145, 146, 147, 148, 152, 153, 157, 160, 163, 164, 166, 168, 171, 172, 176, 177, 178, 198, 209, 210, 212, 213, 218, 219, 220
Hindu culture 43
Hinduism 29, 143
Hippies 33, 93, 94, 95, 96, 98, 99, 100, 101, 104, 225
Horticulture 86, 91, 93, 94, 95, 113, 229

I

Iberian 209, 212
Identity, Distinct 15, 34
Identity, Goan 15, 41, 53, 171, 209, 216
Identity, Goa's 41, 128
Identity, Indian 15, 34, 217
Identity, Indo-Portuguese 43, 209
Identity, Pan-Indian 47
Identity, Unique 34, 41, 58, 209
Income, Per Capita 90
Indian army 15, 26
Indian mass culture 212

Indian soldiers 36
Indian troops 36
Indo-Portuguese 40, 55, 210
Industries 16, 51, 56, 89, 90, 92, 93, 105, 107, 108, 109, 112, 173, 180, 187, 228
Industrialisation 83, 88, 89, 187
Inquisition 20, 21, 22, 23, 27, 28, 69, 115, 121, 123, 139
Iron ore 39, 74, 87, 88, 207
Irrigation 69, 72, 77, 80, 81, 82, 83, 182, 183, 228, 229
Israelis 99

J

Jesuits 20, 21, 23, 123, 124, 126

K

Kakodkar, Shashikala 78, 178
Kamat, Nandkumar 175
Kamath, M V 182
Kannada 182, 184, 186, 200, 220
Kannadiga expansionism 48
Kannadigas 208
Karnataka 21, 63, 126, 175, 176, 182, 184, 186, 207, 208, 221, 224, 225
Kavle mutt 137
Kerala 16, 21, 126, 139, 173, 176, 207, 208, 216, 227
Khazan 71, 76, 77, 127
Kher 71, 76
King 20, 21, 23, 28, 31, 50, 53, 69, 122
Konkani 32, 50, 51, 54, 61, 62, 119, 120, 121, 170, 171, 172, 182, 184, 187, 198, 200, 202, 203, 204, 205, 213, 214, 215, 216, 217, 218, 219, 220, 222
Konkani, Devanagri 120, 171, 172, 219
Konkan Railway 126, 127, 128, 203
Konkan region 50, 126
Konkani, Roman 120, 172, 217, 219

Kshatriya 32, 33

L

Labourers 50, 65, 66, 68, 72, 73, 86, 176, 184, 185, 186, 193, 194, 195, 197, 198, 208, 225, 227
Laity 118, 126, 134, 140, 145, 210
Landlords 32, 50, 53, 68, 72, 73, 76, 77, 78, 93
Landowners 72, 76, 77, 79, 183, 187
Land reforms 68, 75, 79, 82, 97
Land Reform Commission 70, 75, 76, 80
Latin 40
Latin America 29, 32, 126
Liberation 17, 32, 34, 37, 65, 66, 67, 68, 69, 72, 80, 86, 90, 93, 114, 115, 119, 120, 125, 126, 134, 158, 173, 175, 178, 180, 185, 203, 209
Lisbon 20, 31, 72, 125
Luis, Alberto 117, 127, 129
Lusophiles 37, 39, 40, 124, 210

M

Maharashtra 15, 21, 30, 54, 56, 60, 61, 62, 63, 82, 103, 118, 126, 176, 182, 201, 224
Maharashtrians 52, 54
Maharashtrian expansionism 119, 121
Maharashtrawadi 52, 53, 119
Malayalam 200, 220
Mand 47
Mando 211, 212
Mandovi 36, 52
Mansions 29, 210, 211
Mapusa 117, 119, 216, 227
Maratha King 123
Marathi 32, 64, 65, 119, 120, 172, 180, 198, 215, 216, 219
Marathiwadi 172
Margao 90, 159, 160, 175, 223, 227
Mascarenhas, Lambert 177, 178

Meta Strips 131, 132, 133, 203
Migration 30, 175, 227, 228
Migration industry 228
Migrants 16,134, 141, 160, 174, 175, 176, 179, 182, 185, 186, 193, 194, 196, 197, 200, 218, 219, 222, 223, 224, 225, 226, 227
Migrant children 198, 199
Migrant communities 198, 220, 221, 223
Migrant labourers 177, 182, 183, 186, 187, 194, 207, 224
Migrant women 200
Mineowners 43, 65, 89, 224
Mines 66, 67, 74, 87, 88, 89, 180
Mining 74, 87, 88, 89, 90, 92
Mineworkers 75
Miscegenation 30, 31
Missionaries 20, 122, 139, 140, 141, 147
Moraes, Frank 49
Mormugao 71, 88, 91, 167, 173, 178, 193, 222, 223, 228
Morod 76
Mosques 79, 197, 221
Mughul emperor 123
Mundcar 73, 74, 106
Mundcari 72
Muslim 17, 137, 141, 145, 146, 152, 153, 154, 155, 156, 158, 159, 160, 161, 162, 163, 168, 175, 176, 186, 213, 220, 221, 223
Muzawar, Rashida 159, 160, 162, 163

N

Naik, Vasantrao 56, 62
Nair, Mohan 207
Natokk, Konkani 218
Nehru 34, 35, 36, 37, 38, 39, 40, 52, 53, 54, 55, 56, 57, 58, 59, 60, 61, 63, 67, 68, 83, 86, 87, 88
Nehru administration 40, 52, 54, 55
New Conquests 57, 64, 71, 90

NGOs 16, 92, 113, 115, 116, 117, 127, 128, 131, 198, 209
Non-Brahmans 60
Non-Goans 38, 201, 206, 224

O

Officers 38, 39, 102, 123, 195, 203, 204, 205
Old Conquests 20, 21, 22, 57, 71, 90, 115, 119
Opinion Poll 15, 63, 64, 71, 119
Oporto 31

P

Paedophile 198, 199
Paedophilia 190, 191
Panaji 36, 106, 116, 117, 119, 132, 158, 175, 178, 182, 184, 185, 193, 194, 201, 205, 210, 222, 223
Panchayat 110, 180, 187, 202, 223, 225, 226
Parishad, Vishwa Hindu 137
Parrikar, Manohar 204, 205
Partagali mutt 137
Parsis 145, 152, 157
Party, Bharatiya Janata 130, 205, 222
Party, Congress 128, 129, 158, 207, 222
Party, Maharashtrawadi Gomantak 15, 44, 53, 59, 60, 61, 62, 63, 64, 65, 119, 206, 208, 222
Party, United Goans 44, 53, 58, 62, 64, 206
Patil, S K 55, 62
Pernem 112, 208
Persian Gulf 16, 25, 179, 218, 227
Personal law(s) 144, 145, 152, 153, 154, 155, 157, 158, 159, 161
Pollution 92, 101, 102, 109, 132, 226
Pope 28, 121, 122, 124, 125, 126, 136, 137, 141, 142

Port 19, 56, 88, 89, 178, 187, 193, 203, 207, 208, 223, 228
Portugal 19, 20, 25, 28, 30, 122, 124, 125, 145, 146, 211
Portuguese 15, 17, 19, 20, 21, 22, 24, 25, 26, 27, 29, 30, 31, 32, 33, 34, 36, 38, 40, 41, 52, 54, 55, 57, 61, 65, 66, 69, 74, 85, 86, 87, 88, 119, 120, 121, 122, 123, 124, 125, 145, 147, 150, 152, 158, 159, 163, 173, 174, 176, 178, 209, 211, 212, 213, 214, 219
Portuguese administration 39
Portuguese army 36
Portuguese colony 173
Portuguese culture 20
Portuguese dominions 45
Portuguese economy 39
Portuguese government 39
Portuguese influences 120
Portuguese regime 39
Portuguese rule 39, 45
Priolkar, A K 53
Punjabi 213

R

Ramponkars 121
Rao, P V Narasimha 128
Rashtramat 50
Ratzinger, Cardinal Joseph 142
Rebello, Monsignor Francisco 127
Referendum 44, 50, 51, 55, 56, 58, 60, 63, 203

S

Sahyadri 71
Saint Thomas 139
Saint Xavier 41, 125
Salazar 15, 19, 34, 37, 39, 40, 124, 125
Sand dunes 106, 194
Sangh, Rashtriya Swayamsewak 137
Saraswats 50, 52, 54, 64, 66, 119

Saraswat Brahmans 50, 65, 118, 137
Sati 23
Sattari 45
Script, Devnagari 54, 121, 219
Script, Roman 54, 121, 219
Sequeira, Jack 53
Shastri, Lal Bahadur 52, 54, 62
Society of Jesus 21
State cadre 206
State domestic product (SDP) 84, 90, 110, 228
Sudir 32, 33, 74
Sudra 177, 182
Sussegad 33, 178, 182

T
Tamil 220
Tamil Nadu 189
Telugu 220
Temple 21, 22, 29, 47, 71, 73, 79, 118, 123, 133, 137, 197, 220, 222
Tenancy 72, 77, 78, 196
Tenants 15, 50, 66, 68, 71, 72, 73, 74, 75, 76, 77, 78, 79, 82, 83, 97, 98, 189, 224
Tiatr 218
Times, The Navhind 65, 190, 192
Tiwari, D P 222, 223
Tourism 33, 83, 93, 94, 97, 98, 101, 102, 104, 105, 106, 107, 108, 109, 110, 111, 112, 113, 114, 115, 116, 117, 135, 187, 212, 225, 228
Tourism department 105
Tourist 187, 204, 224, 225, 226
Tourists 43, 93, 94, 95, 96, 97, 98, 99, 100, 101, 102, 104, 105, 107, 110, 111, 112, 115, 176, 195, 228
Tourist season 187
Tourist traffic 106

U
Urdu 220
Uttaranchal Society 221, 222
Uttar Pradesh 173, 176, 178, 190, 197, 221, 222

V
Vagator 98
Vasco da Gama 36, 117, 131, 132, 137, 162, 173, 176, 180, 187, 189, 197, 207, 208, 221, 222, 223
Vatican 124, 126, 136, 138, 139, 142, 143, 147, 214
Vaz, Miguel 21
Viceroy 25, 30, 122, 123

Z
Zuari 52, 132